VOLUME

KRAV *MAGA*

ISRAELI SYSTEM OF SELF-DEFENSE

SERGIO NISENBAUM

VOLUME 2

KRAVMAGA

ISRAELI SYSTEM OF SELF-DEFENSE

ADVANCED TECHNIQUES

Editorial advisor: Eduardo Viegas Meirelles Villela

Book design: Sergio Nisenbaum

Cover design: Sergio Nisenbaum

International data of Cataloging in Publication (CIP)
Librarian Juliana Farias Motta CRB7/5880

N724k Nisenbaum, Sergio

Krav Maga a defesa pessoal israelense:
técnicas avançadas / Sérgio Nisenbaum . --
1.ed. -- São Paulo: [s.n], 2021.

230 p.; 6.69 x 9.61 . vol.2

ISBN: 978-65-87369-09-9

1. Krav Maga. 2. Artes marciais. 3.Defesa
pessoal. 4. Luta corporal. I. Título: técnicas
avançadas

CDD 796.8

Índice para catálogo sistemático:

1. Krav Maga   3. Defesa pessoal
2. Artes marciais   4. Luta corporal

For doubts, comments, and further information
about this book, visit the author's Instagram profile:
@kravmaga_sergionisenbaum or email to
sergionisenbaum@gmail.com .

Creating Volume 1 was a significant challenge for me. I used to think that I had reached my limit. However, soon after it was launched, like in the practice of Krav Maga where at each graduation I would try to climb higher and higher, the willingness to face the challenge of moving ahead with a new book came up. Thus, I found strength, inspiration, and determination to create and launch this book.

Sergio Nisenbaum

Dedication

Every page in this book I specially dedicate to my students, who have always helped and supported me both in the best and in the hardest moments of my journey.

Acknowledgment

Despite facing the most challenging moments while writing this book, I am grateful for being able to find enough strength and inspiration to create and complete it. I also thank you, reader, for investing your hard-earned money and precious time to read this book.

Warning

This book is a practical guide fully illustrated with Krav Maga defense and attack techniques, the Israeli art of self-defense. All exercises described here are done by advanced groups and they require the care, safety, and technical supervision of a qualified instructor. Once they are advanced techniques, they may cause physical harm to an opponent. Some include defenses against attacks with weapons. Thus, you should never train with any type of real weapon. It is important to know that this book is only a didactic reference and reading it does not substitute training and practicing with a qualified instructor able to teach Krav Maga in a responsible way. The author, the editor, and the printing house are not and will not be liable for any use of this book's contents, whether mistakenly or otherwise. The information provided and illustrated here should be always used in compliance with the legislation in force. Any damages resulting from inappropriate use will be the user's sole responsibility.

The Creator of Krav Maga

Krav Maga was created in the 1940s by Imi Lichtenfeld and has long been considered a secret weapon of the Israeli armed forces. Imi (Imrich) Sedé Or (Lichtenfeld) was born on May 26, 1910, in Budapest, and grew up in Bratislava in the Austro-Hungarian Empire. His father, who rigorously enforced discipline in their family life, was chief of the secret police and responsible for hand-to-hand combat lessons.

During his youth, Imi was passionate about sports and became a boxing and wrestling champion by the age of 18. As a natural-born leader, Imi formed resistance groups when the fascist and anti-Semitic movement began in Europe; despite being outnumbered against the attackers, he participated in street fights and successfully protected the local community.

In 1939, Imi started thinking about immigrating to the region of Israel, which was under British mandate at the time. In 1940, intending to put his plan into action, he boarded a boat with hundreds of people living in precarious conditions. On the vessel, called Pentcho, Imi acted like a true hero, rescuing everything and everyone falling overboard, but his heroic actions almost cost his life, as the accumulation of liquids in his ear led to extreme inflammation. After the vessel shipwrecked near Greece, Imi was rescued by the British navy in a small rowboat led by volunteers and was rushed to a hospital in Alexandria, Egypt, for an emergency surgery to control his ear infection. Upon recovering, he joined the British Armed Forces, where he served for two years.

In 1942, Imi finally arrived in Israel, where he became head of self-defense for Hagana (one of the groups fighting for independence from Israel), thus creating the future of Krav Maga.

During this time, he developed and refined the most effective, efficient, and dynamic self-defense and attack tactics using instincts. In 1948, Imi became a fitness trainer and Chief Instructor of hand-to-hand combat and self-defense for the Israel Defense Force (IDF). In 1964, he retired from the military and established his first training center for civilians in the city of Natanya. Imi passed away on January 9, 1998, at the age of 87.

The world has lost a great man, who changed the perspective of life, thought, peace, loyalty, and respect.

The Krav Maga learning cycle

Beginners train exhaustively each exercise by repeating the movements. In parallel, they also work the development of speed and burst. The details are improved through practice as time goes by, and students incorporate all movements like reflexes. Actually, Krav Maga's main objective is to respond to an aggression as an instinctive and immediate defensive reflex, because in a real life-threatening situation there is not enough time to calculate or think which of the techniques learned in class should be used. When students achieve their first graduation, because they already have a significant amount of information, they can defend themselves in simpler situations of aggression. When the knowledge has been assimilated, students are ready to learn more complex defenses. In the next phase, they can face several situations involving one or more opponents, and the time spent training brings them self-confidence and more control of the movements. Krav Maga's essence, which is the transfer of the body weight added to the movement's speed and burst, becomes part of their skills. Finally, when students reach maturity in their training, they can understand and make more complex defenses, including those more adequate to situations involving any type of weapon and which require maximum technical skill and mental capacity. Learning Krav Maga is like climbing the steps of a long stair. At each practice, even if repeating for the umpteenth time an exercise already learned, you will always climb one step higher in your knowledge and improvement. A great climb worth every second of effort.

Krav Maga in practice

Krav Maga is a self-defense art where defense and attack take place simultaneously through moves whose objective is to reach the opponent's sensitive and vital points. Basically, while a defensive move is made, attacks are simultaneously made to neutralize the opponent and to prevent he has a second reaction. But it does not mean that reaction can only occur when you are attacked. Let us imagine, for instance, a discussion between two people. Suddenly, one of them squats to grab a piece of pipe on the ground. Instead of waiting for the attack, that is the exact moment for a possible reaction to avoid the aggression. Although it is rather hard, that period of time spent thinking and reacting can be developed in practice, thus avoiding the need of a riskier defense. As in Krav Maga, all types of aggression are simulated, students end up being familiar with aggressive movements, which, in a way, enables their subconscious mind to be prepared, when facing a real threat, to instantly analyze the opponents' stance and movements. I tell my students that they should avoid any type of violent situation as much as possible, but we all know that nobody is fully safe because, even having a defensive purpose, we can be surprised by a dangerous context.

About the Author

Born in São Paulo, the most populated city and the financial center of Brasil, **Sergio Nisenbaum** began his Krav Maga journey in late 1999, where he was afforded the opportunity to learn the Israeli martial art in a responsible and legitimate manner. After 5 years of training, he excelled as a student and was considered a candidate for the instructor course. After a rigorous selection, which was divided into 3 stages: physical, technical, psychological, he was chosen to participate in the training course. After 400 hours consisting of theory, philosophy, and didactics of techniques, he was approved and was given the title of a Krav Maga instructor in August 2005. Since then, he has been teaching students of all ages as well as conducting different types of training designed for specific groups.

How the book was made

Volume 2 follows the same creative line and reasoning of the first book. I made and developed the whole graphic part in a vector application program for layout and illustrations. I did not use any application program or resource to generate ready tridimensional figures because it would not pass on exactly what I wished to express in each drawing. Although it was a much harder path which demanded uncountable working hours to reach the outcome I expected, I chose to develop each one of the illustrations in separate scenes with articulated dummies. Instead of using pictures of people, I chose to do something different from the usual, and much more artistic, in order to record the technical richness of the Krav Maga art. The result has been highly rewarding since Volume 1, and through those futurist robot-style characters I was able to express simply lively movements and technical details.

The pandemic and Krav Maga

Suddenly, the pandemic arrived and everything that had been built for years, with hard work and sweat, seemed torn down. Overnight, I had to stop classes for an indefinite period, something that used to be part of my life routine and which I had never done since 2005, the year I started to teach Krav Maga. Many days, weeks, and months went by, and I was missing everything hard. The pleasure of teaching had become forbidden. Nevertheless, unable to go to the gym and even to leave the house, my rule was never to stop.

The formula to face that period was ready. Physical and mental exercises. In the middle of chaos and uncertainty, I found the right moment to write Volume 2. Class hours were substituted by more hours of physical training and working hours and effort to create this book. Nights and days passed quickly, and in the middle of the pandemic, it was time for a new possibility: online classes. Even if they were classes on a smartphone's small screen, it was very joyful and satisfactory to be able to resume teaching and mainly to see my students again.

The book was completed in the middle of the pandemic and, still facing many problems, such as opening and shutting down the gym, among others, I did not allow myself to neglect the knowledge and discipline acquired during many years practicing Krav Maga. Certainly, that was what kept me focused and with the objective of moving ahead with the same determination that has brought me to where I am now.

Safety Hints

Krav Maga brings students the ability to know how to defend themselves against any type of aggression, but to develop a defensive stance is also part of the learning. However, it is a fact that even taking the necessary precautions within a preventive and defensive stance, it is rather difficult and uncertain to be one hundred percent safe. Nowadays, just reading or watching any media is enough to learn daily news about violence, and that these events happen in all places, with people from different socioeconomic classes and genders.

Small changes in habits and stances can avoid, or at least decrease, chances of you, and whoever is with you, of being involved in a robbery, theft, or assault. Find below some hints of safety and prevention.

When entering a new environment, find and be aware of where emergency exits are.

If you are at a place where a fight starts, leave immediately.

Avoid walking on empty and badly lit streets; choose streets with people, even if the route is longer.

Choose to walk in the opposite direction to the flow of the cars.

Keep your hands free from any objects and avoid using a cell phone while you walk down the street. If it is an urgent matter, get into a commercial establishment where you can talk safely.

Be always attentive and trust your intuition. If you suspect anyone's stance and attitude, do not wait to see what is going to happen.

Keep your wallet or cell phone in the front pockets.

Pay attention to people's movements when you are leaving or arriving a place, even if it is your home.

If you are in restaurants, bars, etc., do not leave your cell phone lying exposed on the table or counter.

Time for you

If you were working in a company where a meeting is scheduled every week at the same weekday and time, you would do your best not to miss it because you could put your job at risk. But if you had to schedule a meeting with yourself every week to take care of your wellbeing, would you do the same effort to attend it? Krav Maga brings benefits well beyond learning how to defend yourself. Working body and mind help improving the quality of your life and, consequently, improves your yield at work and in your studies. What I can say after so many years practicing and teaching Krav Maga is that the personal benefit compensates all the efforts and dedication to the practice. It does not matter which physical activity you enjoy doing, see it always as a pleasure, not a task.

Krav Maga physical exercises

Some physical exercises can help Krav Maga students improve their physical and muscle resistance. An actual situation of aggression requires a fast and bursting response which demands a high discharge of energy. That is why aerobic exercises, such as running, for instance, are excellent to keep you fit, and to improve breathing. Strength exercises can also improve the body control and muscle stiffening necessary for the hand and leg moves. Find below some suggestions of exercises.

Before starting any physical activity always have a medical evaluation. To execute well each exercise below, look for a qualified physical education professional.

Running

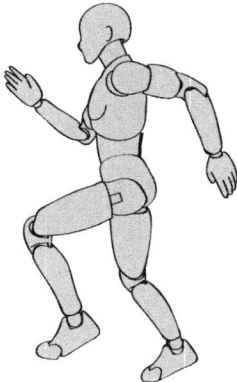

Parallel bar

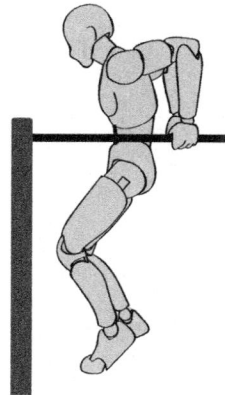

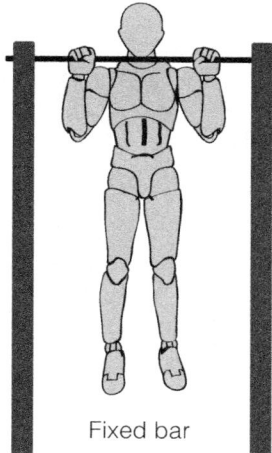

Fixed bar

Abdominals

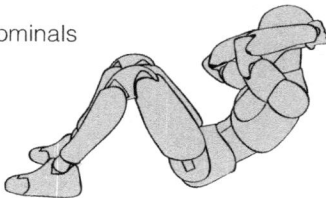

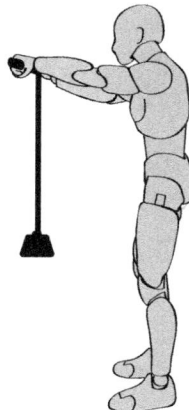

Wrist and forearm weight

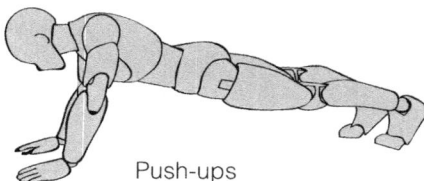

Push-ups

Clarification

The word "opponent" is used in this book to characterize the one who attacks, who is actually the aggressor.

Sergio Nisenbaum

Table of Contents

Sensitive and Vital Points
Safety Perimeters
Defensive Stances
"Live" Side and "Dead" Side
Technical Exercises

Defense Against Kicks

Immobilizations

Defense Against Grabs

Defenses Against Attacks on the Ground

Defenses Against Hair Grabs

Using a Stick in Attacks and Defenses

Defense Against Gun Threats

Sergio Nisenbaum

Sensitive and Vital Points

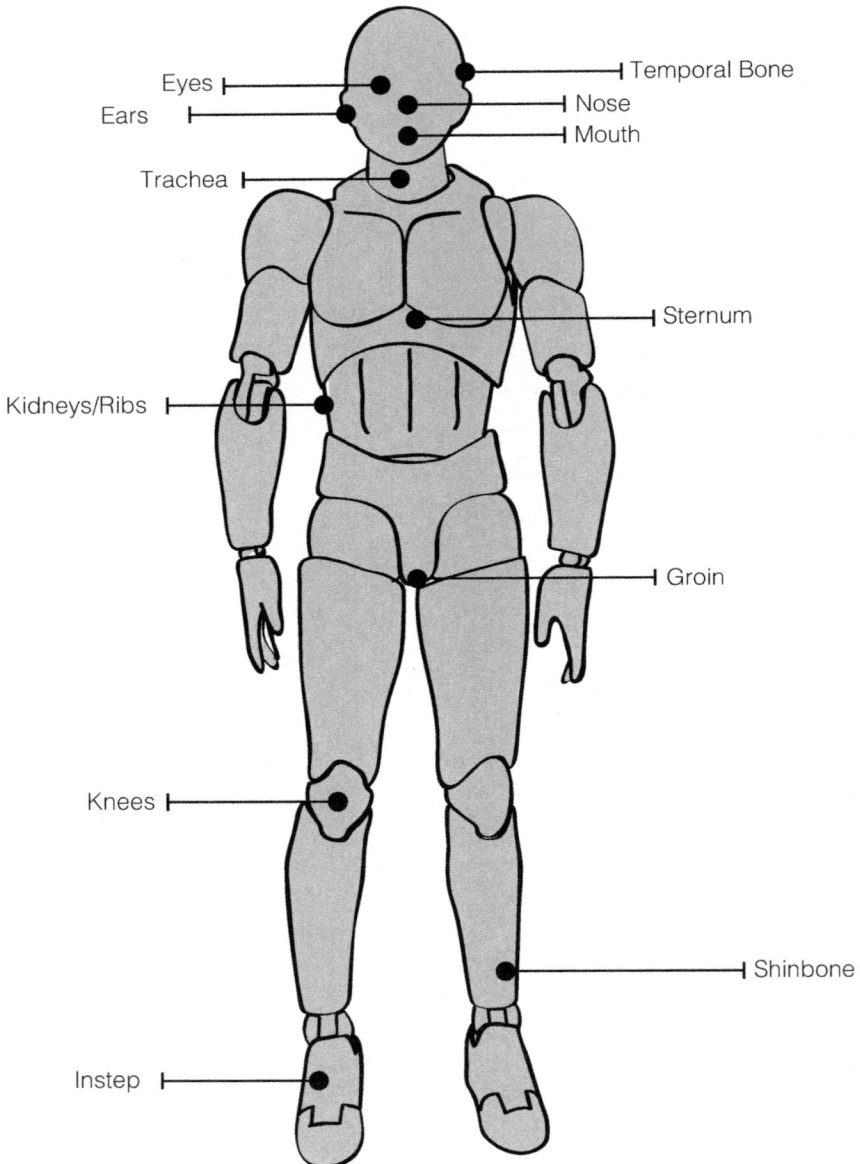

Eyes — Temporal Bone — Nose — Ears — Mouth — Trachea — Sternum — Kidneys/Ribs — Groin — Knees — Shinbone — Instep

A well-executed defense, combined with an attack that hits a sensitive and vital point, can immediately neutralize an opponent. In Krav Maga, any defense and attack movement have the aim of hitting one of these points.

Safety Perimeters

The Safety Perimeter is a natural distance that we keep when we get closer to somebody, or when somebody gets closer to us. In Krav Maga the safety perimeter is divided in three parts: short, medium and long distance.

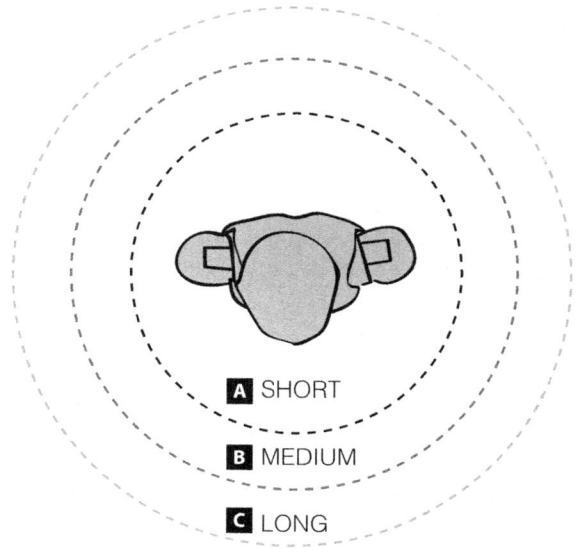

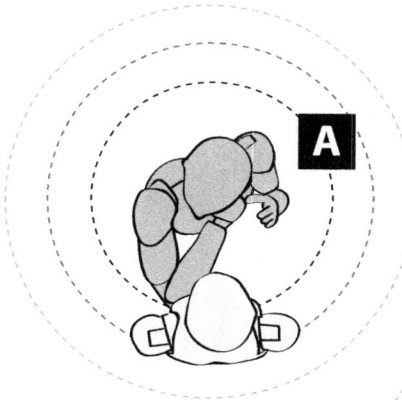

A SHORT

B MEDIUM

C LONG

A At short distances, we use strikes such as: Elbow Strikes, Hammer Strike Forward, Knee Strikes, etc.

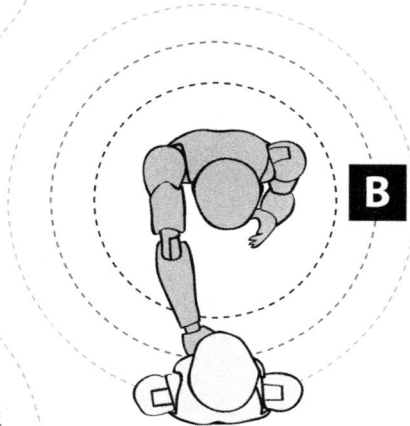

B At medium distances, we use strikes such as: Boxing Strike, Knife-hand Strike, Hammer Strikes, Kick Strikes, etc.

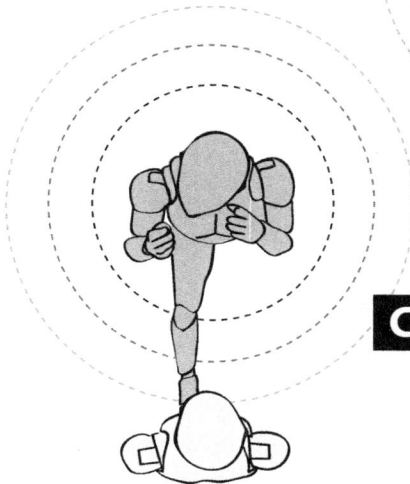

C At long distances, we use strikes such as: Kick Strikes and others in which our body moves towards the target.

Defensive Stances

In Krav Maga, the Defensive Stances vary significantly and the ones more generally used during practice are: Regular Stance (or the same stance inverted) and Parallel Stance. And there are also variations where the hands are kept open or closed, and at different heights. In the daily practice, the stances help a lot the technical development which enables students to understand how each exercise is done, but in the reality of the streets not always you can be ready to prepare a defensive stance, mainly in the first moment when you realize that you are going to be attacked. Therefore, any attack can be defended virtually in any position. With the arms down, crossed, when sitting, standing, or even lying down, you can defend yourself successfully.

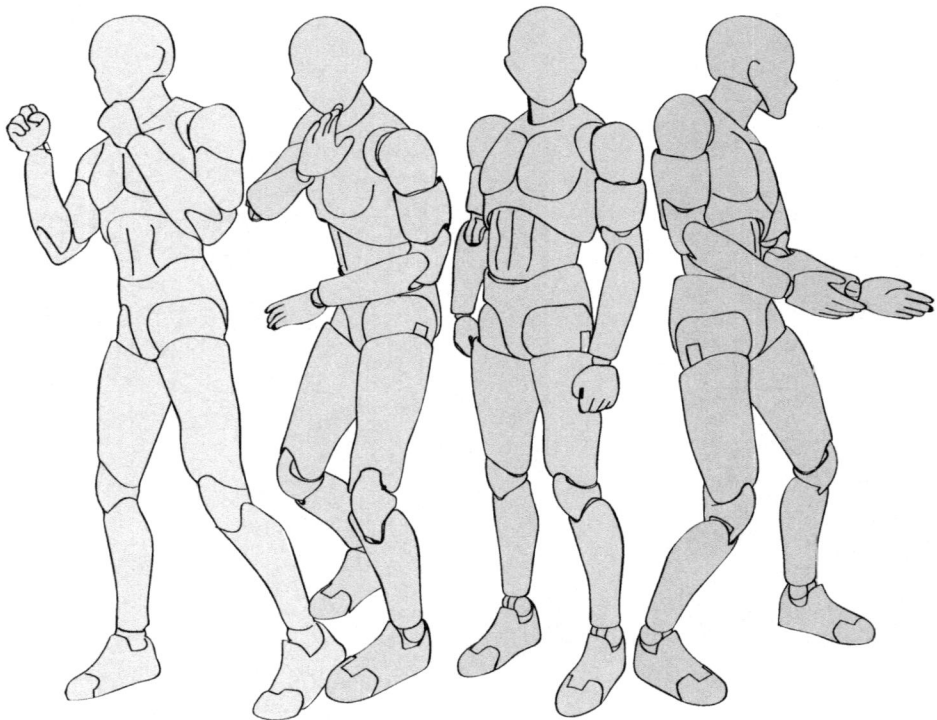

"Live" Side and "Dead" Side

You can defend yourself in several directions. The "dead" side is deemed the opponent's outside, and the "live" side, his inside. The example below shows the same type of stick attack from above being defended in both sides.

In the first example, defense is done in the opponent's "live" side (A), and it is done virtually in front of the opponent and between his arms. In the second example, defense is done on his "dead" side (B) and on the opponent's side. Although they look very much alike, facts such as distance and position change the technical form of the defense and, consequently, the continuations are also different in both cases.

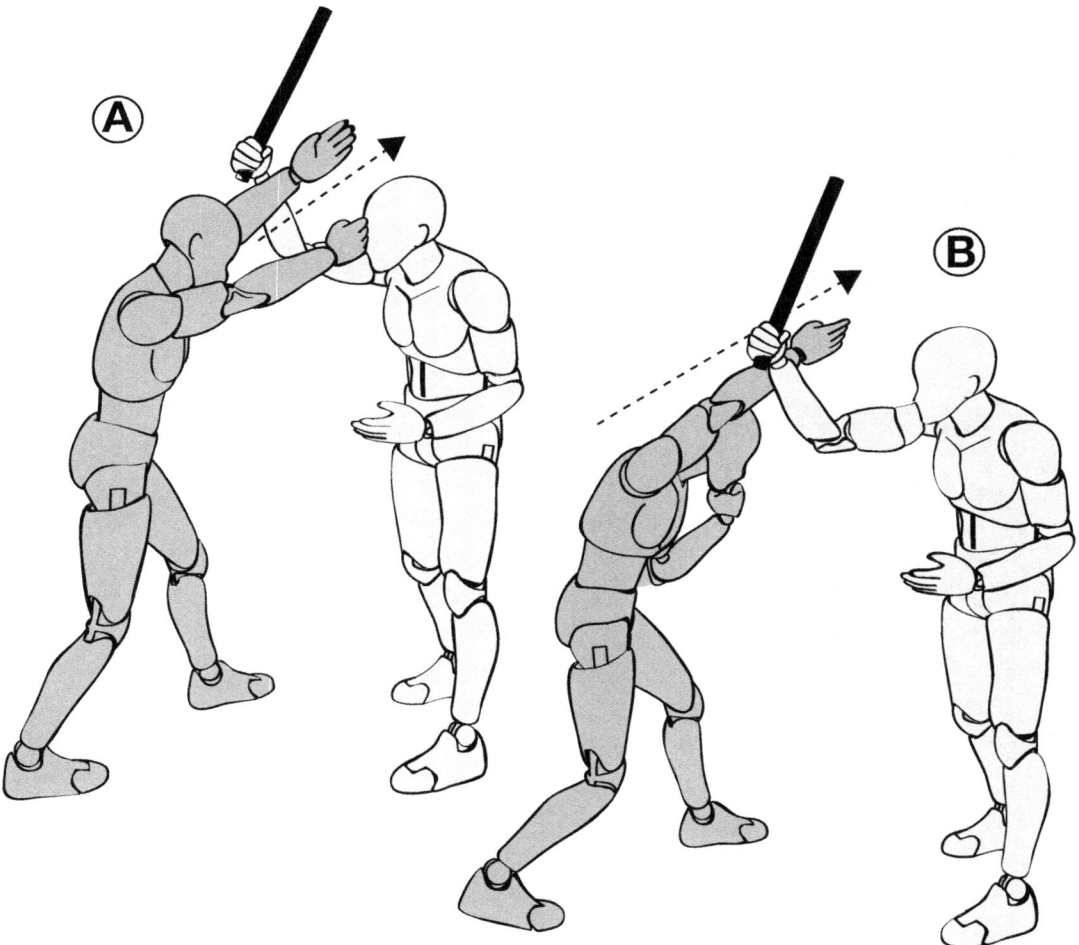

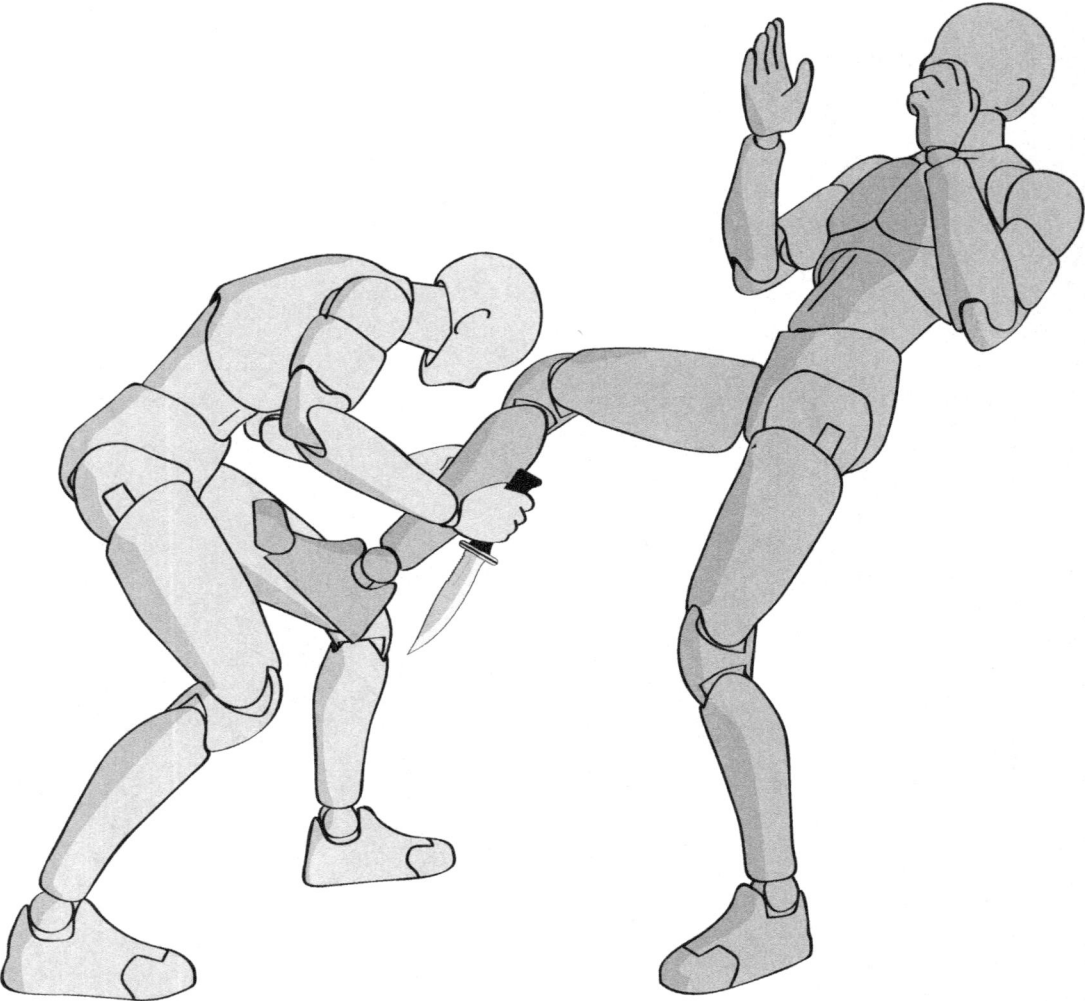

Technical Exercises

All exercises described next are done by advanced groups with enough technical knowledge to respect the necessary safety limits in the practice. Many defenses reach the opponent's sensitive and vital points, and they can cause permanent physical damages. That is why they should be practiced carefully, responsibly, with self-control, and under technical supervision of a duly qualified Krav Maga instructor. Observe warning notices in some specific exercises aimed at increasing safety during practice. The description of every exercise refers to each one of the illustrations and, in some situations, the same defense can be made in an inverted way to defend attacks from the other side.

To watch video demonstrations of the
techniques presented in the book,
access the author's YouTube channel
using the QR Code below.

1 Sequence of Attacks

In Krav Maga, Sequences of Attacks are called continuations, and they are delivered right after the main defense has been done. In a certain exercise, for instance, a defense against a knife attack, the main objective is to be able to defend yourself from the attack and not to be hurt. Soon after that, sequences of attacks are delivered to fully eliminate a second reaction by the opponent.

But as far as should continuations continue to be delivered? The answer comes in two ways: the first one, up to the moment when the opponent no longer represents a threat; and the second is linked to self-control, which means knowing when to stop and according to what the situation requires.

Every movement is made combined with the next one, i.e., a movement triggers the other, and they are delivered in a natural flow. It is not possible to forecast which types of sequences of continuations will be necessary because they also depend on the opponent's distance and position, among other factors, such as obstacles, confined environments, or situations involving more than one opponent. This is the importance of having technical knowledge of each exercise practiced in Krav Maga since the initial phase, with boxing strikes, hammer fists, elbow and knee strikes, kicks, etc. All those movements are excessively and continually practiced even by more advanced groups because they are part of all defenses.

In Volume 1 I have didactically described each one of the exercises you will see in combinations of sequences of attacks. If you have any doubts about how to perform these basic techniques, I recommend you read the first book.

The suggestions can be practiced individually, and the same attacks can be repeated more than once on the same side, inverted, or alternating between regular or parallel stances.

A

Left Boxing Strike	Right Boxing Strike	Lower Sickle Boxing Strike	Upper Sickle Boxing Strike	Hook Boxing Strike

   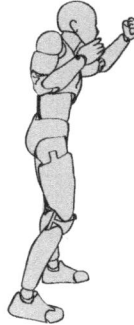 

B

Regular Kick	Left Boxing Strike	Right Boxing Strike	Sickle Kick

C

Knee Strike	Elbow Strike Forward	Elbow Strike Upwards	Left Boxing Strike	Right Boxing Strike

  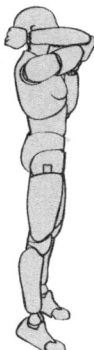  

Sergio Nisenbaum

D

Hammer Strike
Forward

Left Boxing
Strike

Right Boxing
Strike

Regular
Kick

E

Left Boxing
Strike

Right Boxing
Strike

Regular
Kick

Hammer Strike
Downwards

F

Golpe de Cotovelo
para Frente

Joelhada
para Cima

Golpe de Cotovelo
para Baixo

G

Knee Strike   Hammer Strike Forward   Left Boxing Strike   Defense Kick Forward

H

Elbow Strike Sideways   Heel Kick to the Knee   Hammer Strike Sideways

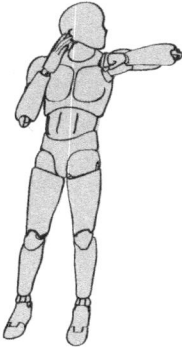

I

Left Boxing Strike   Right Boxing Strike   Regular Kick   Regular Kick Upwards

Sergio Nisenbaum

J

| Knee Strike Sideways | Hammer Strike Forward | Regular Kick | Left Boxing Strike | Righft Boxing Strike |

 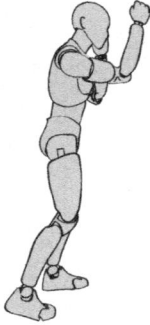   

K

| Regular Kick | Sickle Kick | Hammer Strike Sideways | Heel Kick to the Knee |

L

| Heel Kick to the Knee | Hammer Strike Sideways | Left Boxing Strike | Regular Kick |

M

Regular Kick Heel Kick to the Knee Knife-hand Strike Outward

N

Knife-hand Strike Inward Hammer Strike Forward Left Boxing Strike Righft Boxing Strike

O

Left Boxing Strike Lower Sickle Boxing Strike Upper Sickle Boxing Strike Regular Kick

P

Lower Boxing Strikes

Lower Sickle Boxing Strike

Hook Boxing Strike

Left Boxing Strike

Right Boxing Strike

Q

Elbow Strike Backwards

Elbow Strike Outward

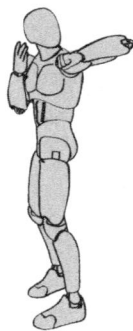

Regular Kick

Defense Kick Forward

R

Regular Kick Backwards

Regular Kick

Left Boxing Strike

Right Boxing Strike

2 Backward fall break

It is particularly important to learn how to fall safely. A backward fall can result from several factors, including due to an attack where you can be pushed or hit. A fall can lead to serious lesions, such as fractures and even loss of consciousness, which is extremely dangerous in a situation of aggression.

(A)

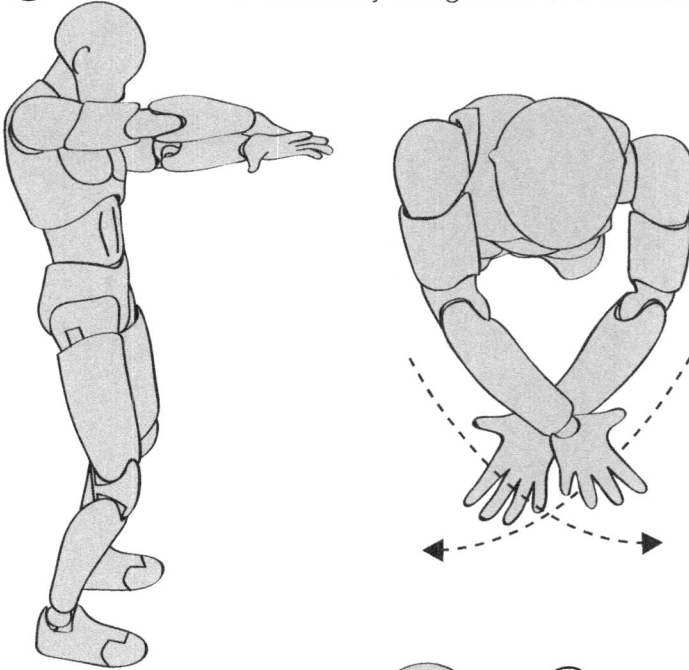

Two things should happen simultaneously during a fall: the impact is muffled with the forearms and the chin rests on the chest to avoid the effect of hitting the head on the ground when you fall.
Arms remain crossed (A).

(B)

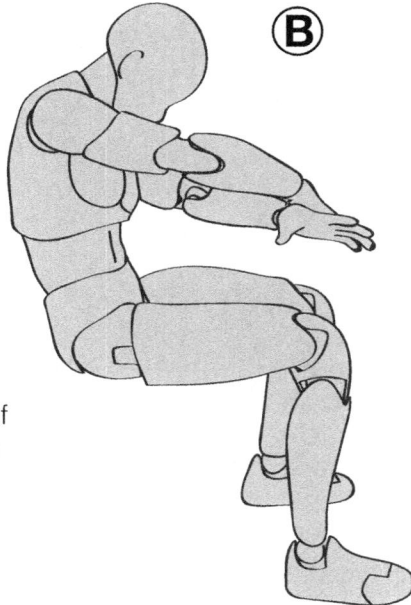

To reduce the height of the fall, flex the knees as if you were going to sit down (B).

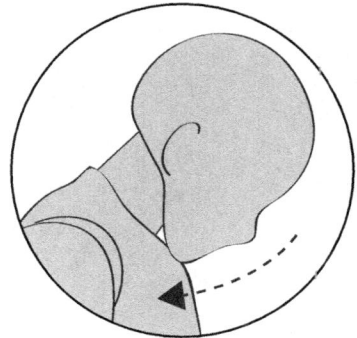

The chin rests on the chest until the end of the fall to avoid hitting the ground with the head.

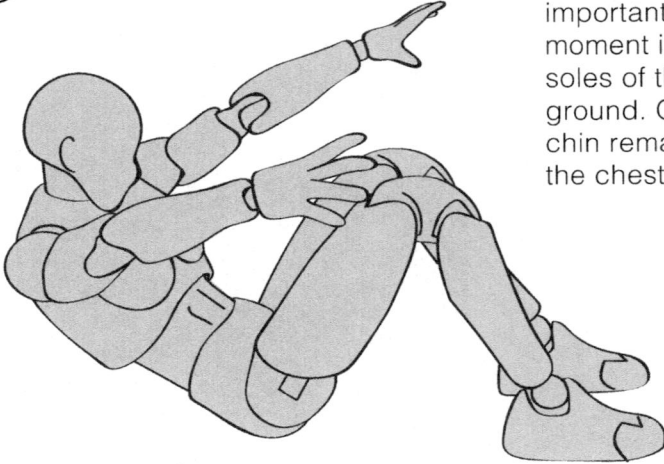

The glutes must contact the ground first, and the forearms are uncrossed to muffle the impact to the spine (C). Another important thing in this moment is to keep the soles of the feet on the ground. Observe that the chin remains resting on the chest.

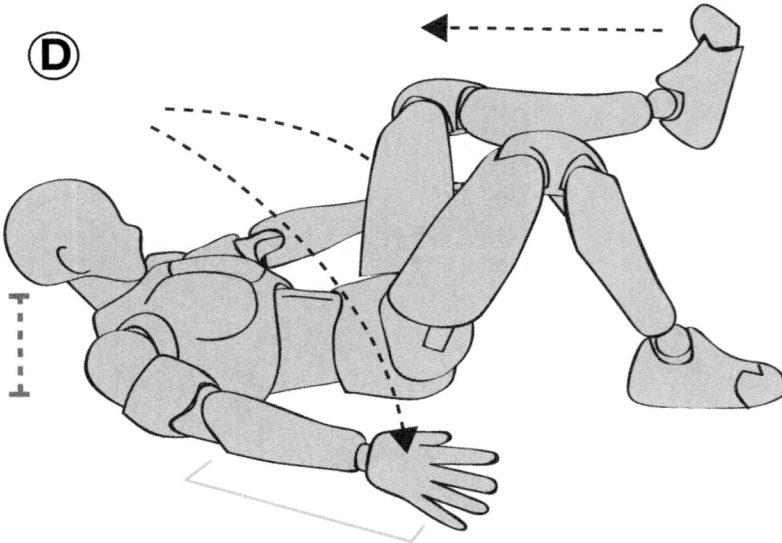

In the final phase (D), lying down, with the forearms and heels of the hands you break the impact of the fall, and the left foot is retracted to be in a defensive stance. You should remember that when there is a situation of aggression, even if you are lying down you are still fully able to defend yourself.

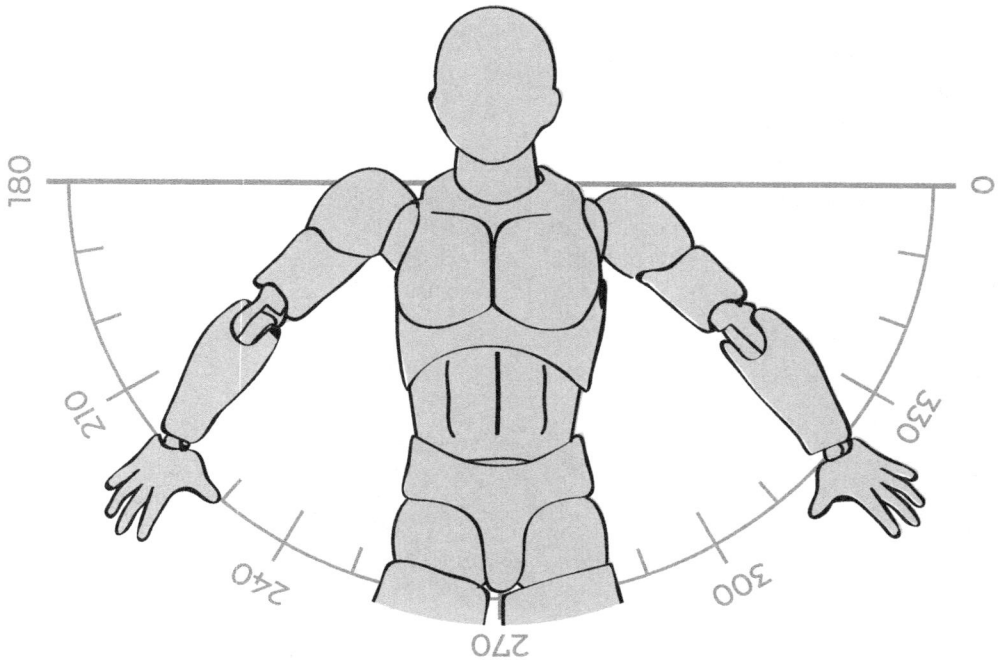

The ideal angle to break a fall is having the arms neither too closed nor too open. Never hit the ground with the heel of your hand first because the forearm and the hand must simultaneously break the fall to avoid overcharging the shoulders and the impact on the elbows.

From right to left, see a step-by-step summary of how to fall. Arms stretched and crossed, the knees start to flex, the glutes make the first contact with the ground, and, finally, the arms break the fall, thus positioning the body in a defensive stance. Next, do the defense on the ground after a fall.

Ⓔ

In the position of defense on the ground, the forearms and the right foot work as support and help the body rotating at any angle, if the opponent change directions. The left foot raised can prevent the opponent from coming closer (E).

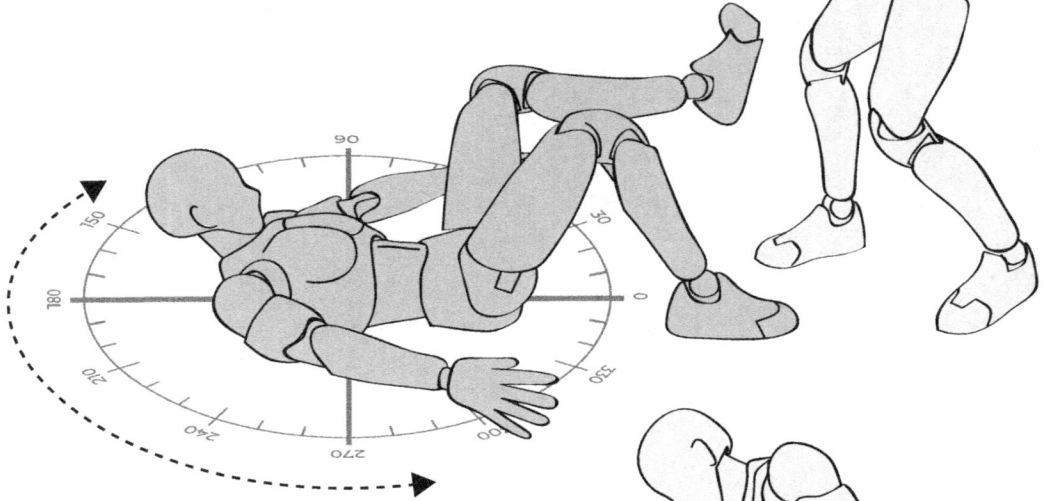

If the opponent does come closer, the left foot, which was in a defensive position, strikes regular kicks to reach the opponent's groins and even his face (F).

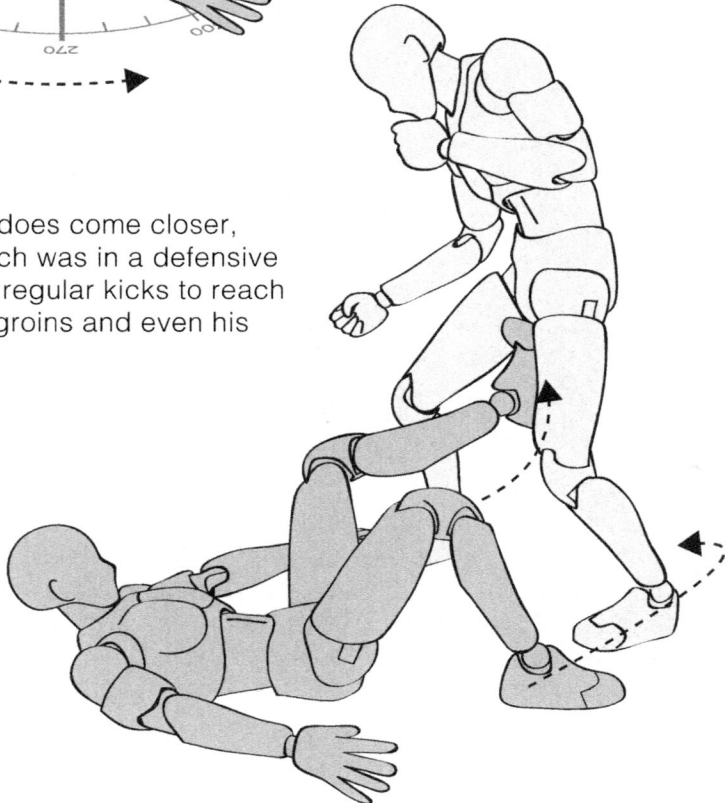

Ⓕ

(G)

After one or more regular kicks you can make a lever from behind the opponent's ankle, in this case with the instep of the right foot, and the left foot delivers heel kicks on the opponent's knee. The movement is simultaneous and with opposing forces: at the same time, while the right foot pulls to one direction, the left pulls to the other (G).

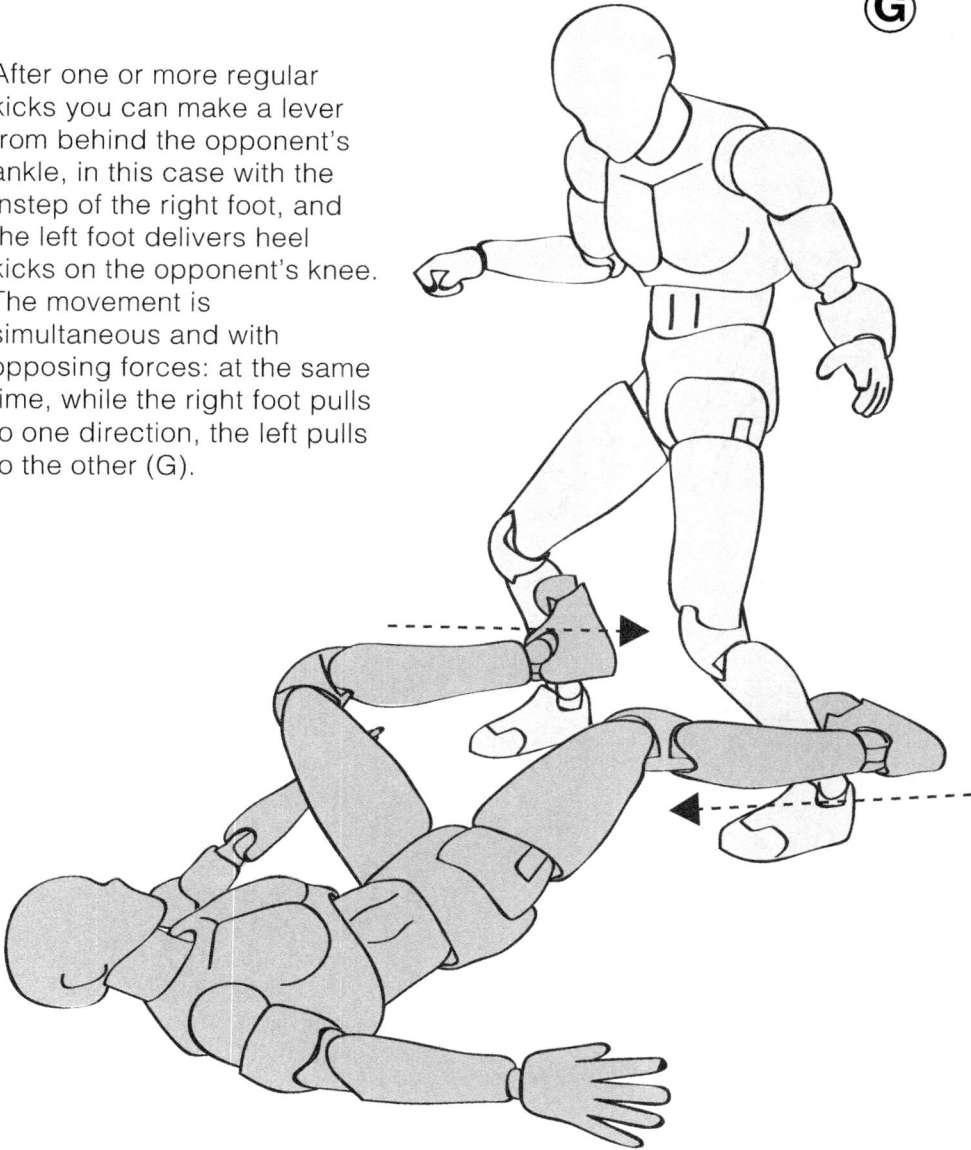

The Backward Fall is part of several defenses practiced in Krav Maga because many defensive situations and attack continuations end up by making the opponent fall on the ground.

Sergio Nisenbaum

Defense
Against Kicks

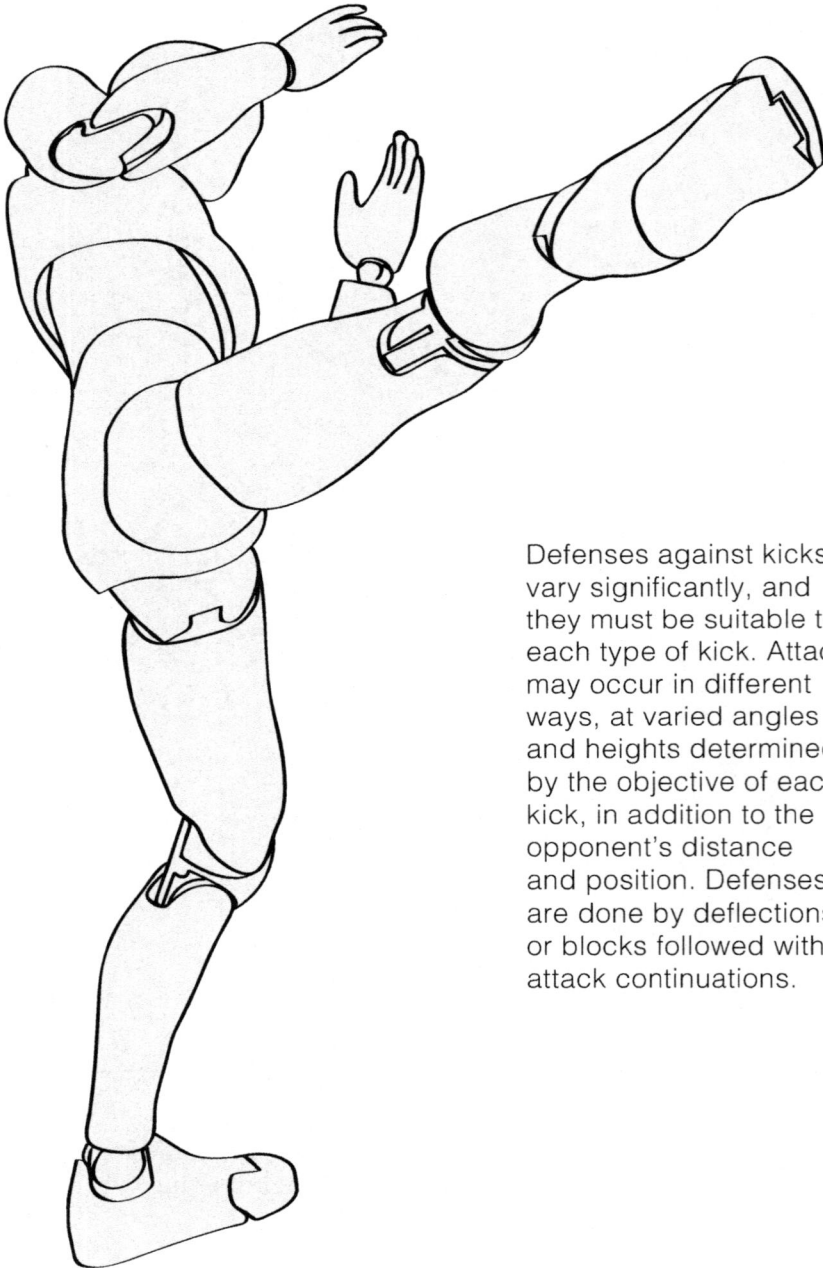

Defenses against kicks vary significantly, and they must be suitable to each type of kick. Attacks may occur in different ways, at varied angles and heights determined by the objective of each kick, in addition to the opponent's distance and position. Defenses are done by deflections or blocks followed with attack continuations.

3 Defense Against a Regular Kick with Deflection N°1

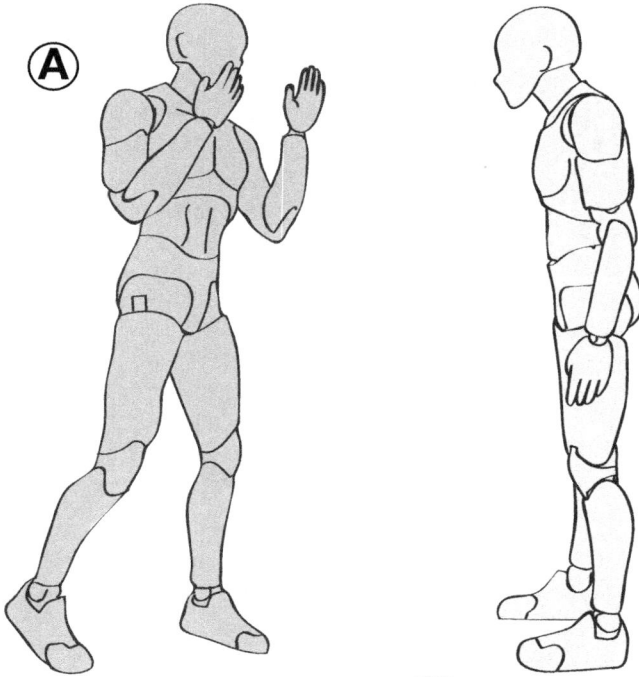

(A)

The defense against a Regular Kick with Deflection N°1 deflects the kick with the area between the tibia and ankle. The deflection happens virtually at the beginning of the opponent's kick. The defense can be done in the regular or in the parallel stance (A).

At the same time, the opponent's right leg starts to go up to kick, the left leg that is going to defend is already preparing the defense by going up as if it were also going to kick (B).

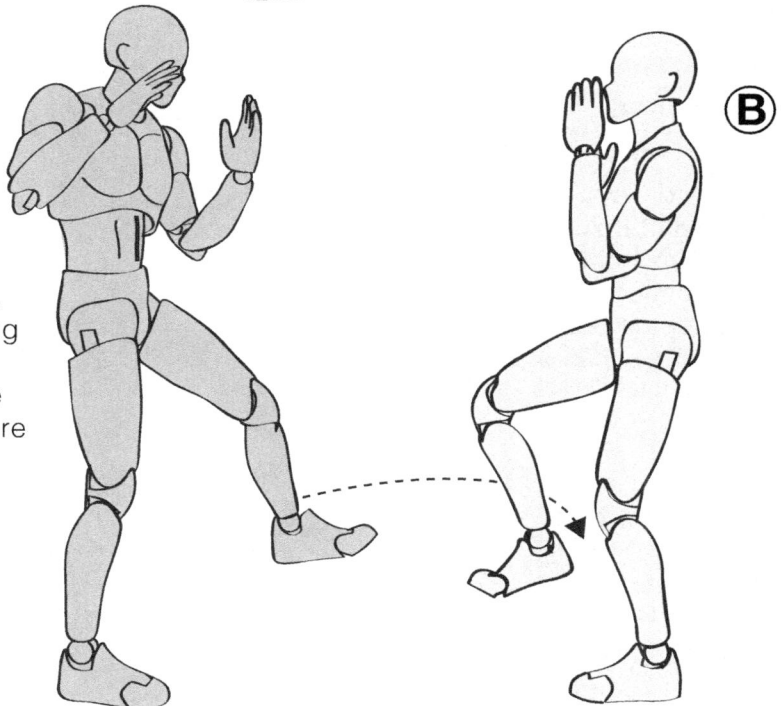

(B)

Ⓒ

The deflection is a short movement and much faster than the kick, and it is done toward the inside and from behind the opponent's leg, in the area near the ankle. In the moment of the defense, the angle of the left foot's position, which deflects the kick, stays pointing at 2 or 3 o'clock, having as reference the hands of a clock (C).

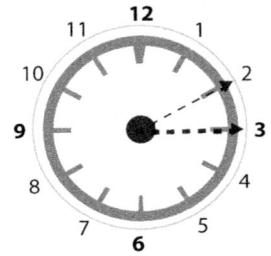

Ⓓ

After the deflection, deliver a Left-Hand Boxing Strike (D) and, as from there, do random continuations, which are the Sequences of Attacks seen in exercise 1.

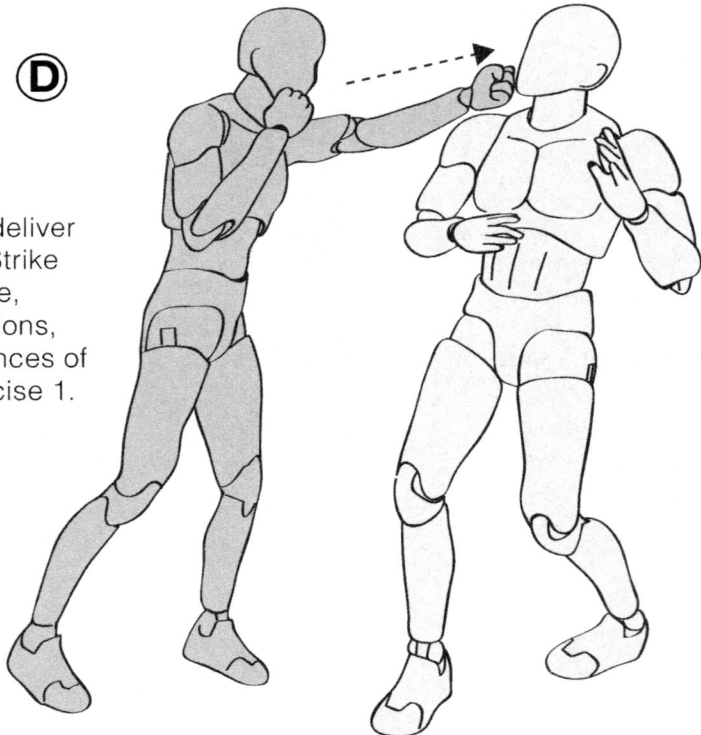

4 Defense Against a Regular Kick with Deflection N°2

In the Defense Against a Regular Kick with Deflection N°2, the kick is deflected just like explained before. What changes now is that the deflection happens from inside out. As the previous defense, the defending leg will go up fast as if it were going to kick (A).

(A)

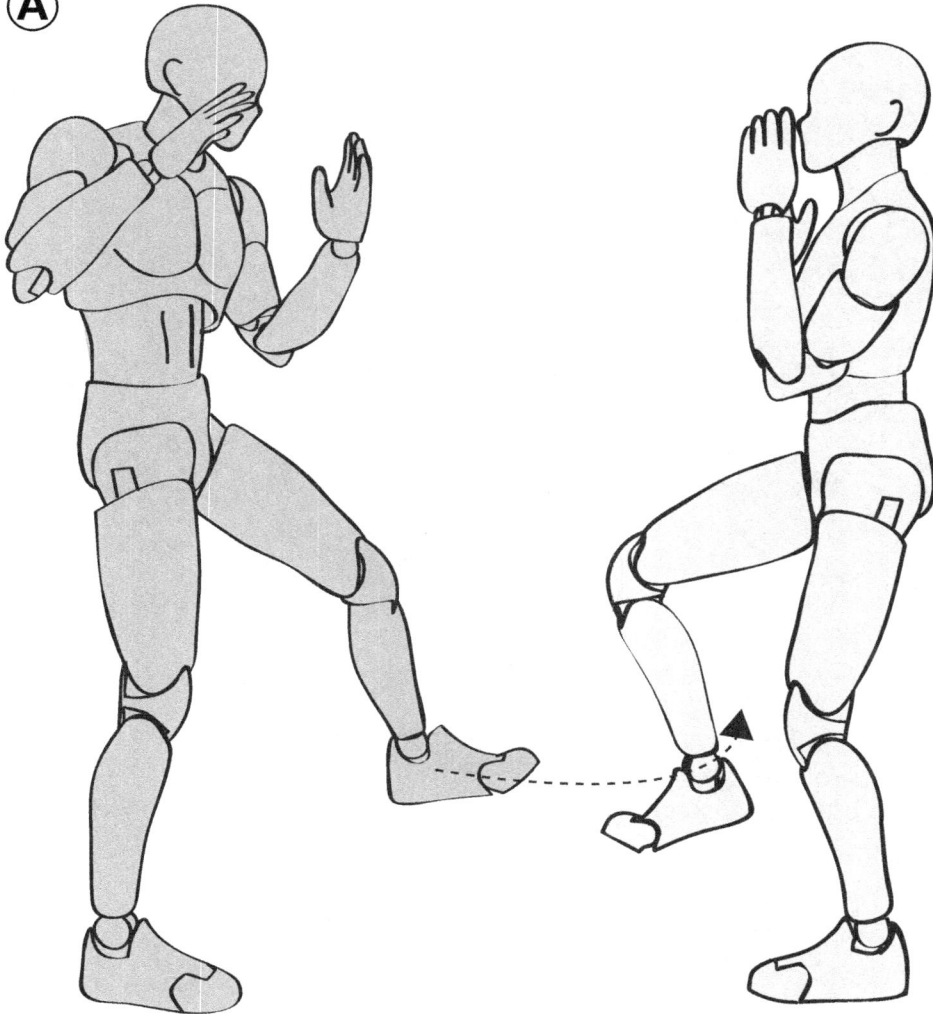

B

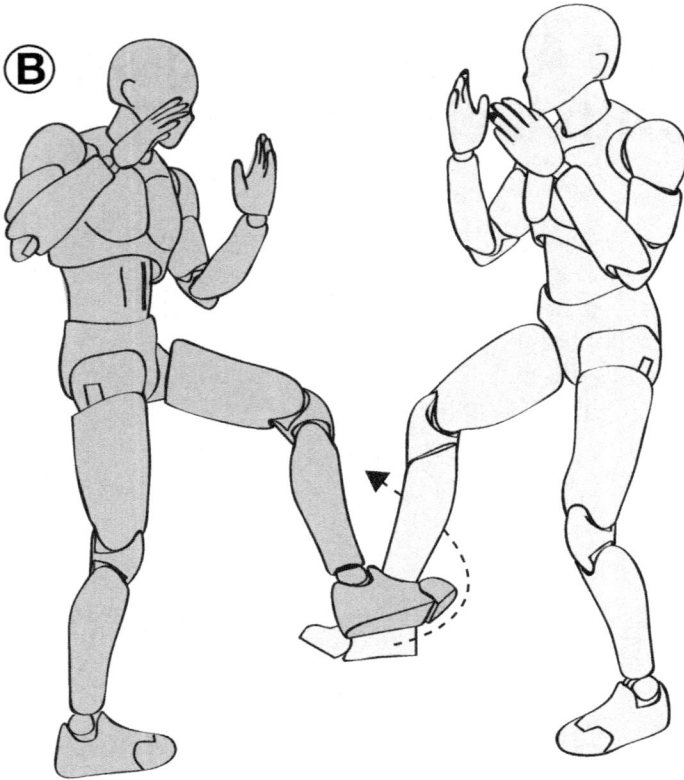

Differently from the previous defense, the reference for the angle of the left foot, which deflects the kick, is as if it were pointing at 11 o'clock (B).

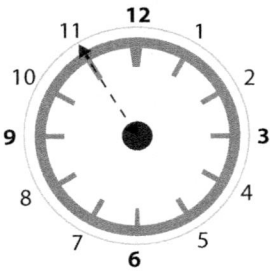

C

After the deflection, launch an attack of Right-Hand Boxing Strike and go ahead with the continuations (C).

5 Defense Against a High Regular Kick

The High Regular Kick's objective is to hit areas on the opponent's chest and face (A). The defense is done with two simultaneous movements: one step to deflect the body and the deflection of the kick. The step is taken forward, diagonally, toward the opponent's "dead" side.

At the same time, the left forearm's central area deflects the kick (B). Next, a boxing hammer fist (C) is delivered aimed at the opponent's face. As from there, the continuations start with more attacks.

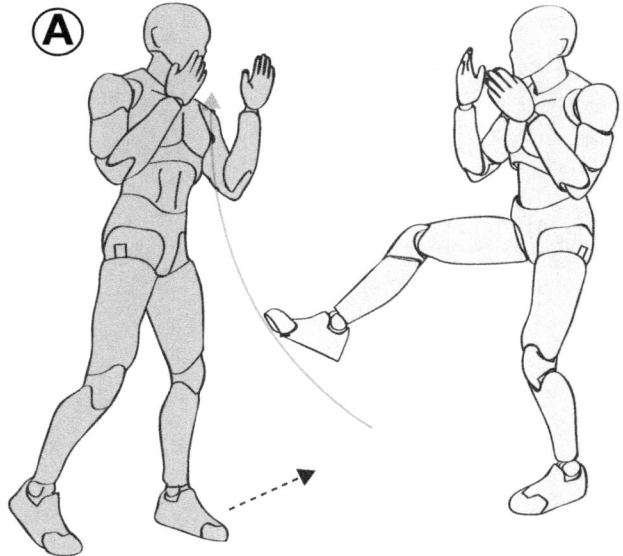

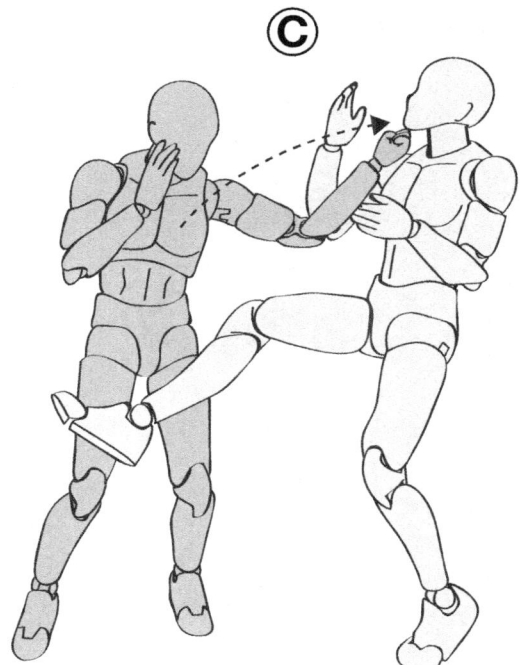

6 Sitting Defense Against a Regular Kick N°1

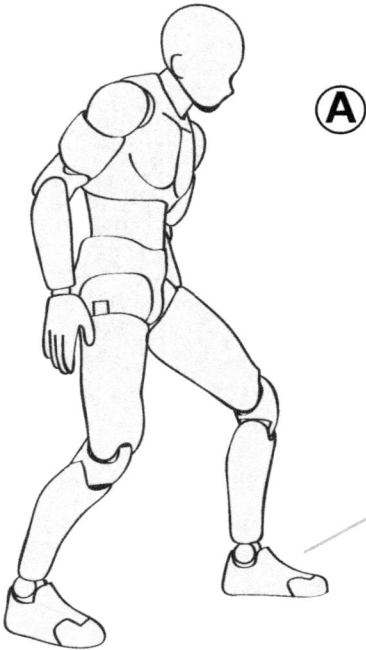

A

In the Sitting Defense Against a Regular Kick N°1, the opponent comes close to kick with the left leg (A).

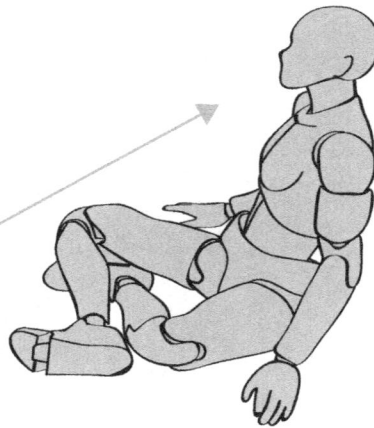

B

The kick is deflected with the left forearm and, at the same time, the very defense helps boosting and deflecting the body to the side opposed to the kick (B). Even while sitting, the hip rotates to get out of the line of attack, thus easing the deflection.

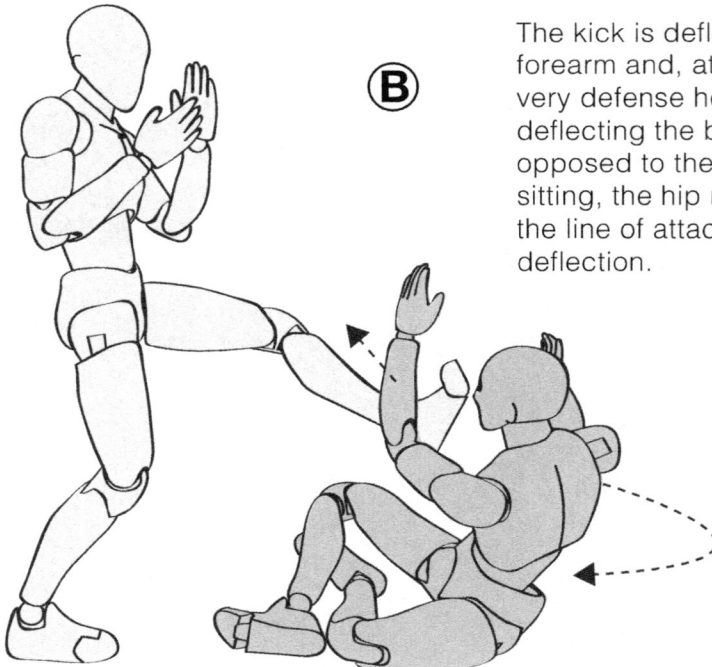

With the strength of the impact of the kick deflection with the forearm plus the deflection done by rotating the hip (B), the body naturally goes to the left side and, so, for the defense to continue and to prevent a second attack by the opponent, the heel of the left hand makes a support on the ground and, at the same time, a Regular kick is delivered in the opponent's groins (C).

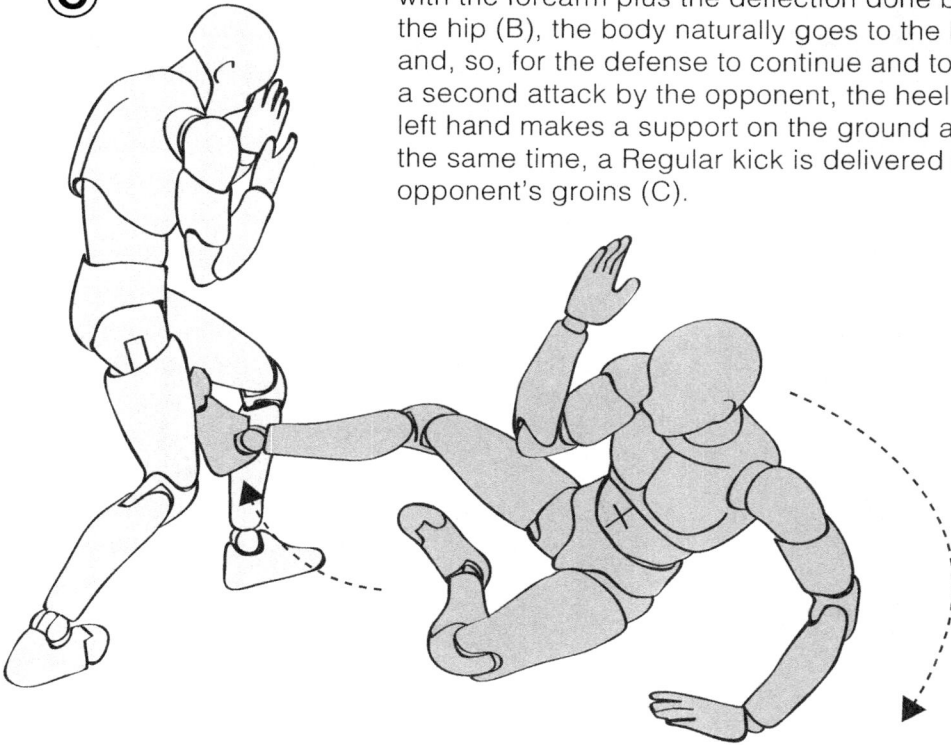

The heel of the left hand continues on the ground together with the left knee so that a heel kick is struck in the opponent's knee (D). Supported by the hand and the knee on the floor, now it is possible to get up easily (D).

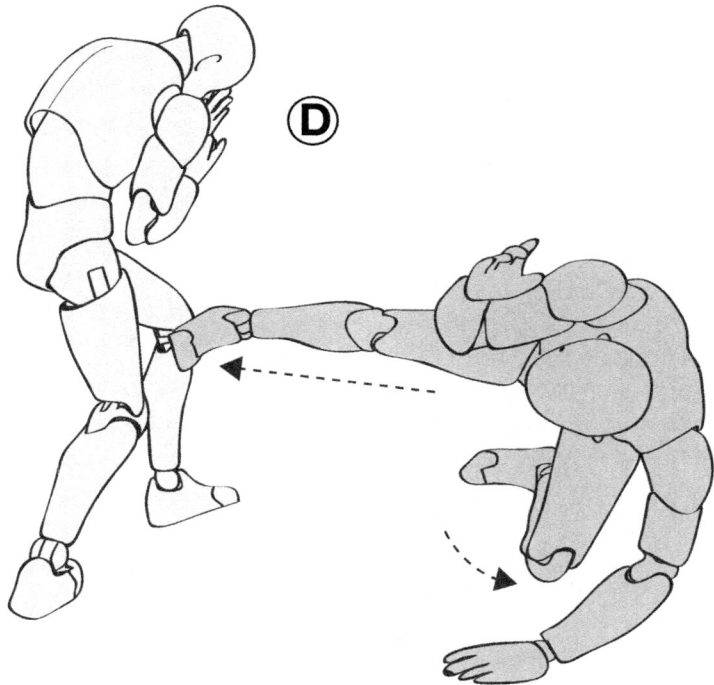

Sergio Nisenbaum

7 Sitting Defense Against a Regular Kick N°2

In the Sitting Defense Against a
Regular Kick N°2, the opponent
comes closer to kick with the
right leg (A).

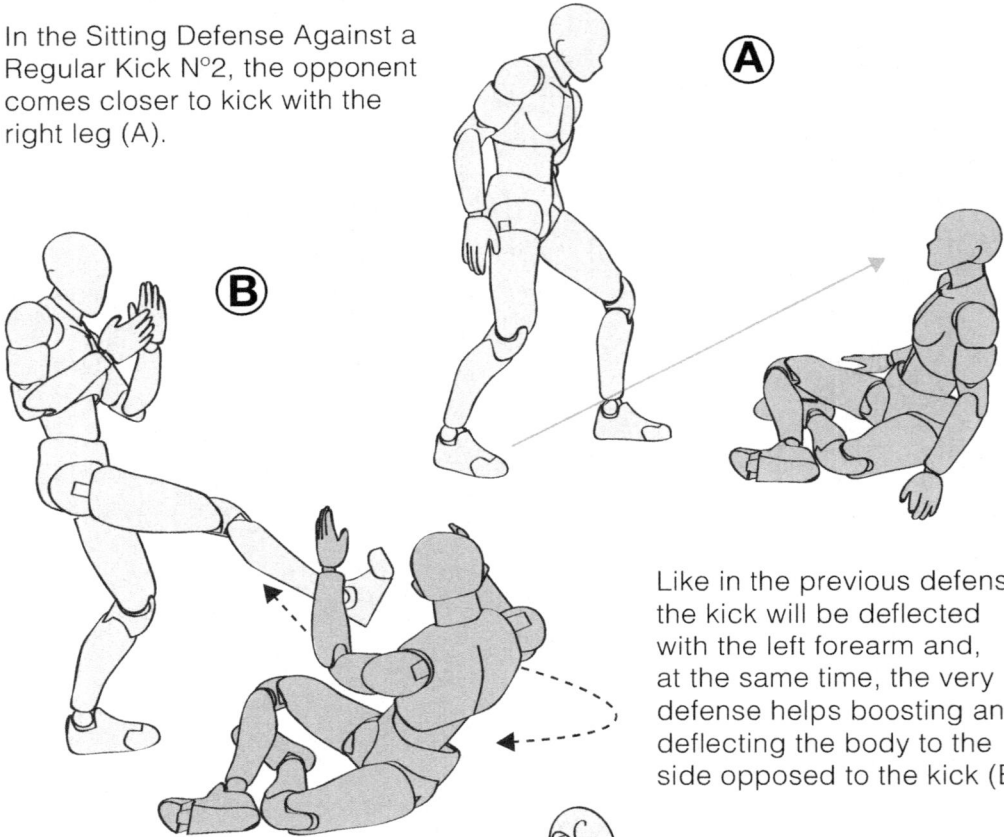

Ⓐ

Ⓑ

Like in the previous defense,
the kick will be deflected
with the left forearm and,
at the same time, the very
defense helps boosting and
deflecting the body to the
side opposed to the kick (B).

However, here is the big
difference related to the
previous defense: support
is offered by a larger area,
which includes the heel of
the hand and the left forearm,
and virtually the whole side of
the left leg. The body is lying
sideways, and a heel kick on
the knee will be delivered on
the opponent's left leg. This
position also eases getting
up (C).

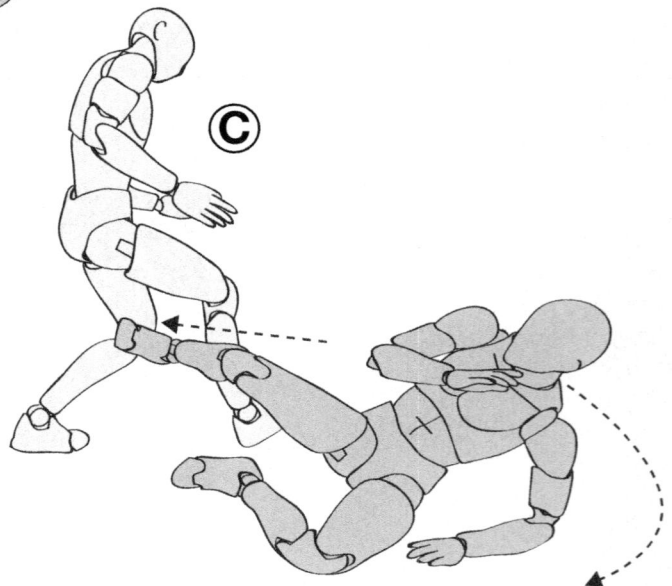

Ⓒ

8 Defense Against a Heel Kick N°1

In this situation, the opponent is standing on the side to kick with his right leg at the level of the knees (A). The Defense Against a Heel Kick N°1 happens with three simultaneous movements.

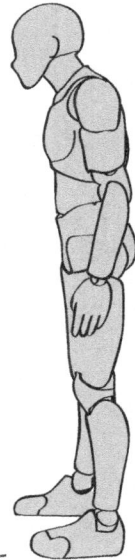

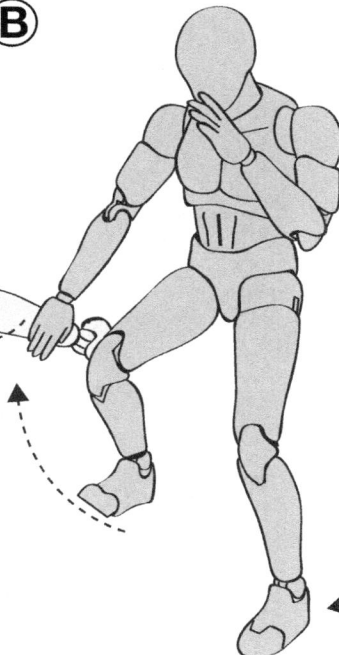

The three movements happen as follows: the left foot advances diagonally to the left and, at the same time, the right knee is raised to get out of the line of attack of the kick, and the heel of the right hand deflects the kick. The body ends up by lying virtually on the back turned to the line of the opponent's kick (B).

At this moment, after the deflection, the right foot is still raised, and it must go down to the ground. By taking advantage of the position of the right leg with the knee raised and the body lying on the back (B), deliver a heel kick from behind the opponent's left or right knee (C).

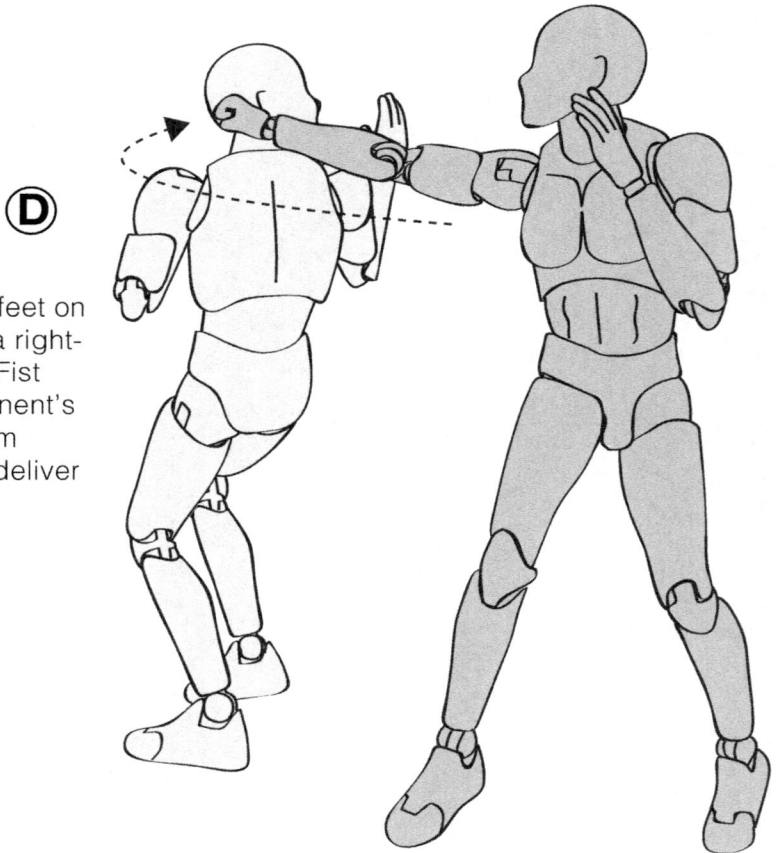

Finally, with the two feet on the ground, launch a right-hand Side Hammer Fist (D) toward the opponent's face or nape. As from there, if necessary, deliver more continuations.

9 Defense Against a Heel Kick N°2

In the Defense against a Hill Kick N°2, the defense is the same as N°1, but now, the opponent is positioned on the side to kick with the left leg at the knees' level. As much as in the previous defense, three simultaneous movements are made.

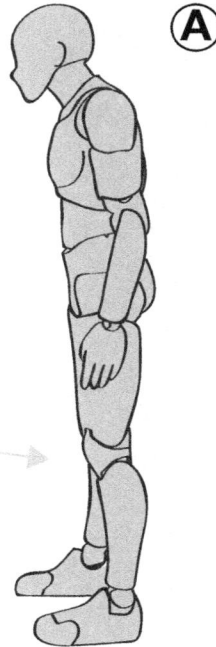

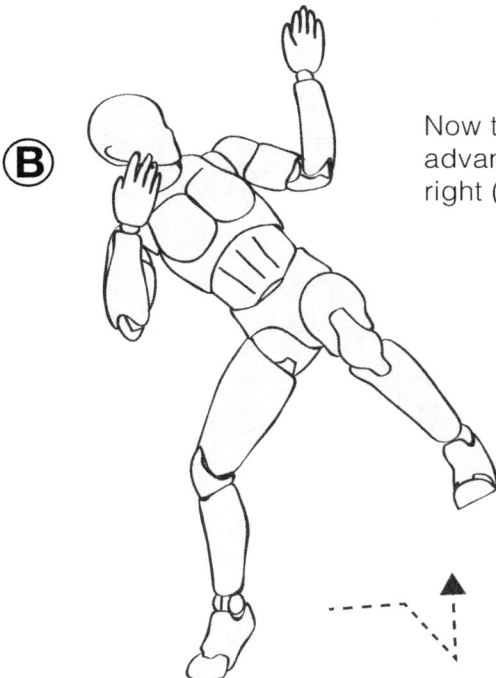

Ⓐ

Now the right foot will advance diagonally to the right (B).

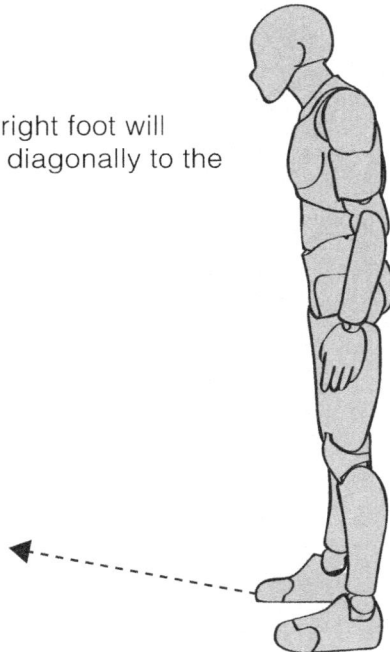

Ⓑ

(C)

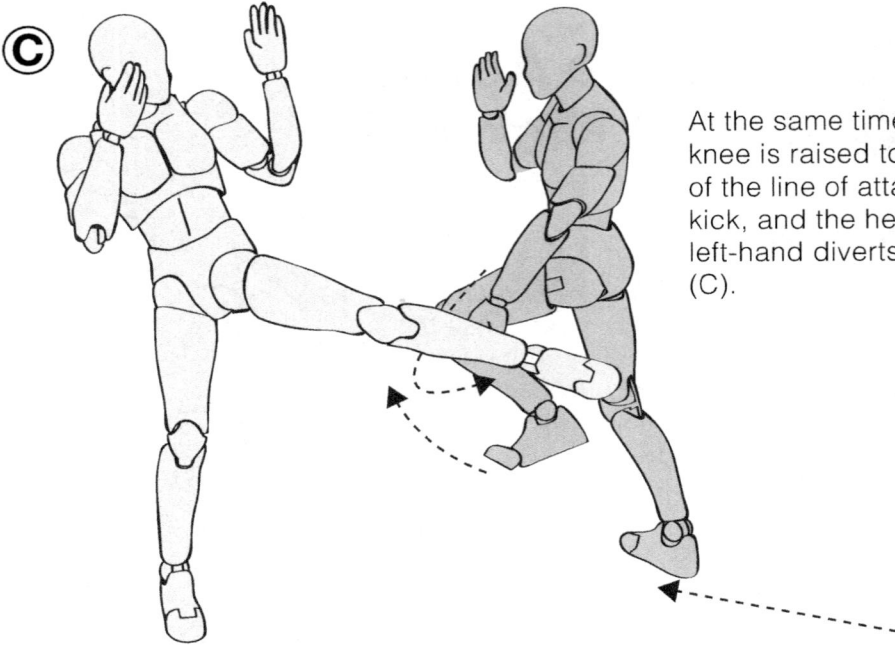

At the same time, the left knee is raised to get out of the line of attack of the kick, and the heel of the left-hand diverts the kick (C).

(D)

The body also ends up by being virtually with the back turned to the line of the opponent's kick (D).

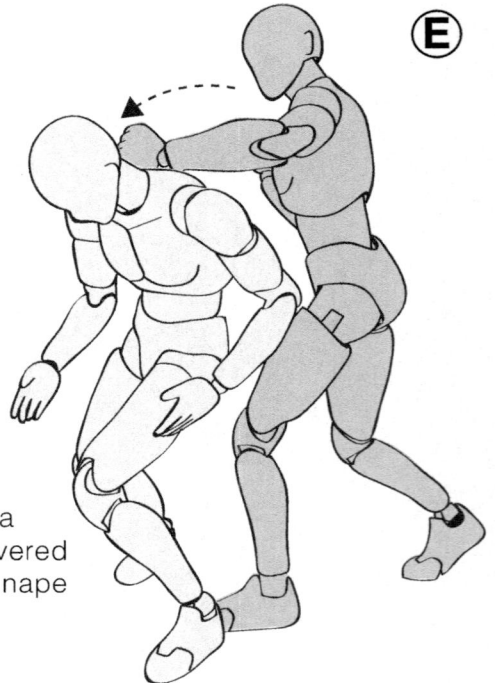

(E)

With both feet firm on the ground, a left-hand Side Hammer Fist is delivered toward the area of the opponent's nape (E).

10 Defense Against a Heel Kick Nº3

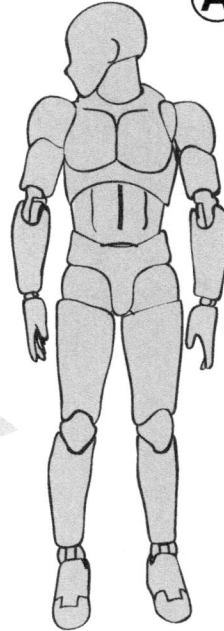

In the Defense Against a Heel Kick Nº3 both adversaries are positioned sideways (A). The intention now is to prevent the opponent from starting the kick.

The knee goes up to get out and away from the line of attack, but mainly for the purpose of interrupting and blocking the opponent's kick (B).

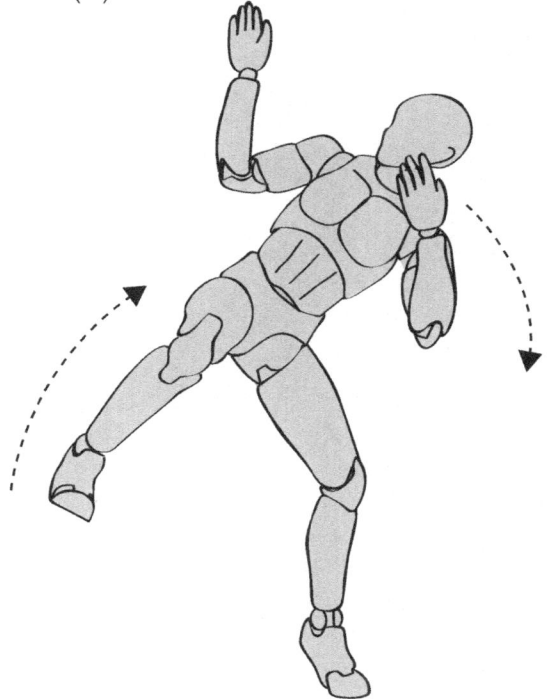

The block is also made with a heel kick on the opponent's left knee (C).

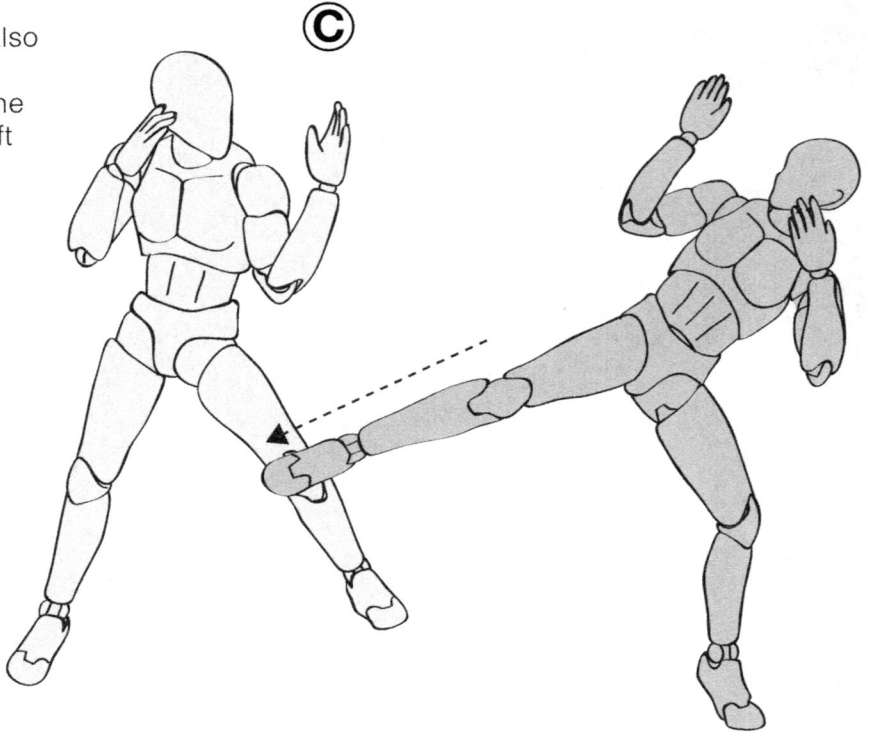

Ⓒ

Ⓓ

Next, soon after the block and with both feet already on the ground, a right-hand Side Hammer Fist is delivered (D) toward the opponent's face.

11 Defense Against a Defense Kick N°1

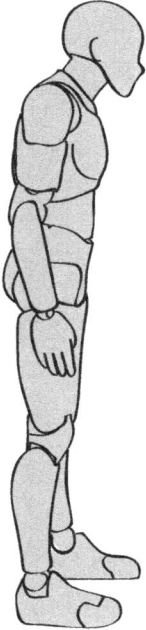

(A)

As the Defense Kick is a kick at the chest level, it is considered high and, so, it can be defended like in the Defense Against a High Regular Kick (Exercise N°5). The opponent's distance to deliver the kick can be a bit longer than that in the High Regular Kick (A).

To get out of the line of attack it is necessary to take a diagonal step forward with the left foot (B), thus getting out toward the opponent's "dead" side.

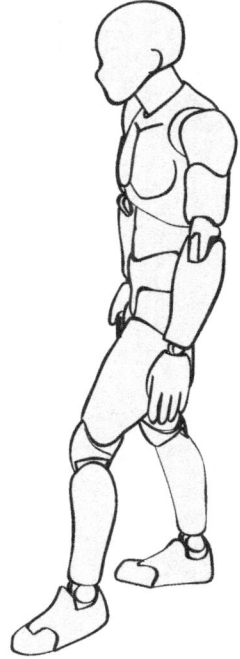

(B)

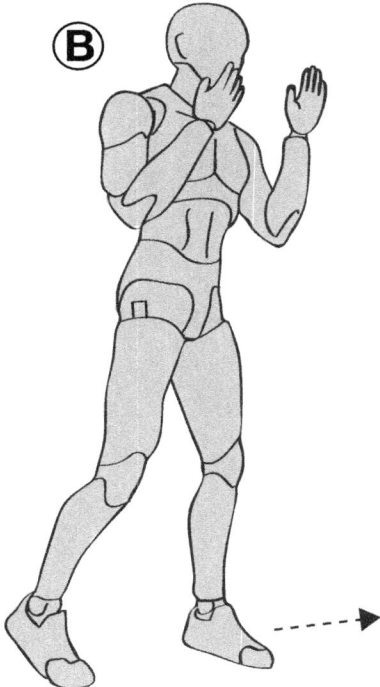

C

Distance

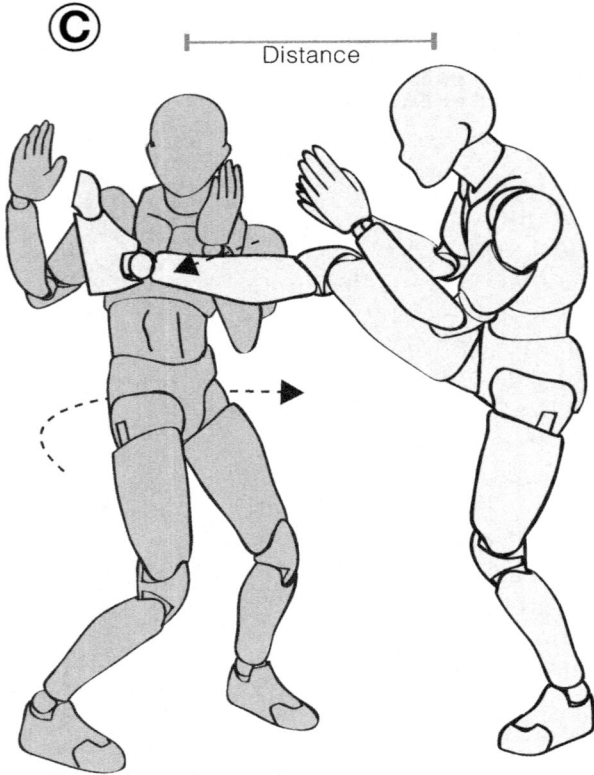

The difference between the Defense Against a High Regular Kick and this defense happens at this moment because the Defense Kick is delivered virtually in a straight line. The set of three simultaneous movements, the diagonal step, and the strong rotation of the hips together with the left forearm, which deflects the kick, help moving fully out of the line of attack (C).

D

Next, a Hammer Fist (D) is delivered aiming at reaching the opponent's face. As from there, start the continuations with more attacks.

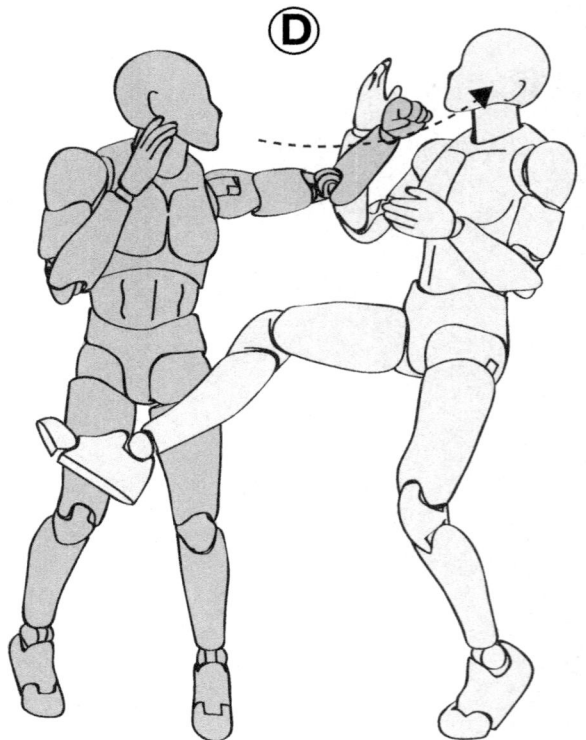

12 Defense Against a Defense Kick N°2

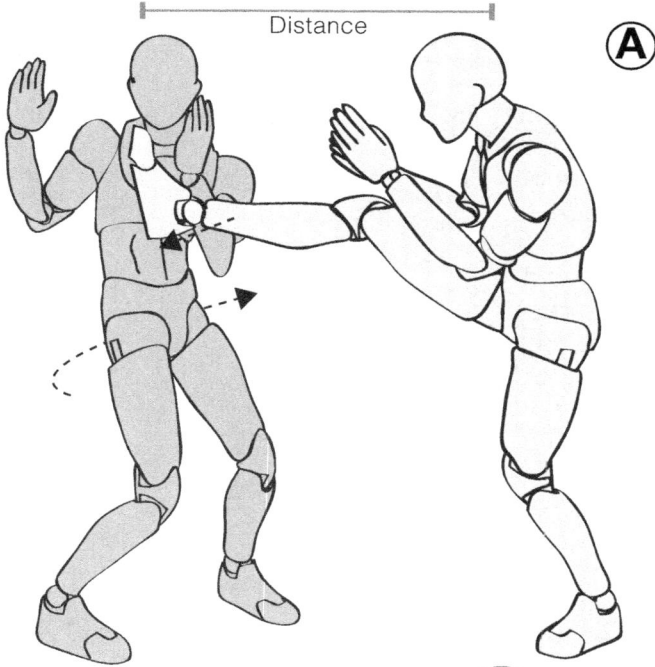

Distance

(A)

The Defense Against a Defense Kick N°2 is done like in the Defense Against a Defense Kick N°1. The difference here is that the diagonal step to get out of the line of attack is more open (A), thus creating a bigger distance to the line of attack, and making it impossible that a Side Hammer Fist, like in the previous exercise, reaches the target efficiently.

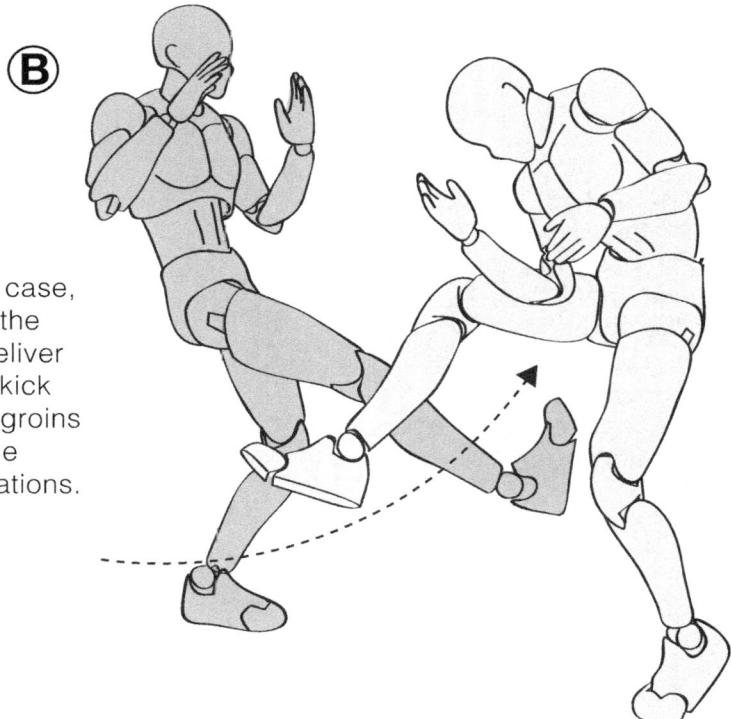

(B)

That is why, in this case, take advantage of the long-distance to deliver a right-leg regular kick on the opponent's groins (B), and then do the necessary continuations.

13 Defense Against a Sickle N°1

(A)

In the Defense Against a Sickle Kick N°1, the movement to move out of the line of attack is also especially important and should be done quickly. The objective of the circular movement of the Sickle Kick is to hit you on the side. In this case, the defense is against a high Sickle Kick.

(B)

Starting from the Regular Stance (A), deflection has two objectives: the first is to move away from the kick, and the second, to protect with the forearms the head and neck area (B).

C

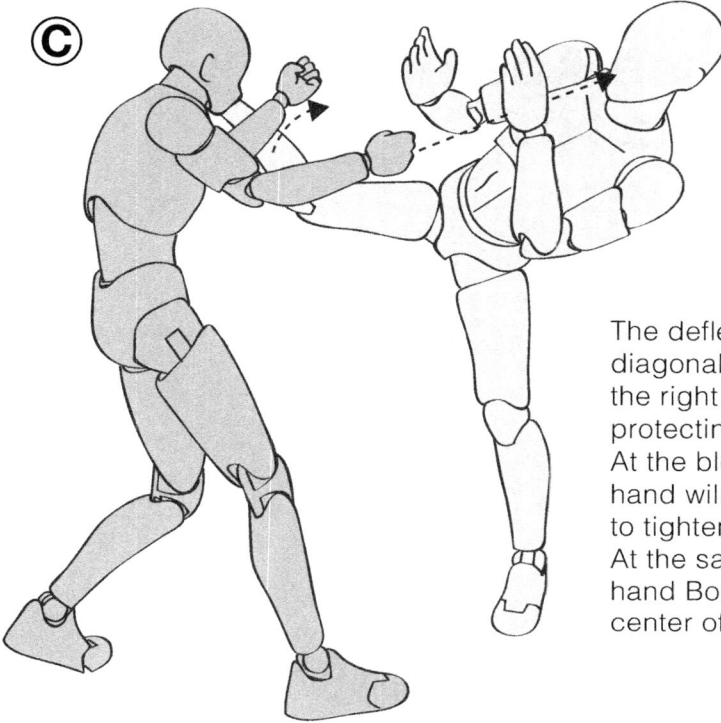

The deflection is done by taking a diagonal step to the right side with the right foot, and by blocking and protecting with the left forearm. At the blocking moment, the left hand will be closed and locked to tighten the forearm's muscles. At the same time, deliver a right-hand Boxing Strike toward the center of the opponent's face (C).

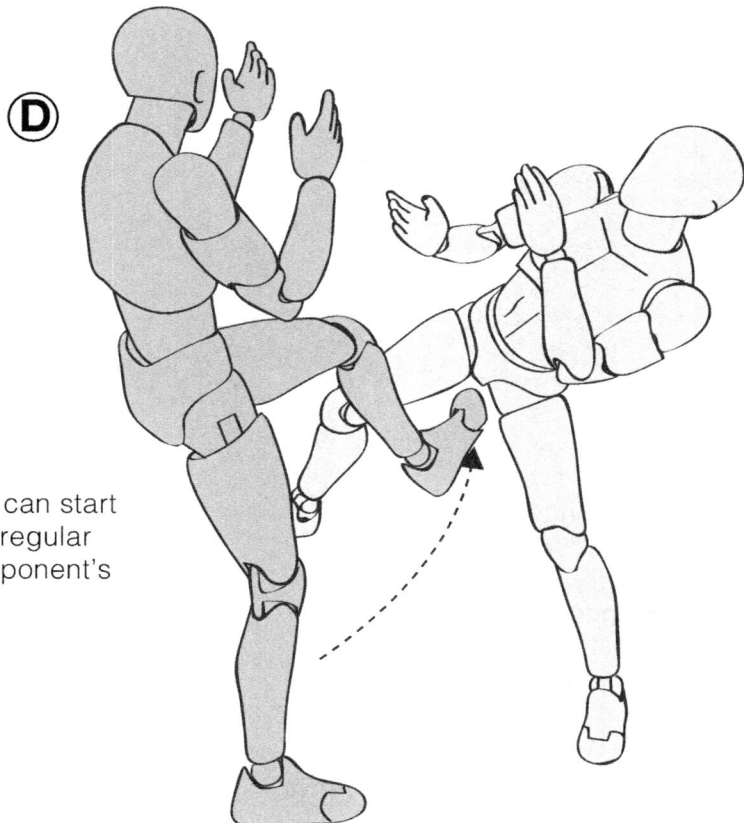

D

Continuations can start with a left-leg regular kick on the opponent's groins (D).

Sergio Nisenbaum

14 Defense Against a Sickle N°2

A

In the Defense Against a Sickle Kick N°2, the deflection is done with a step taken more to the side than diagonally, like in the previous defense. The block and protection are also made with the left forearm (A).

B

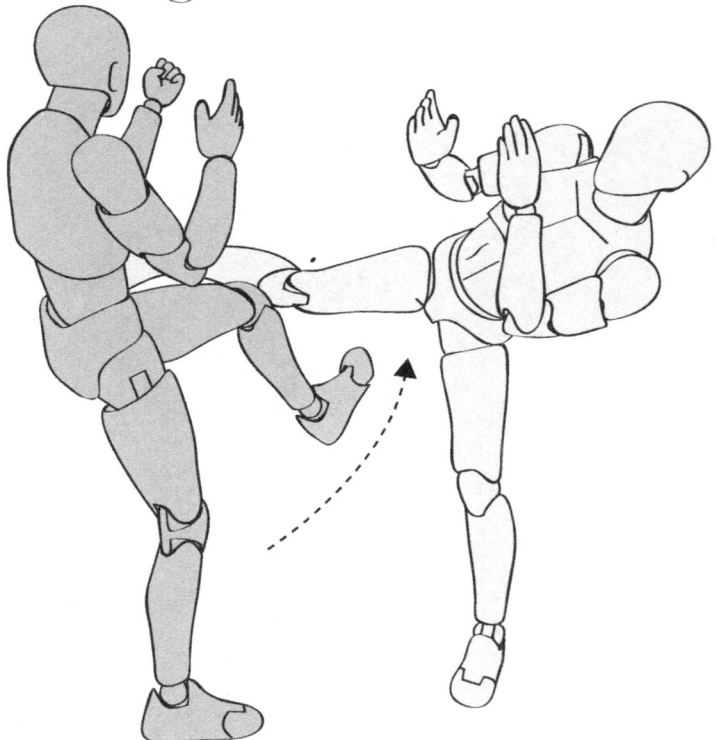

Once here the deflection is more sideways and the distance related to the opponent is longer, you should deliver a left-leg Regular Kick (B).

Immobilizations

Immobilizations will be mainly used to control the opponent by means of torsion and pressure. They cause extreme pain in sensitive points of the joints, mainly in the wrist and shoulder. As a figurative example, imagine a film scene divided into beginning, middle, and end. In Krav Maga, immobilizations are not recommended at the beginning of a situation of aggression. It is awfully hard to try to immobilize someone fully altered and aggressive without doing something before. But does it mean that you must wait for being attacked to defend yourself and be able to immobilize the opponent? The answer is no. A simple hand move in the opponent's groins already makes room for immobilization. So, let us now go to the middle of the scene. The opponent has tried to hit you with a Boxing Strike, you defend it, launches a regular kick in his groin and then you immobilize him. Finally, as from this point where you are in control, you take the opponent to another place or, if necessary, you can take him to the ground to keep him immobilized longer. To do that, sometimes it is necessary to change from one type of immobilization to another.

Next, you will see the immobilizations didactically presented. Pay attention to the varied positions of the feet and the sides of hand grabs.

You will also see how to defend against immobilizations known as Chokehold and Full Nelson.

15 Immobilization N°1

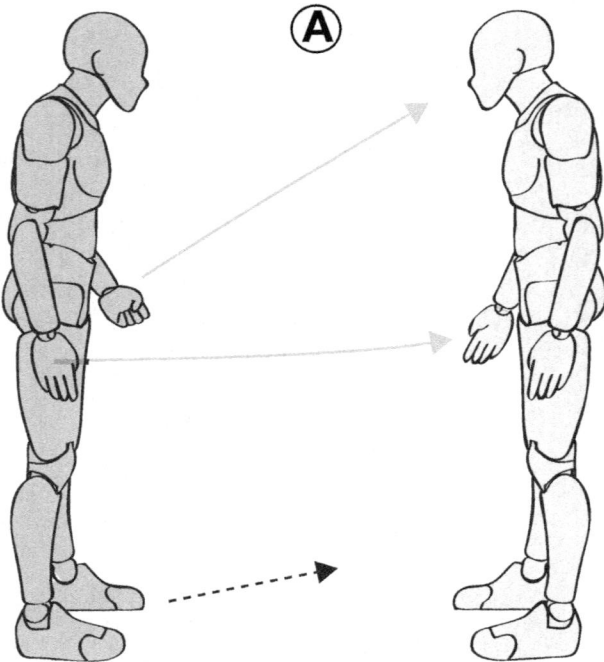

A

Immobilization N°1 happens in a very quick sequence of a set of movements. Firstly, the right hand grabs the opponent's right hand (A).

B

While grabbing the hand, you take a step toward the opponent's side for the purpose of launching a left-hand boxing strike and, at the same time, the right hand pulls the opponent's arm in the direction opposed to that of the boxing strike (B).

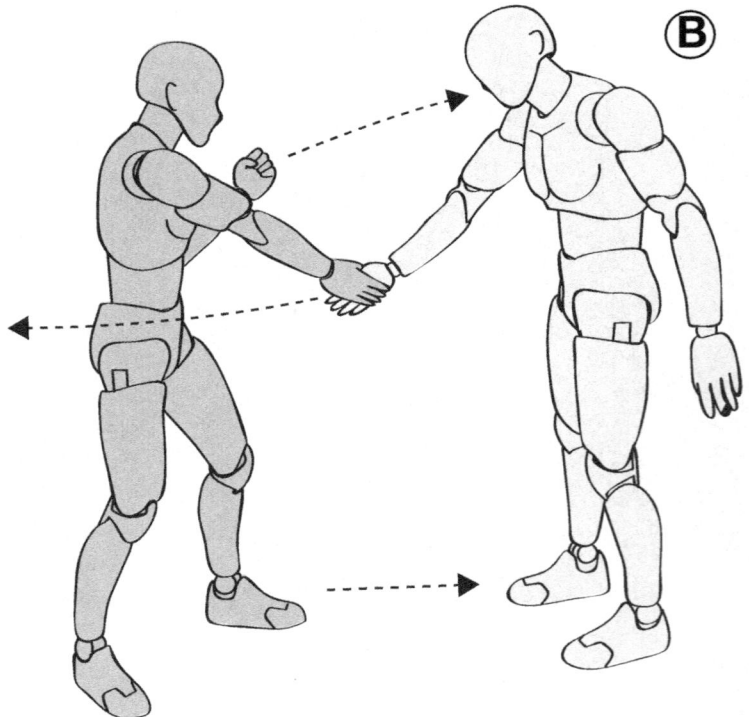

Ⓒ

1

2

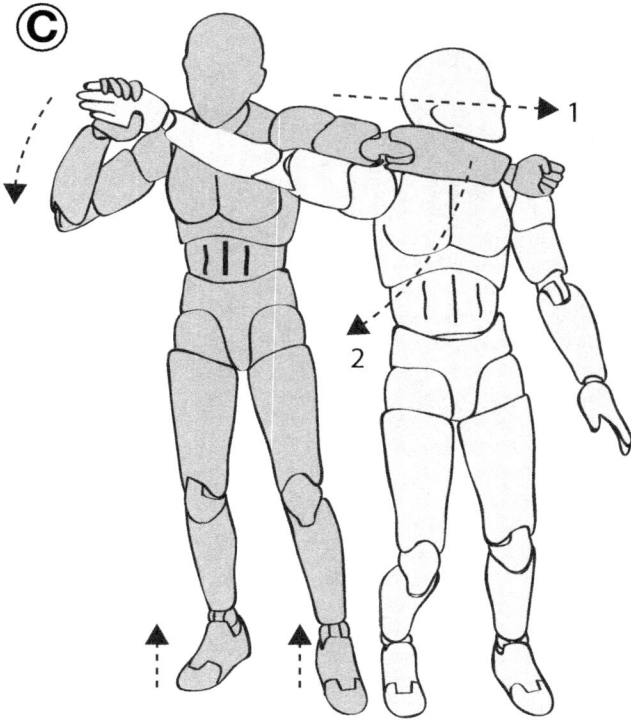

The arm that delivered the left-hand Boxing Strike (1) passes the forearm under the opponent's arm (2). At this point, to strengthen the final immobilization, stand on tiptoes (C).

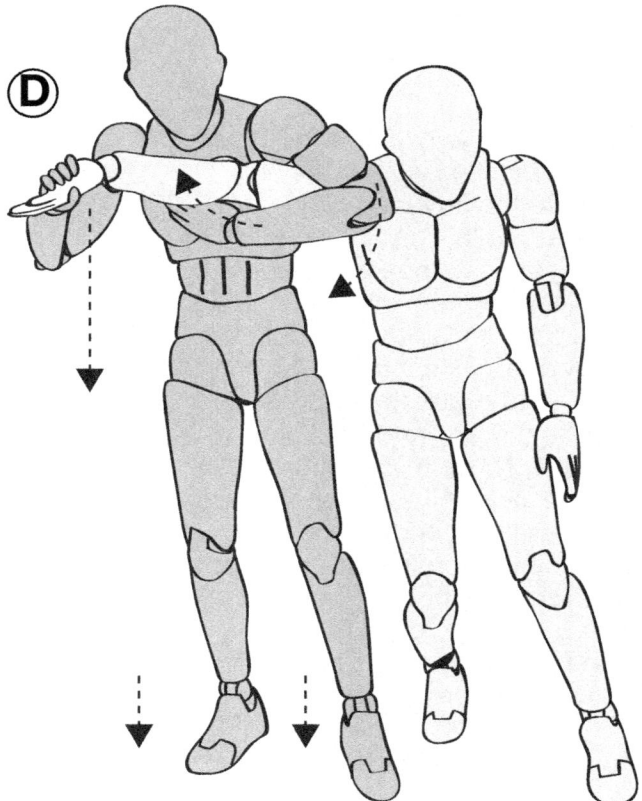

Ⓓ

The left forearm offers support to make a lever under the opponent's elbow, while the right hand twists the wrist downward.
Finally, the feet go down to lift the body weight and strengthen the immobilization pressure (D).

Sergio Nisenbaum

16 Immobilization Nº2

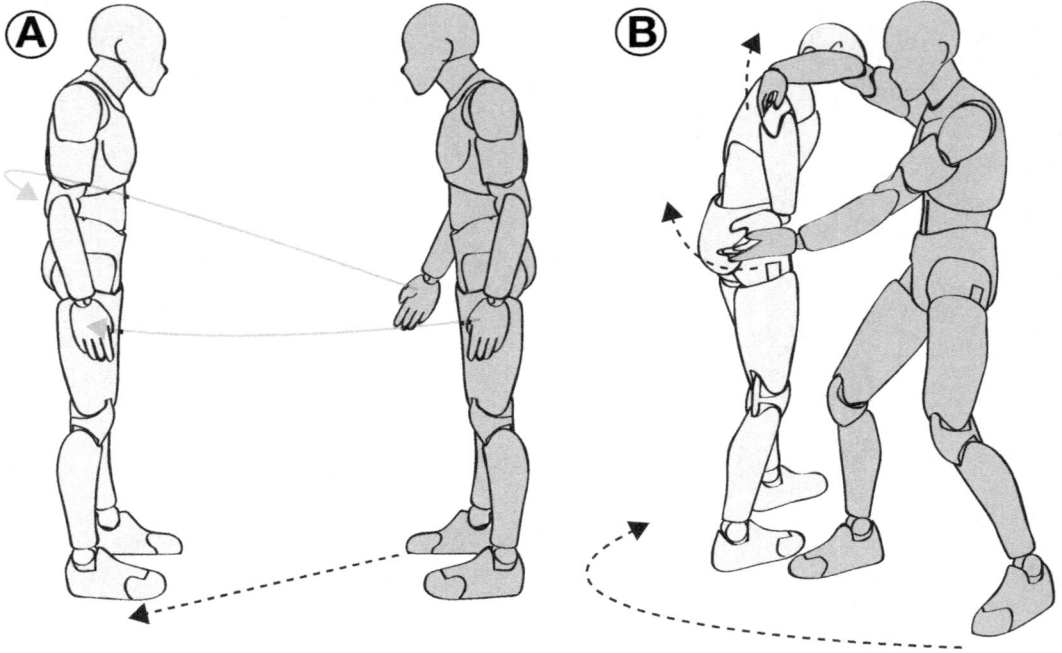

A

B

Immobilization Nº2, among all those described in the book, is the only one where the advance of the foot is crossed. In this case, the right foot advances to the left side (A). Simultaneously with the step, the right hand grabs behind the opponent's right elbow pulling it upwards, and the left hand grabs the opponent's back of the right hand and takes it backward. These movements break the resistance of the opponent's arms (B). To position yourself and complete the immobilization, the left foot goes to the right side behind the opponent. At this point, the right hand keeps on holding the elbow pressing it to the left side while the left hand rotates upward and to the right, twisting the opponent's right wrist (C).

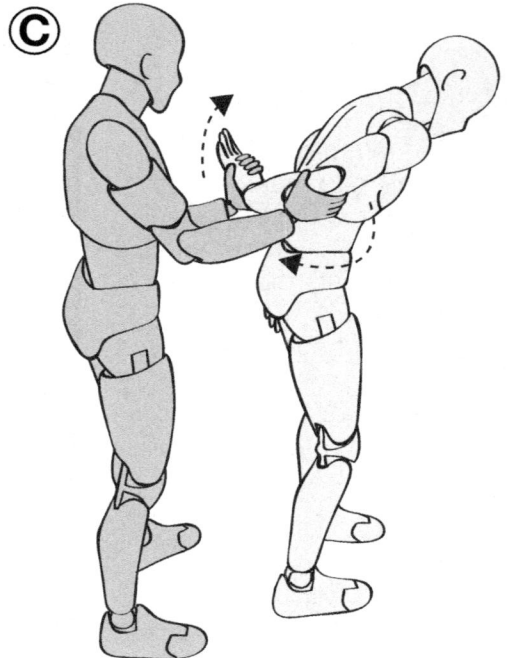

C

17 Immobilization Nº3

(A)

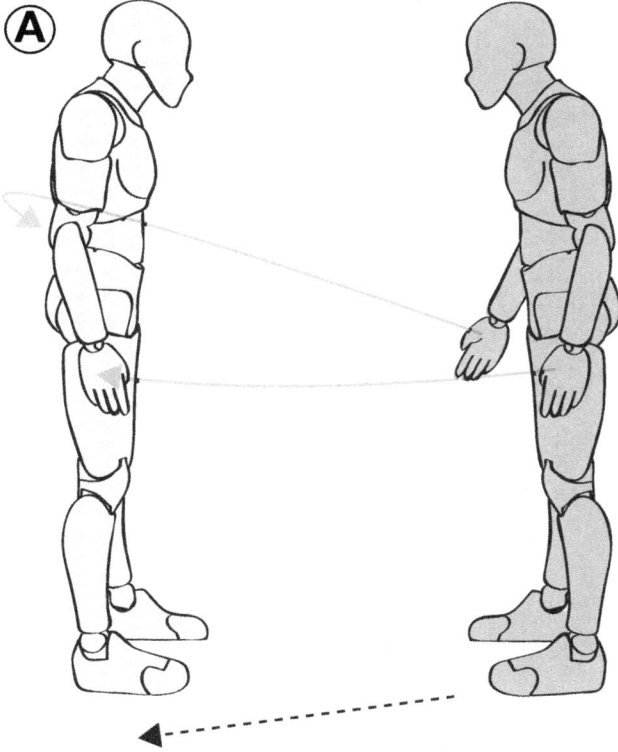

Immobilization Nº3 looks very much alike the previous one. Observe that small positioning details fully change the result. Here, the objective is to take the opponent to the ground. Different from Immobilization Nº2, the left foot advances to the left side (A).

(B)

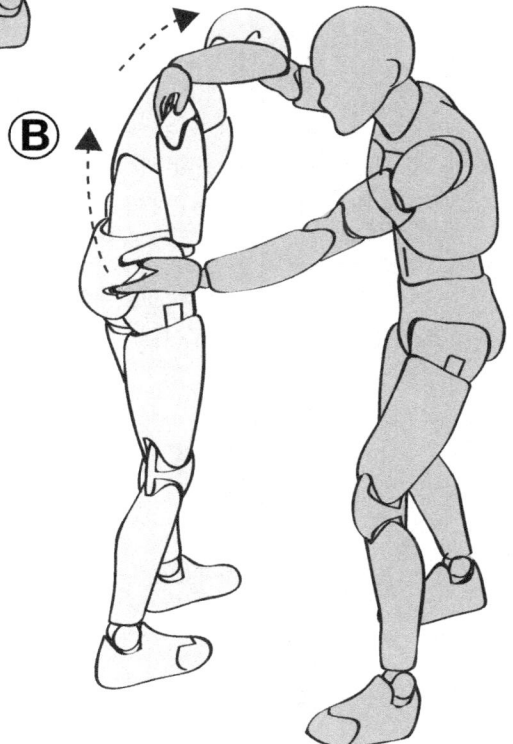

Simultaneously to the step, the right hand grabs the right elbow from behind and pulls it upwards, and the left hand holds the back of the opponent's right hand and take it upwards as well (B).

Ⓒ

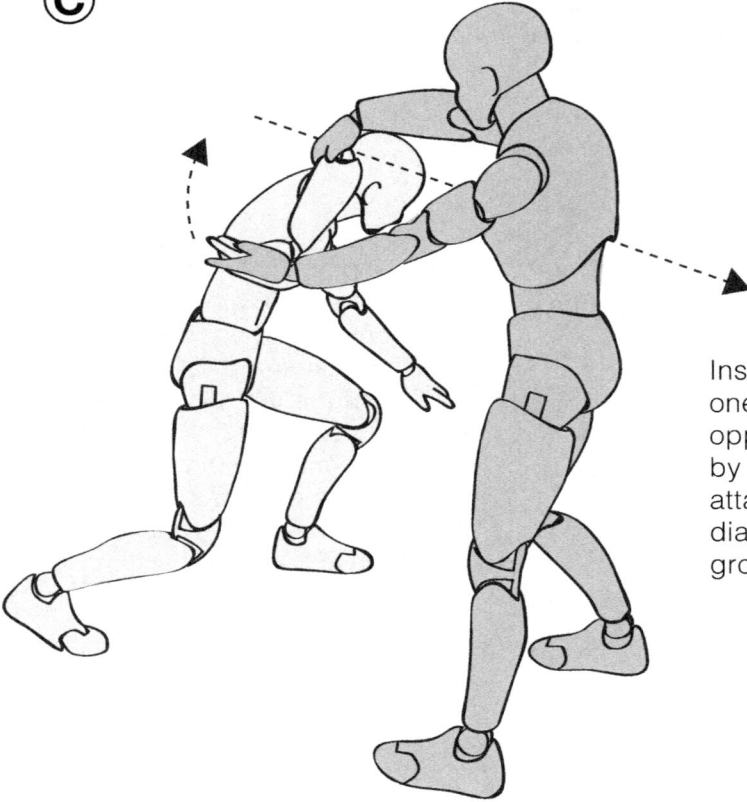

Instead of positioning oneself behind the opponent, you must stay by his side and point the attacker's right elbow diagonally toward the ground (C).

Ⓓ

To take the opponent to the ground, move sideways, maintaining the elbow and the hand under control until the opponent is completely lying on the ground (D).

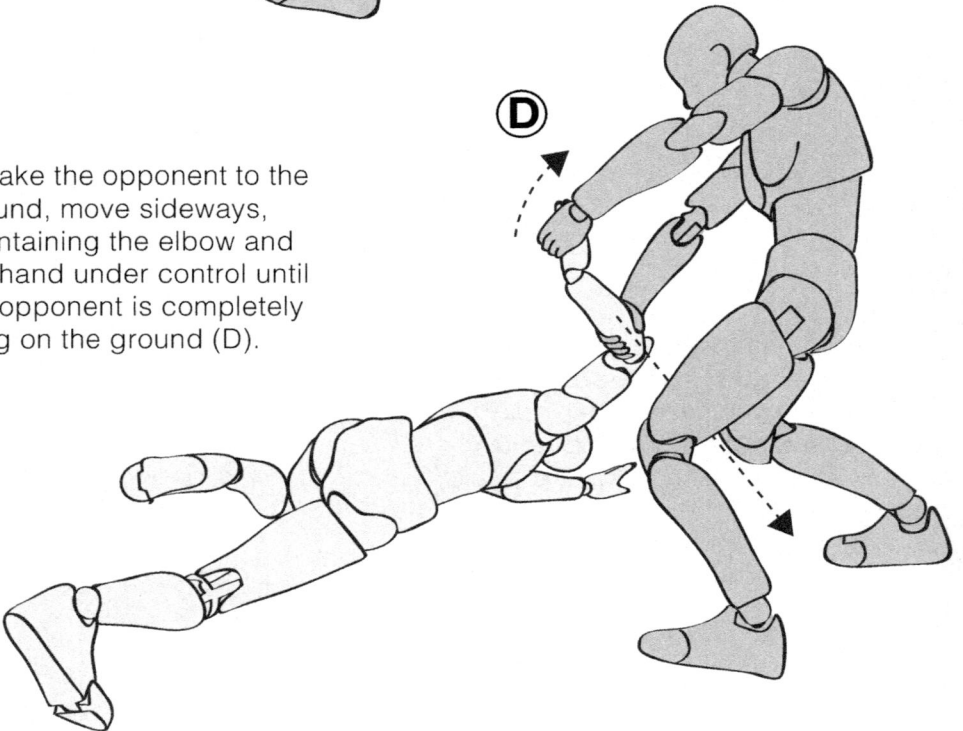

18 Immobilization N°4

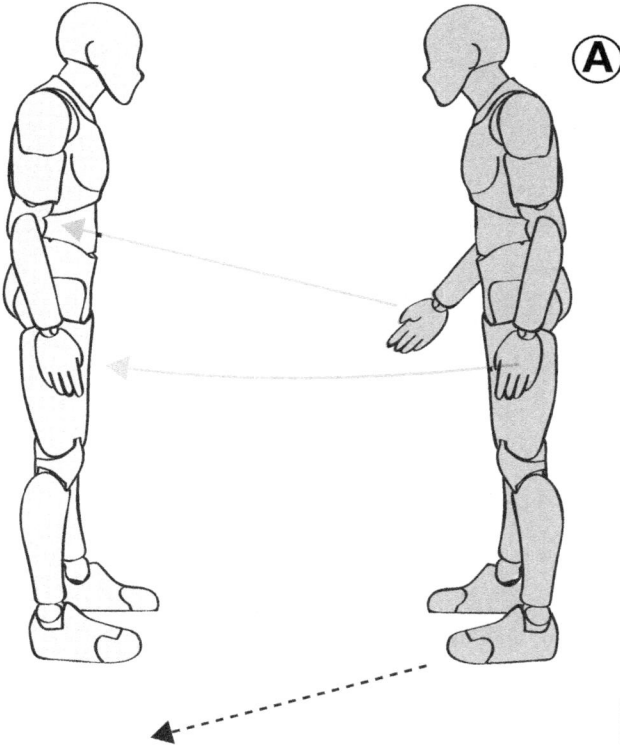

(A)

In Immobilization N°4 the left foot advances to the left side, the right hand grabs the opponent's right elbow and the left hand grabs his right hand (A).

(B)

When grabbing the elbow, and to break the resistance of the arms, the tip of the thumb of the right hand strikes the opponent's elbow fold, while the left hand helps raising his right hand behind his back. When advancing to the left, position yourself by the opponent's side (B).

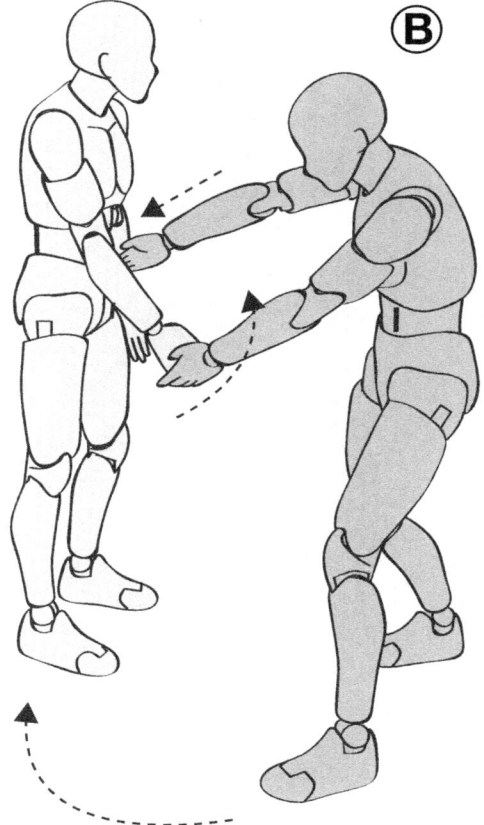

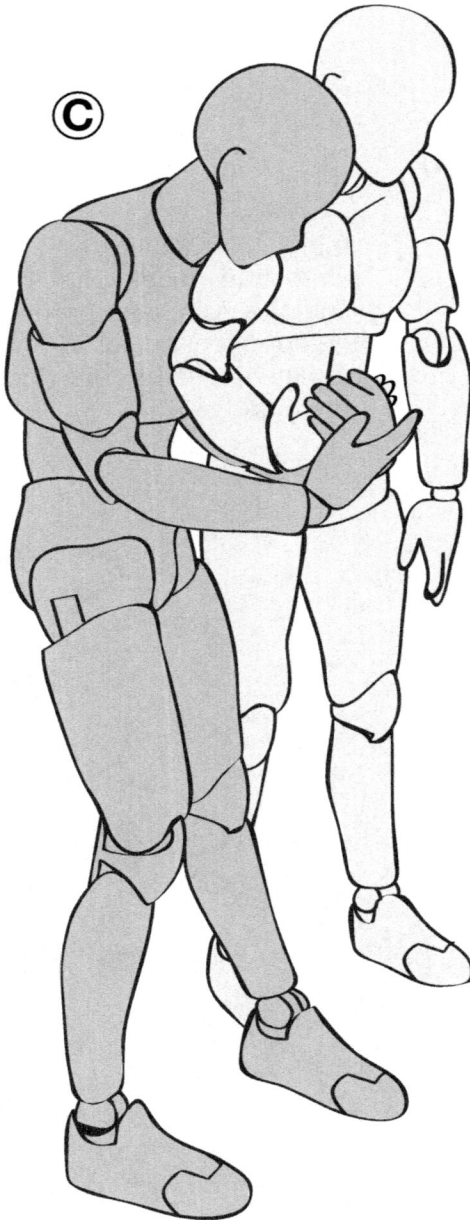

Already positioned by the opponent's side, the opponent's elbow is supported on the body, while both hands simultaneously make a strong pressure and twist the wrist of his right hand (C).

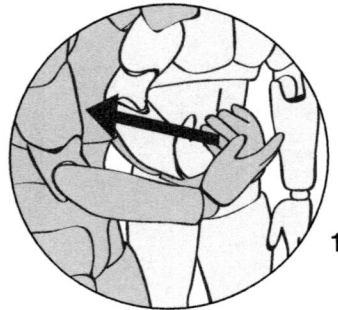

The left hand presses inward toward the support of the elbow on the body (1).

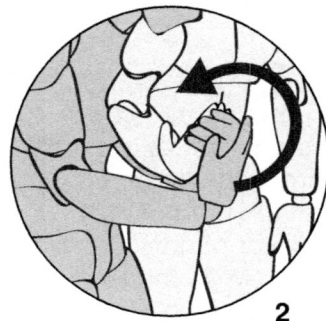

At the same time, the right hand stays on the left hand and rotates to the right (2).

19 Immobilization N°5

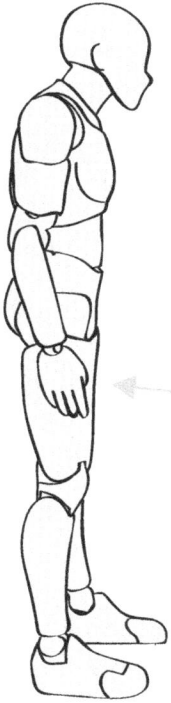

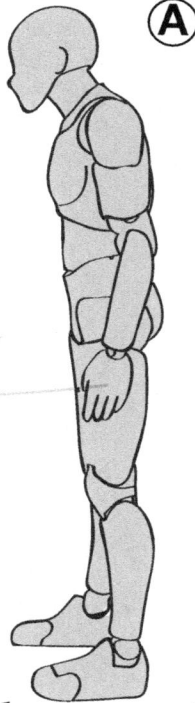

Ⓐ Carefully observe the details in the next three immobilizations. The beginning of each one is rather similar, but the positions the hands take are quite different and change the final objectives of each one of them. In Immobilization N°5 the left hand grabs the opponent's right hand while taking a diagonal step forward with the left foot (A).

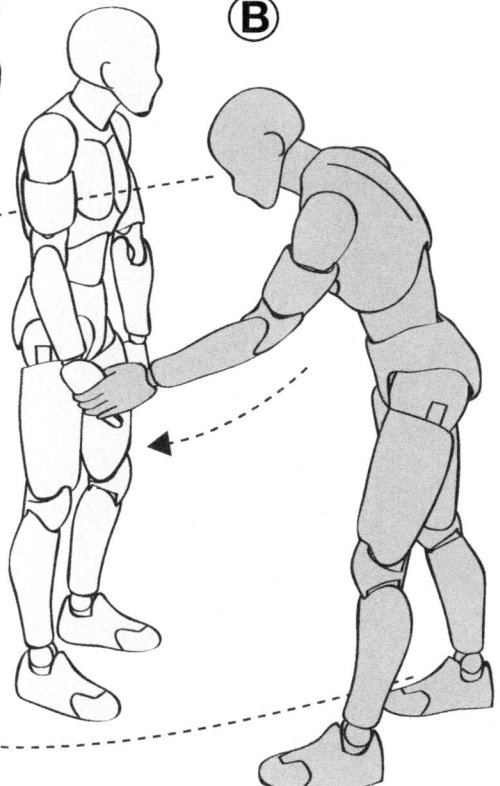

Ⓑ

Already holding the hand, another step with the right foot is necessary to go under the opponent's arm (B).

Ⓒ

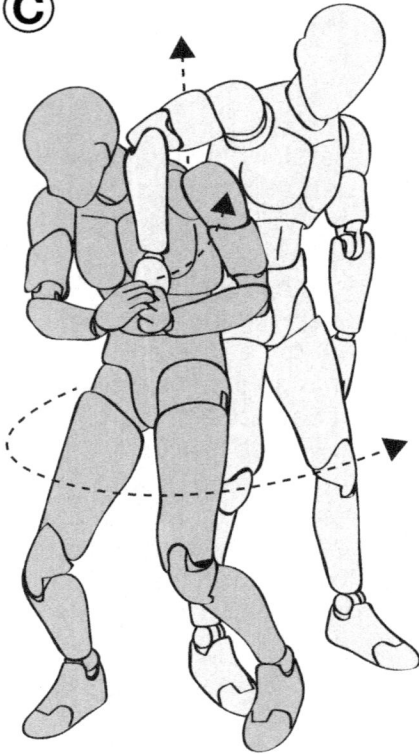

To pass under the arm, the body is positioned sideways with the back turned to the opponent's side. As already seen in some of the previous immobilizations, here the resistance of the arms is broken with a quick raise where the left shoulder hits under the opponent's armpit. The right hand grabs the opposing part of the left hand. Now you rotate your body, which will position you practically in front of the opponent (C).

Ⓓ

Jointly with the rotation, the opponent's arm is raised with the elbow pointing upward. The hands should be at least at the armpit level. Both hands twist the opponent's wrist with a rotation counterclockwise (D).

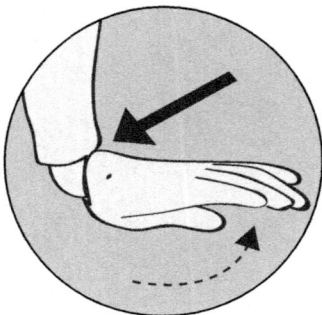

The wrist is twisted with the heel of the opponent's hand positioned downward.

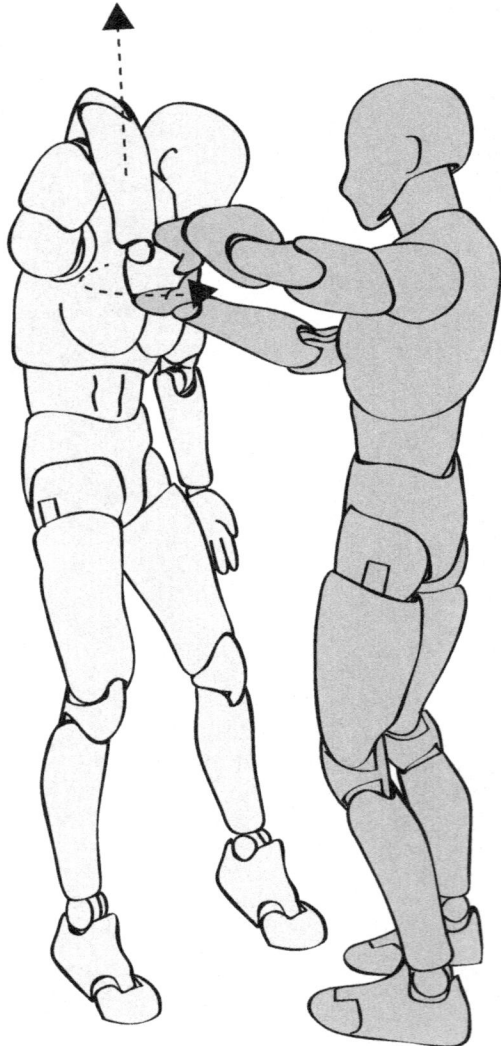

20 Immobilization N°6

In Immobilization N°6 your right hand grabs the opponent's right hand and you take a diagonal step forward with the left foot (A).

As in the previous immobilization, another step is taken with the right foot to pass under the opponent's arm (B).

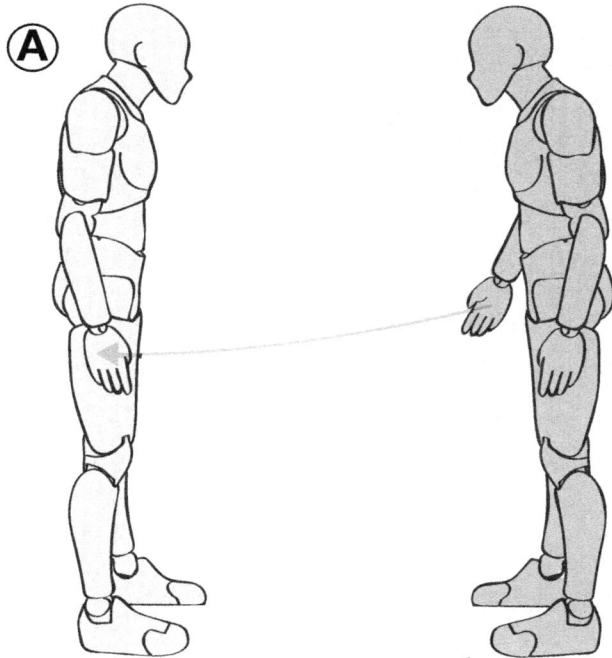

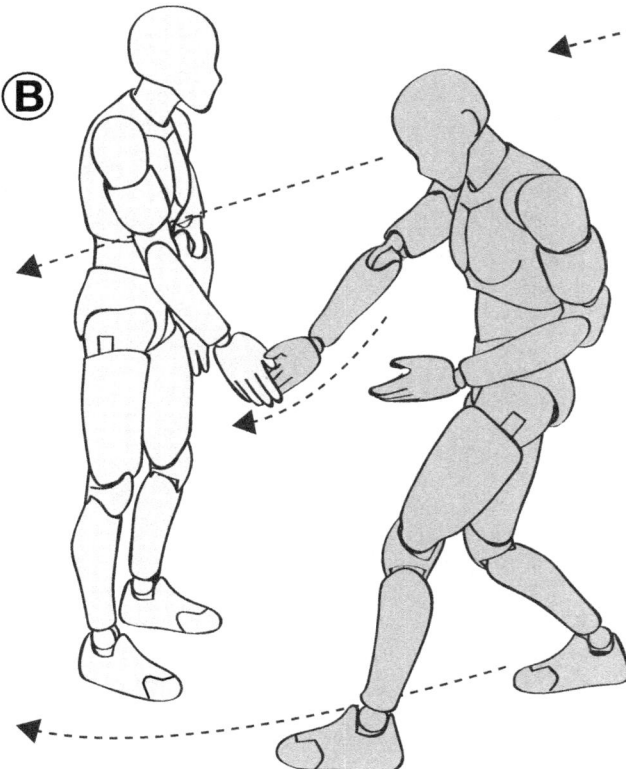

To pass under the arm, the body is positioned sideways, with the back turned to the opponent's side. As much as seen in Immobilization N°5, the left elbow passes quickly under the opponent's armpit. The left hand grabs the opposing part of the opponent's right hand. (C).

C

D

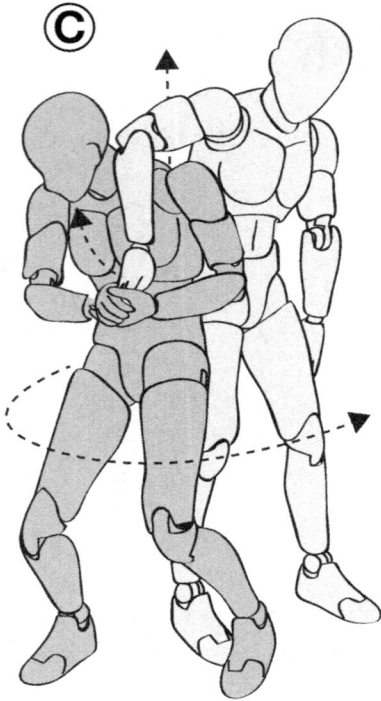

Now you rotate your body so that you are positioned practically by the opponent's side. At the same time, it is possible to twist the opponent's wrist with the left hand, holding it and turning it counterclockwise while the right hand supports and controls the elbow (D).

E

Another alternative is to twist the opponent's wrist with both hands, but remember that in neither alternatives the opponent's elbow stays below the line of the chin (E).

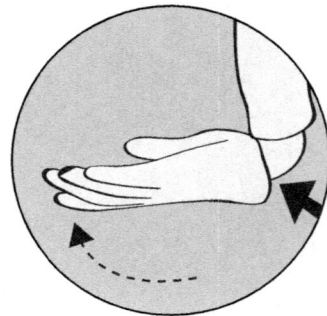

Twist the wrist with the heel of the opponent's hand turned upwards.

21 Immobilization N°7

Immobilization N°7 is called Carrousel Immobilization and it begins virtually in the same way than the Immobilization N°5. Your left hand also grabs the opponent's right hand and you take a diagonal step forward with the left foot (A).

Already holding the hand, you now must take another step with the right foot to pass under the opponent's arm (B).

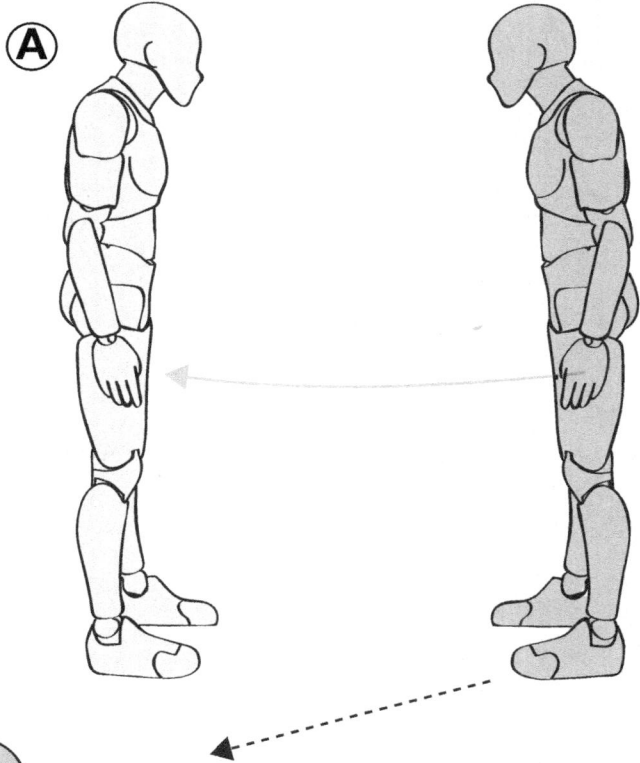

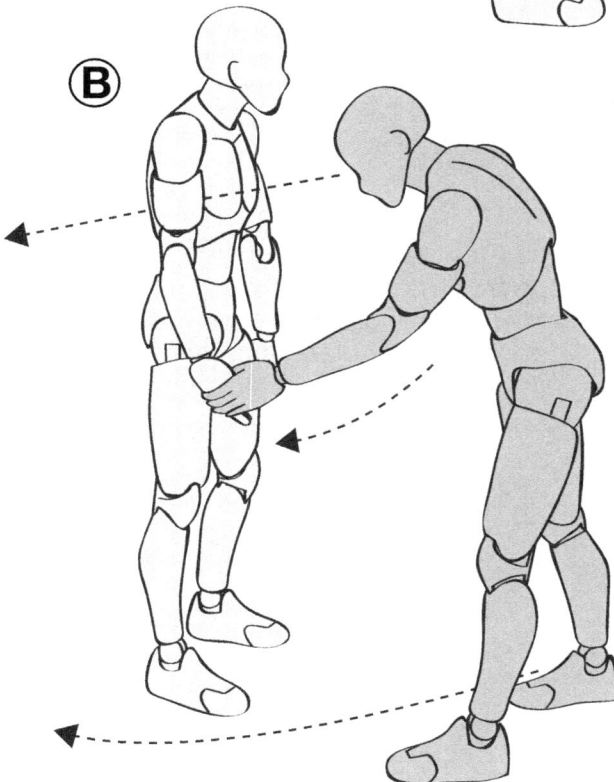

Ⓐ

Ⓑ

At this point the differences related to Immobilization N°5 start.
The movement of transition from figure (C) to figure (D) happens quite fast.
While passing under the opponent's arm, the right hand grabs the opposing part of the left hand. Now a rotation is done to position yourself practically in front of the opponent (C).

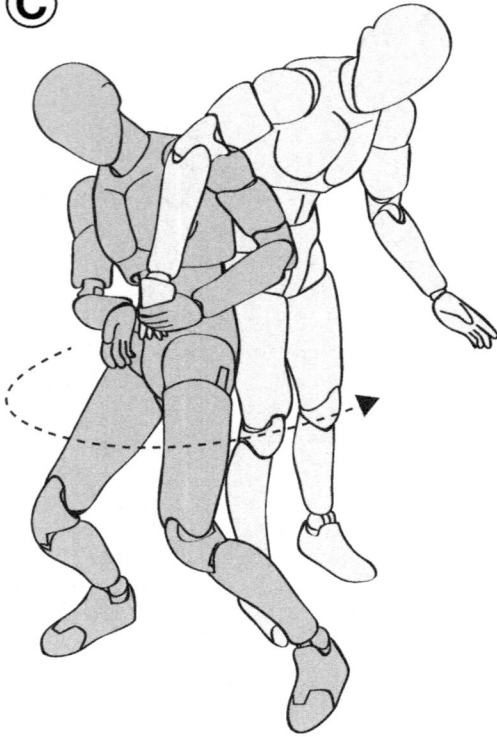

C

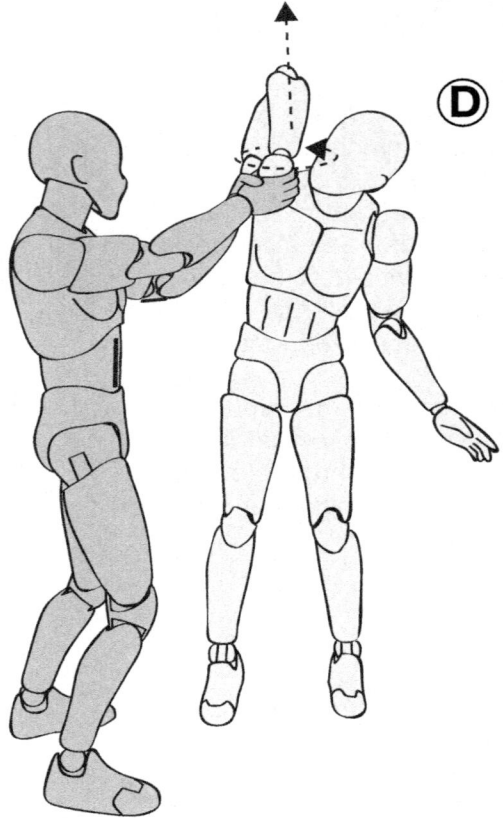

D

The opponent's arm goes up with the elbow pointing upwards (D).

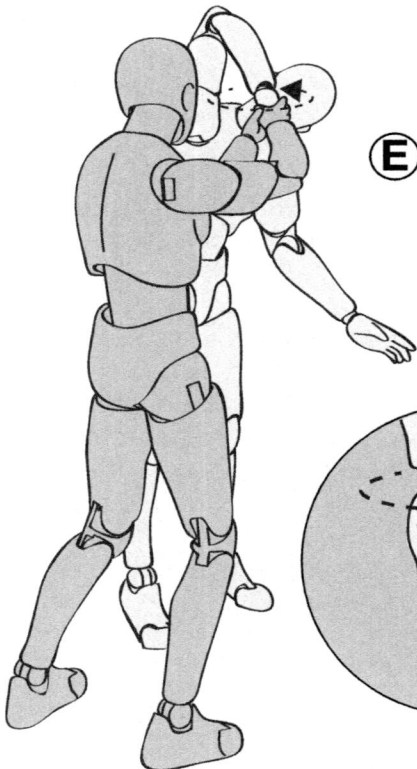

E

The two hands that are holding the opponent's right hand rotate the wrist anticlockwise (E). The twist makes the opponent also rotate, and that is why this immobilization is called Carrousel.

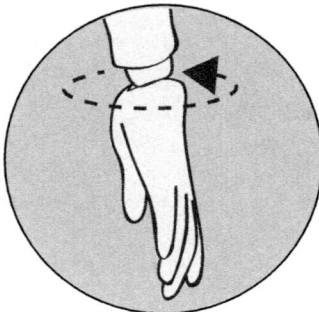

The wrist is twisted with the heel of the opponent's hand positioned vertically.

22 Escape from a Side Chokehold

Ⓐ

The Chokehold is a type of immobilization that, through pressure made on arm and forearm, choking is attempted. Once the neck is an area with vital points, the reaction must be very quick. An attack with a Chokehold Immobilization can come as a surprise exactly because the opponent may be positioned behind you (A). To escape a Side Chokehold, even if the opponent starts his attack from behind, position yourself sideways.

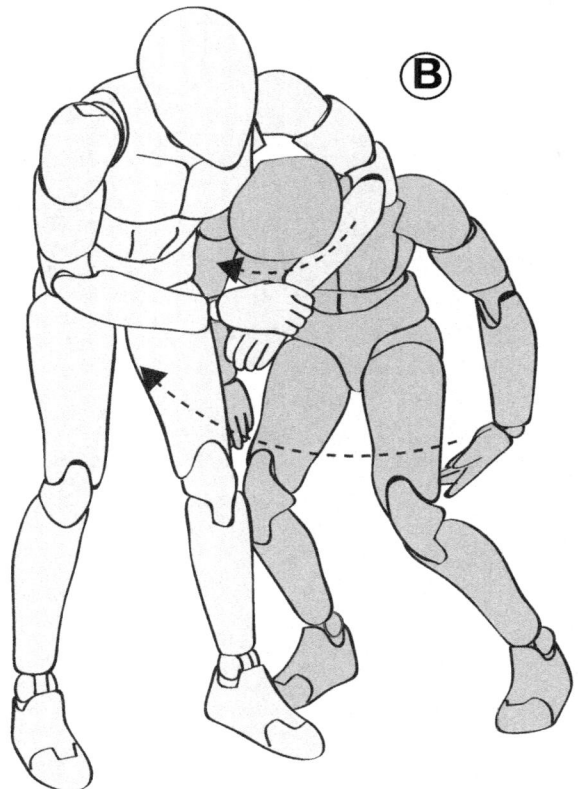

Ⓑ

The opponent holds your neck with his left arm with the help of his right arm. To prevent pressure on the trachea region and the choke, the neck must turn to the right and the left hand must be prepared to deliver an openhand move on the opponent's groins (B). In this position, it is also possible to bite the area of the opponent's ribs.

1

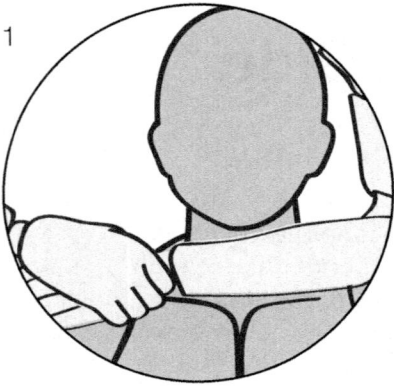

The forearms press the trachea.

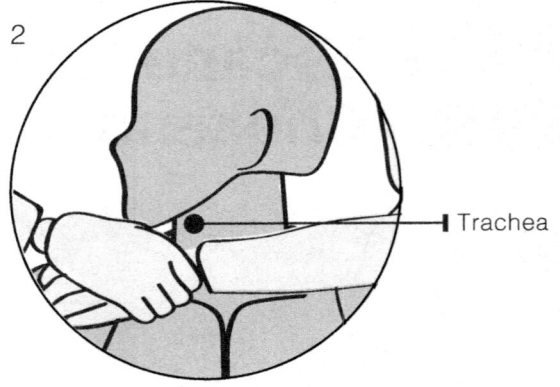

2

Trachea

The head turns sideways to alleviate the pressure on the trachea.

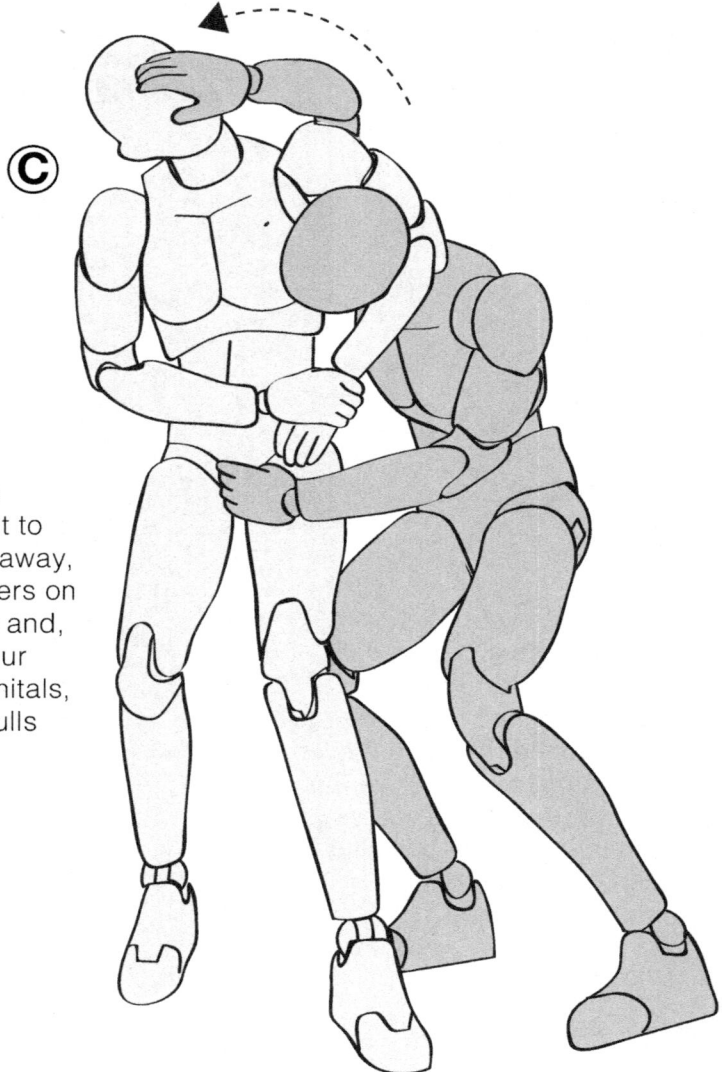

©

The right hand goes behind the opponent to move the opponent away, then places the fingers on his eyeballs or nose and, at the same time, your left hand hits his genitals, grabs tightly, and pulls (C).

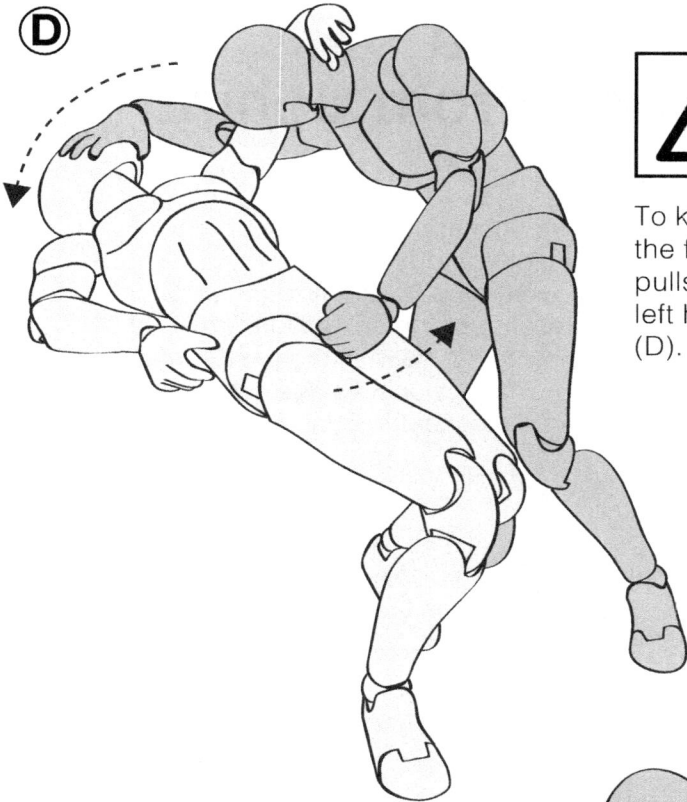

To knock down the opponent,
the finger on the eyeballs or nose
pulls the head backward and the
left hand continues to hold tight
(D).

The opponent goes
down and at this point, if
necessary, continue with
attacks with Boxing Strikes
and Regular Kicks (E).

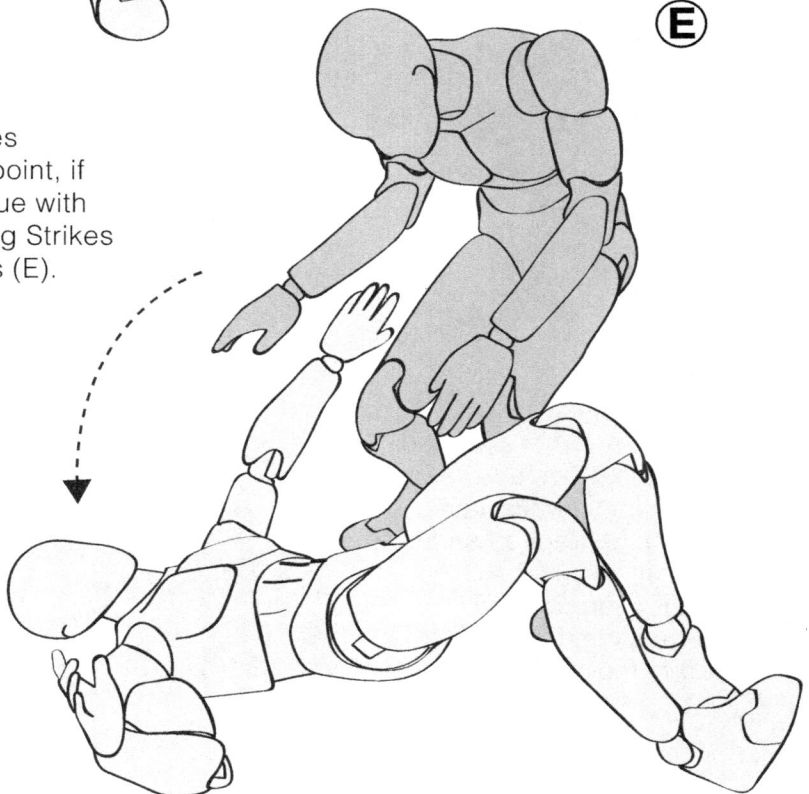

Sergio Nisenbaum

23 Escape from a Chokehold from Behind

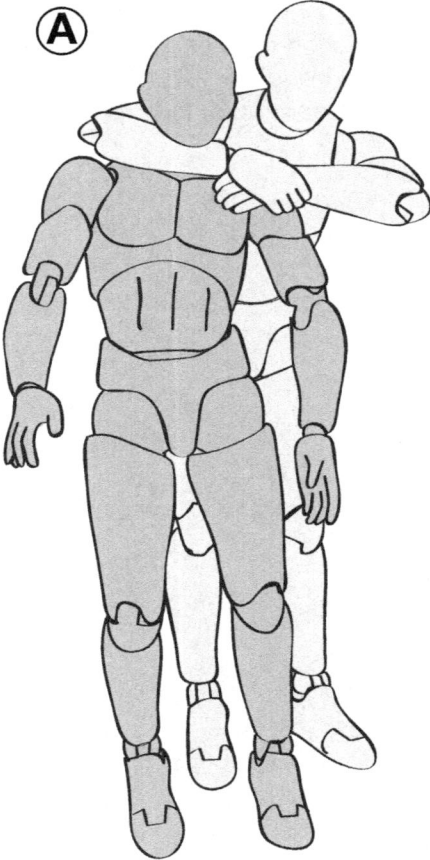

(A)

When escaping from a Chokehold from Behind the opponent makes the same movement of immobilization and puts pressure of the arm or forearm to cause choking, as seen in the previous exercise. Now the opponent's final position is completely behind you (A).

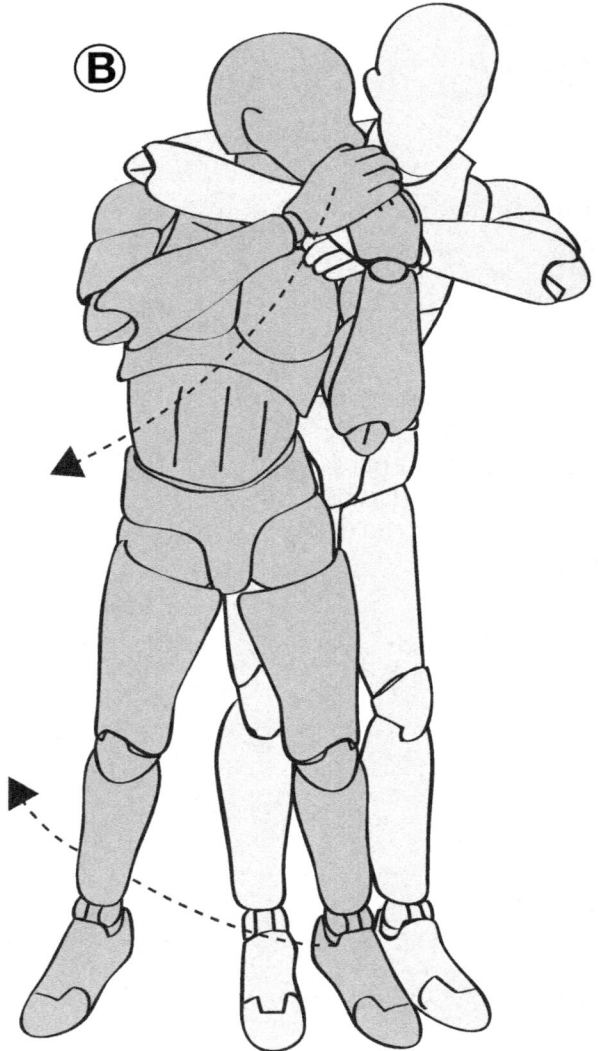

(B)

As seen in the previous exercise, the head rotates to alleviate the pressure on the trachea and both hands together must hold the opponent's hand upward.
At the same time, the left foot is prepared to move backward (B).

Ⓒ

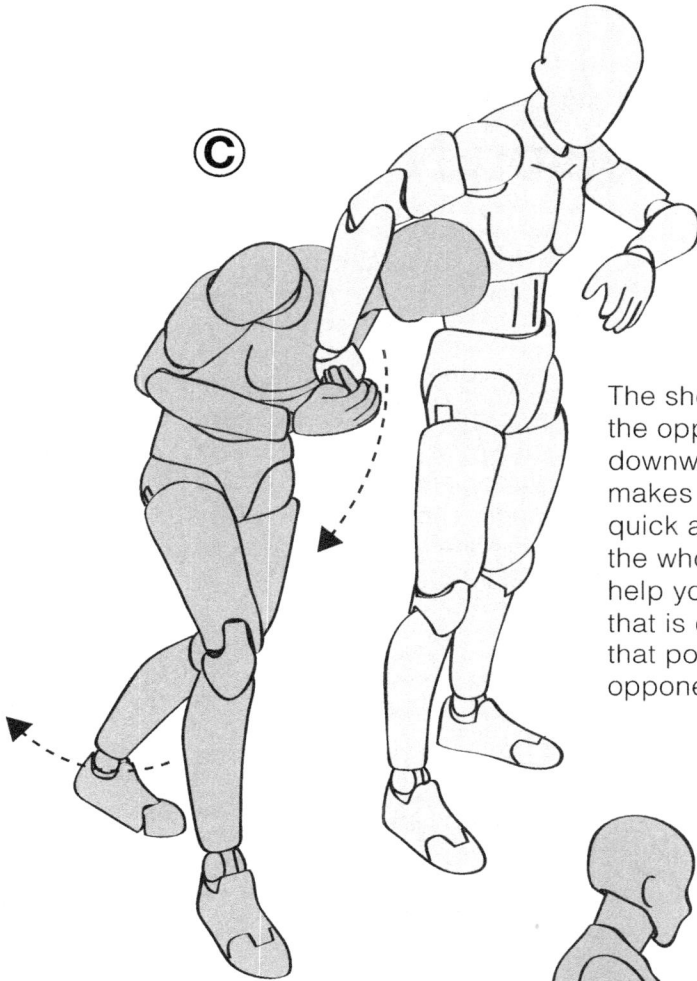

The shoulder that is on the opponent's side points downward, and the left leg makes a movement backward, quick and strong, to transfer the whole body weight and to help you escape from the arm that is doing the chokehold. At that point, you can also bite the opponent (C).

Ⓓ

Even after being released from the immobilization, the hands do not lose touch with the opponent's arm and hand and, thus, it is possible to do Immobilization N°2 seen in Exercise 16 (D). If necessary, instead of immobilizing, you can use the continuations.

Sergio Nisenbaum

24 Defense Against a Full Nelson N°1

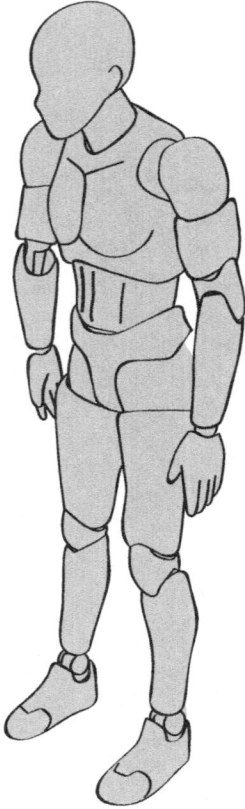

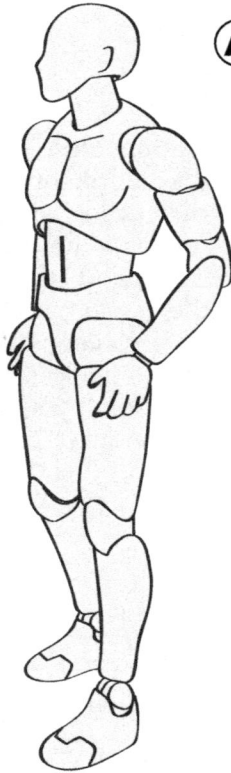

(A)

Called Full Nelson, this immobilization occurs when the opponent comes from behind to grab and lift both your arms supported by his two hands on your neck. The attack can also come as a surprise, and it requires a quite quick response (A).

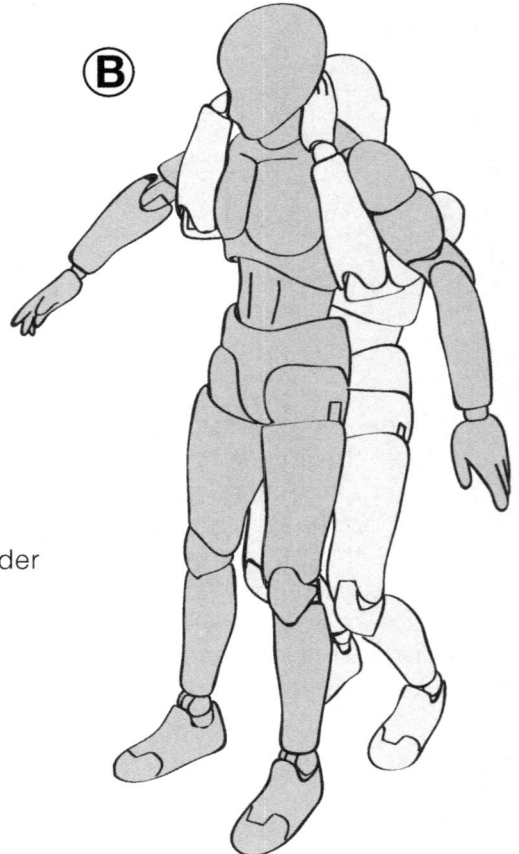

(B)

The support of the Full Nelson immobilization happens with a lock under the armpits together with the hands' support on the neck (B).

If the opponent is pulling backward, the first movement is to try to hit the region of his temple with the hands locked and closed.
The second movement is to take a step sideways raising mainly the right foot behind the opponent's left ankle (C).

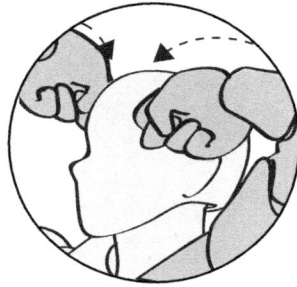

The middle finger hits the opponent's temple.

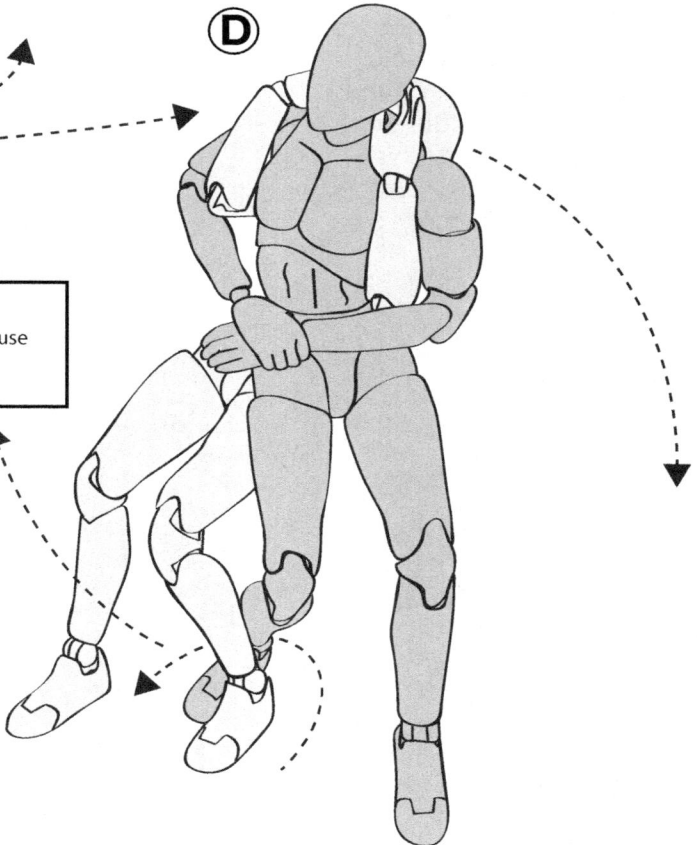

WARNING
This technique may cause a high-impact fall to the opponent.

The arms go down and both hands are crossed to lock the opponent's arms. The right foot is already supported behind the ankle and now the body tilts backward fast to overthrow the opponent (D).

E

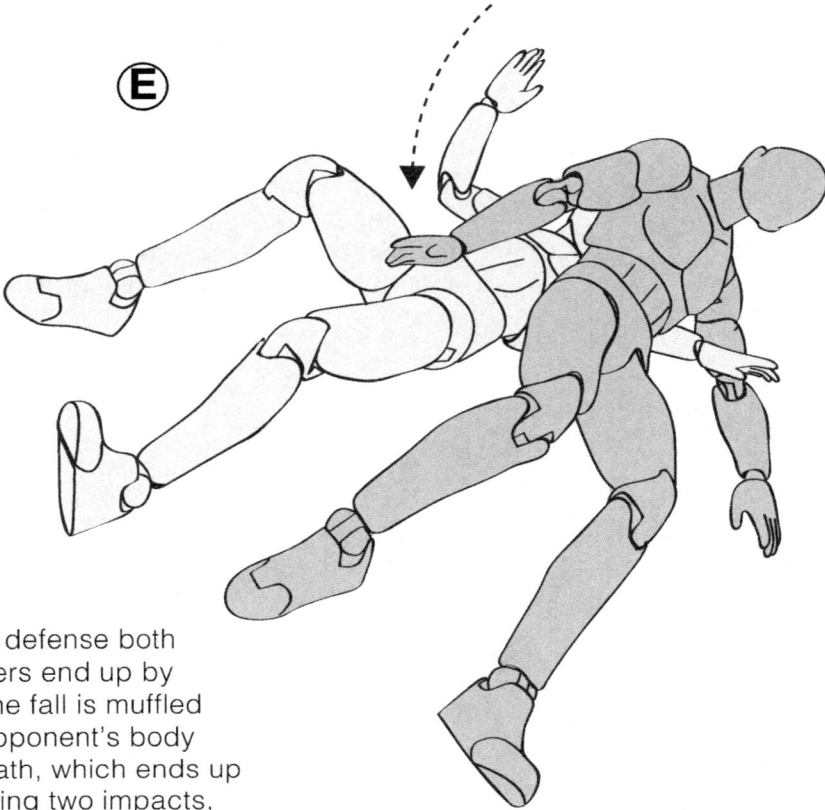

With this defense both contenders end up by falling, the fall is muffled by the opponent's body underneath, which ends up by suffering two impacts, that of his own fall and that of muffling the weight of your body on his. At this point, the arms are released to deliver a hand move on the groins (E).

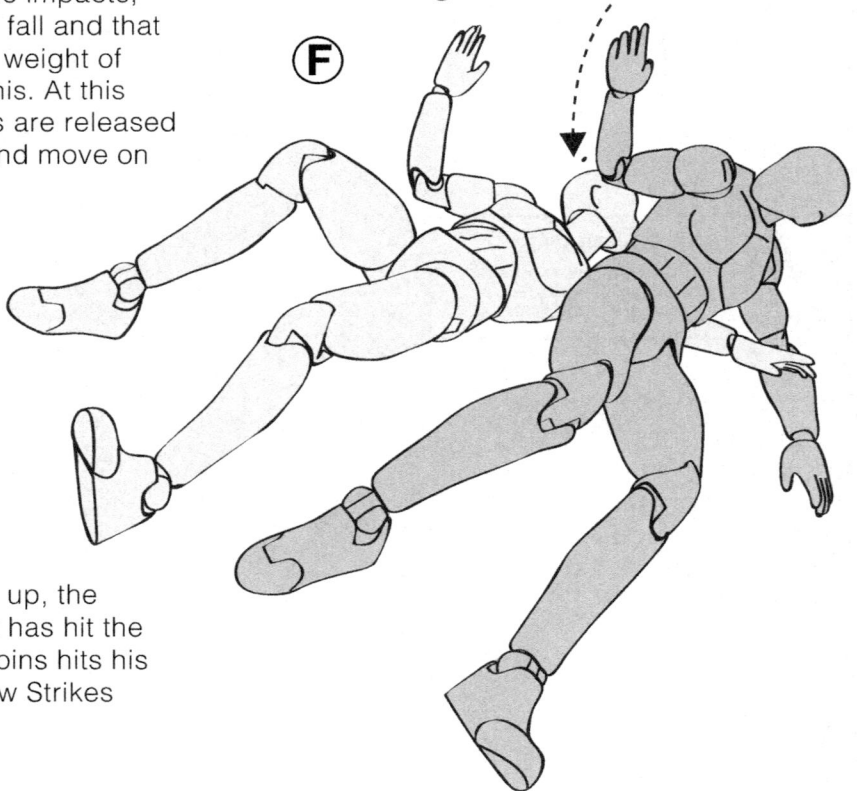

F

Before getting up, the same arm that has hit the opponent's groins hits his face with Elbow Strikes (F).

25 Defense Against a Full Nelson N°2

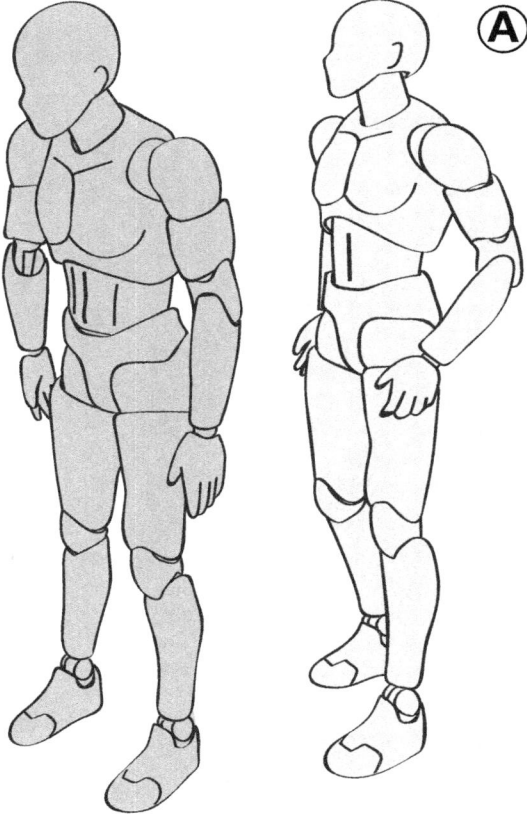

(A)

In the Defense Against Full Nelson N°2, the attack happens in the same way than the previous exercise. What changes is the time of reaction (A).

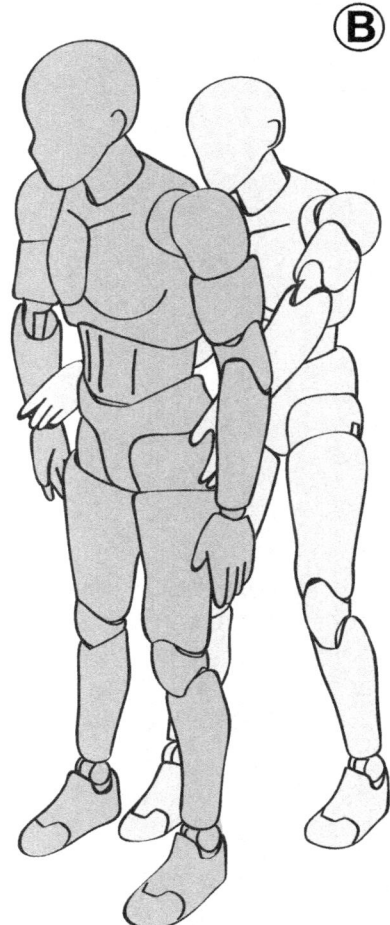

(B)

The opponent tries to do the same immobilization by passing the hands between your arms to lift and lock them with both hands behind your nape (B). It is exactly at that moment that the defensive reaction must take place.

C

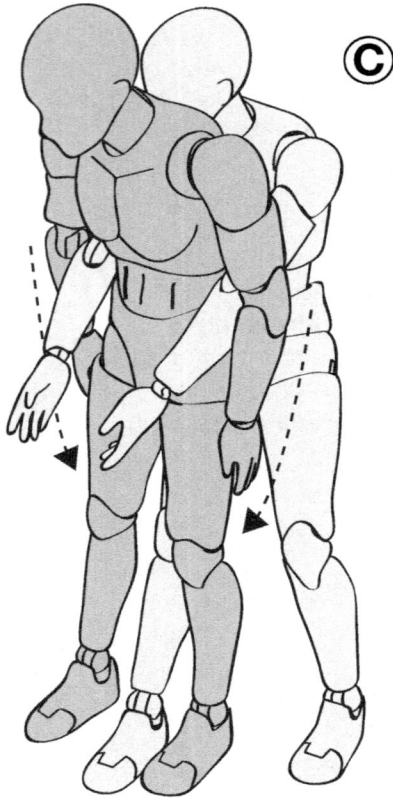

To void the beginning of the immobilization, when you feel the opponent's hands on you, the arms must contract and close to remain near the body as much as possible. The opponent's arms are not able to lift them up and lock (C).

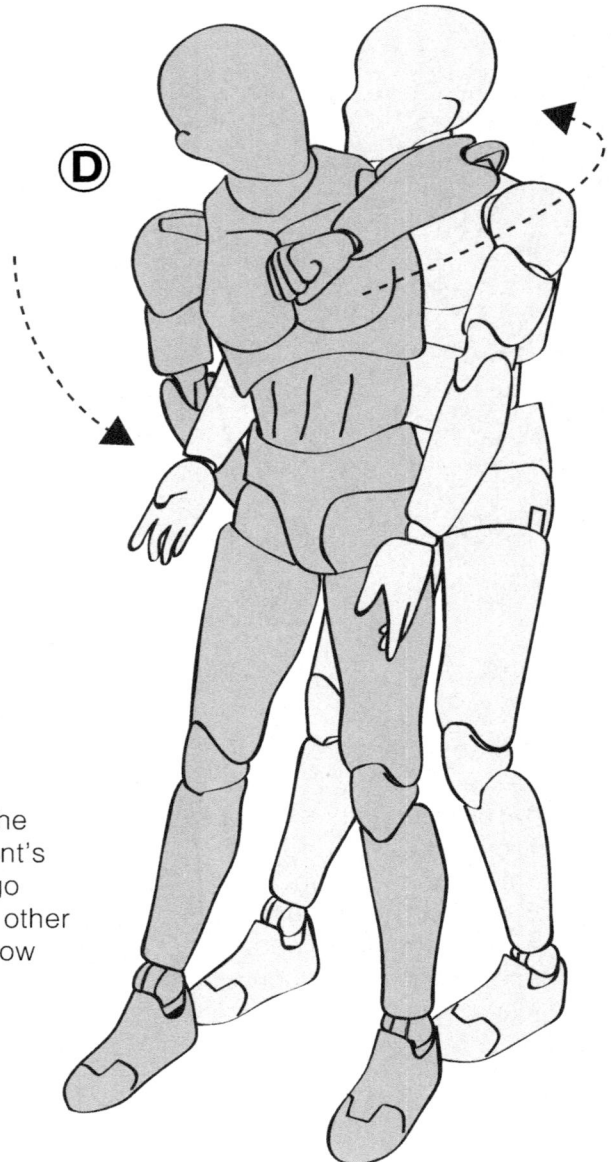

D

To continue the defense, the right hand hits the opponent's genitals and does not let go and, at the same time, the other arm delivers a left-arm Elbow Strike (D).

26 Defense Against a Full Nelson N°3

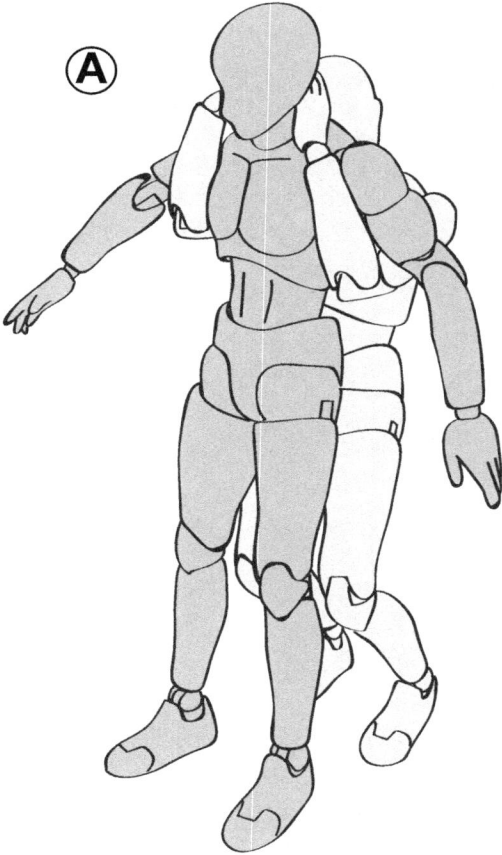

(A)

This immobilization is the same as the previous ones (A). What changes is that when the opponent is already doing the immobilization, you can hit his temple region with both hands and do the Defense Against Full Nelson N°1, or you can go straight to the Defense Against a Full Nelson N°3 (B).

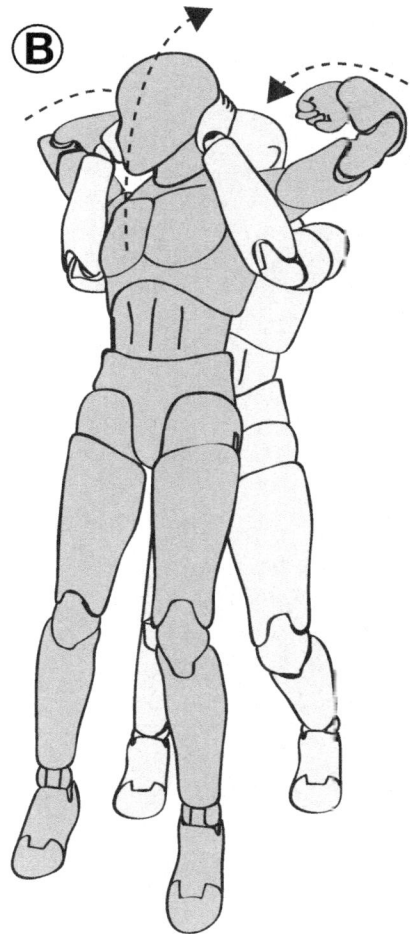

(B)

When the opponent supports his hands behind your head, another situation is also possible, where he forces the head forward and down, making it impossible for you to hit his temple with the hands, which eliminates the option of Defense Against the Full Nelson N°1.

C

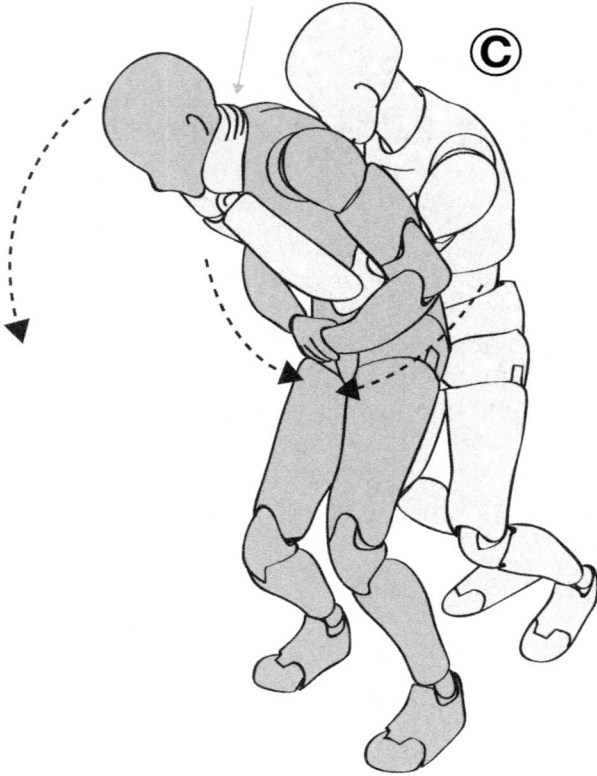

Regardless of whether the opponent is making pressure to move your head downward, in this defense, it may be done intentionally. The arms go down and both hands cross to lock the opponent's arms and the knees flex for the body to tilt forward and down (C).

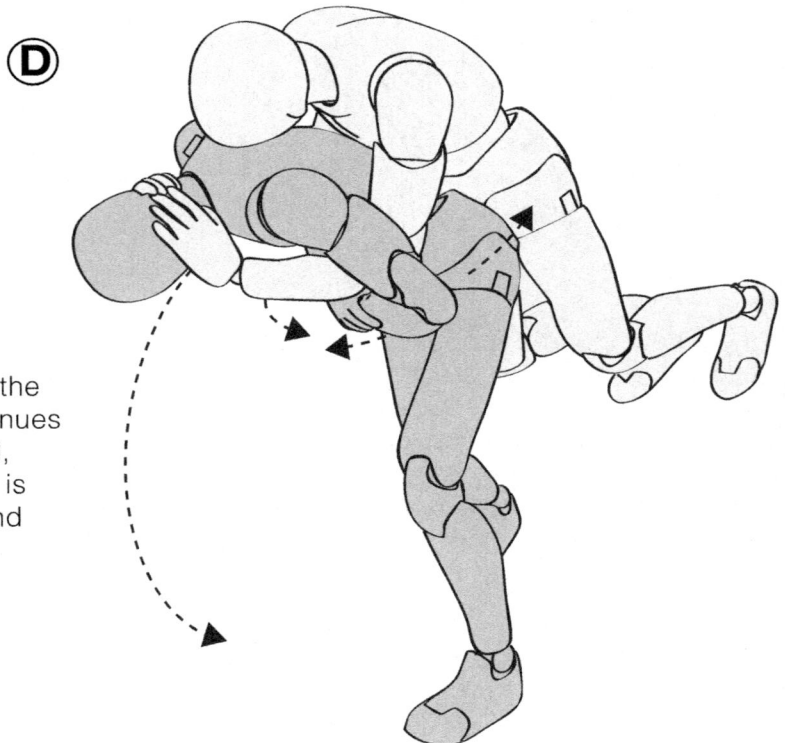

D

The hips fit in under the opponent, who continues with the arms locked, and his body weight is projected forward and down (D).

Ⓔ

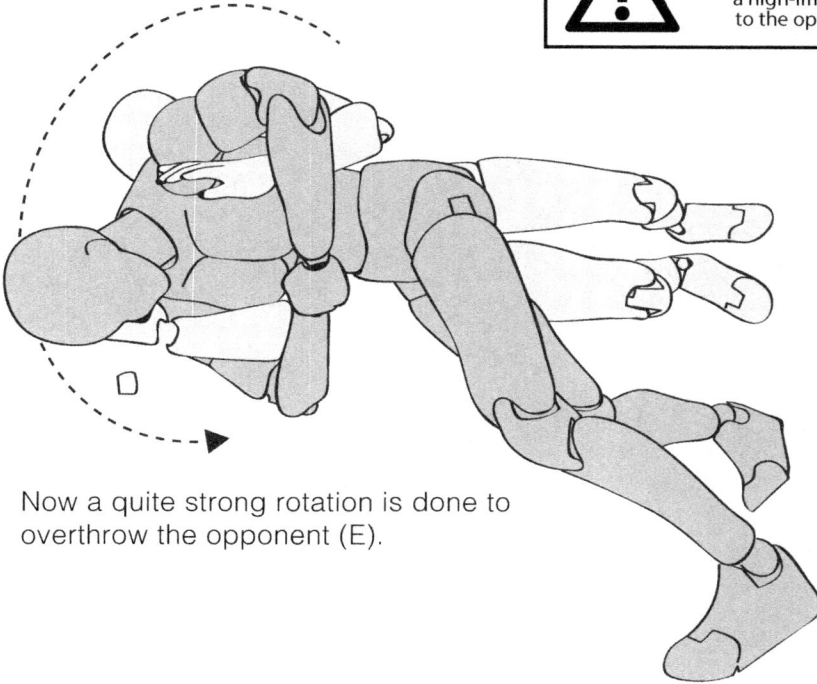

Now a quite strong rotation is done to overthrow the opponent (E).

Ⓕ

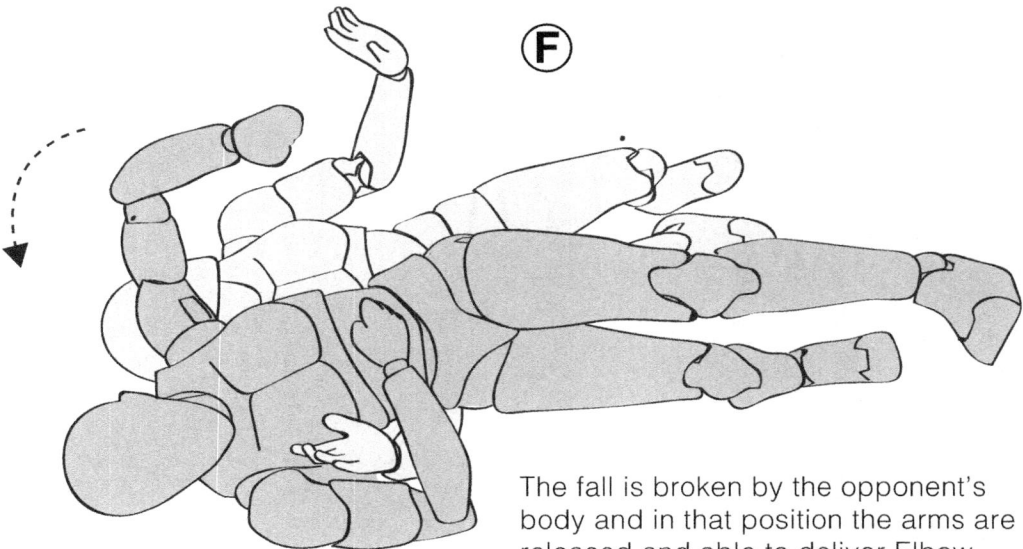

The fall is broken by the opponent's body and in that position the arms are released and able to deliver Elbow Strikes (F).

Defense Against Grabs

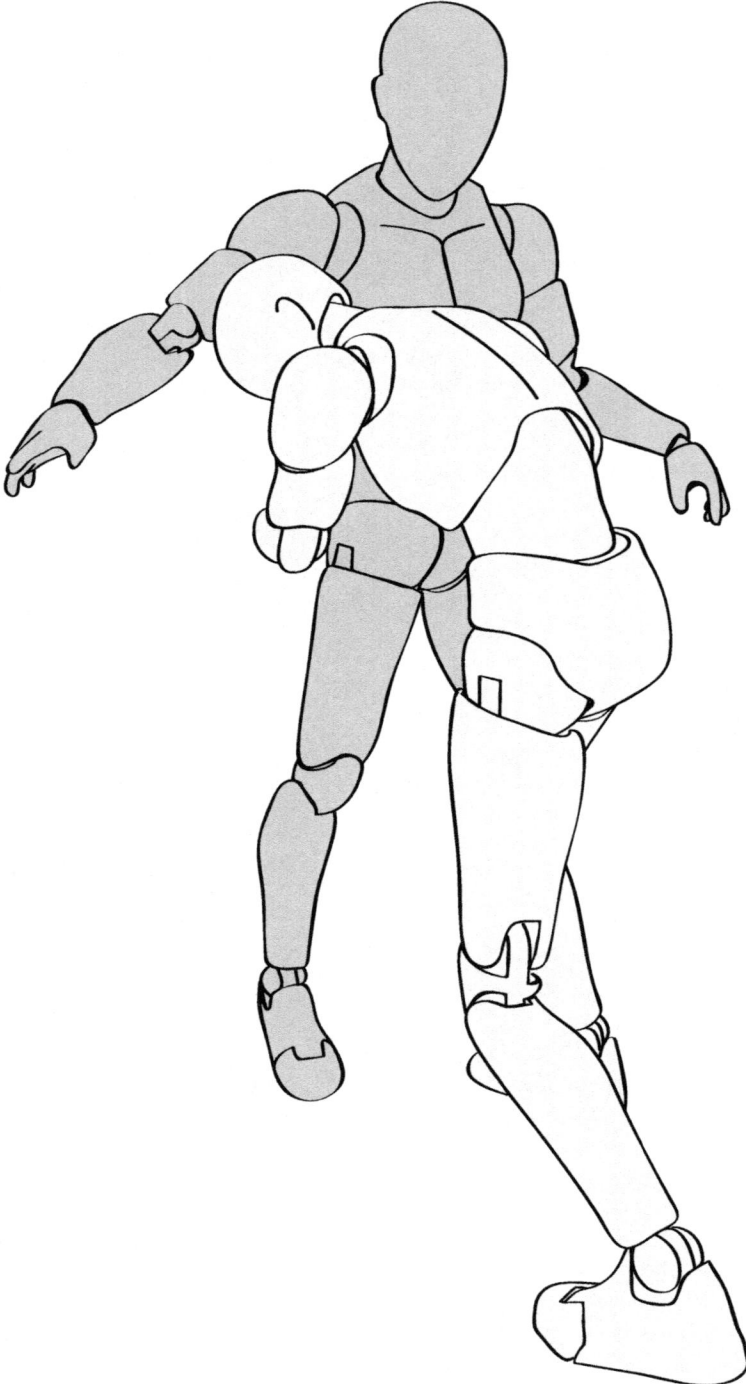

The practice of Defense Against Grabs is rather extensive. There are several different situations that may involve this type of aggression. The defense must be very quick, and it can happen in different moments of the attack, such as, for instance, when the opponent is coming close to start the attack and he is already grabbing you to try to knock you down or lift you up.

In the next exercises, you will see a variety of those situations with different types of grabs that may come from the front or from behind, with the arms locked or free.

27 Defense Against a Front Grab

With hands free N°1

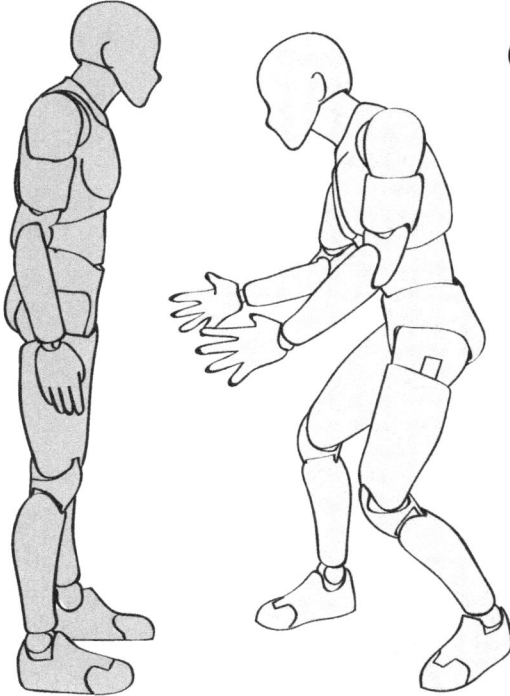

(A)

In this defense, the opponent comes to grab at your trunk level, leaving your hands free (A).

(B)

⚠ WARNING

Twisting the neck is dangerous.

While your right hand makes the block and supports the chin, the left hand tries to grab the opponent's head at his forehead level or to grab his hair. The left foot moves backward (B).

C While the right hand pushes the chin, the left hand rotates the head. The result is a twist in the opponent's neck caused by a quick rotation movement of the head supported by the hands (C).

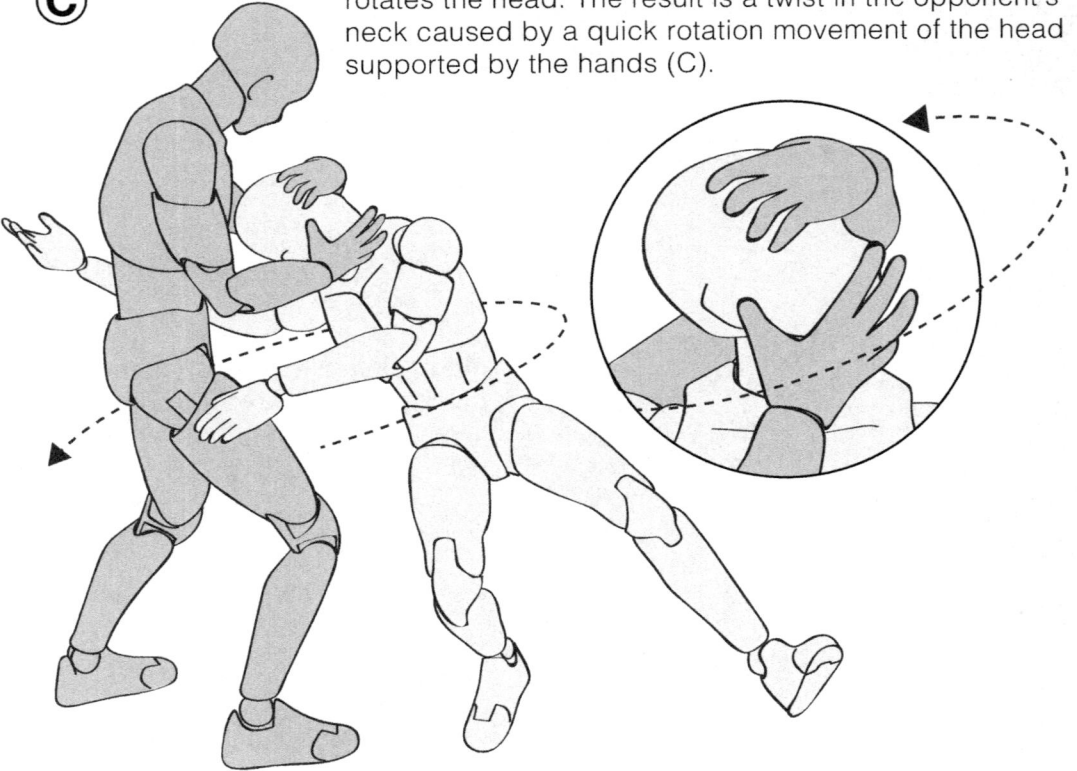

D

WARNING
This technique may cause a high-impact fall to the opponent.

The rotation of the opponent's head continues until it makes him fall (D).

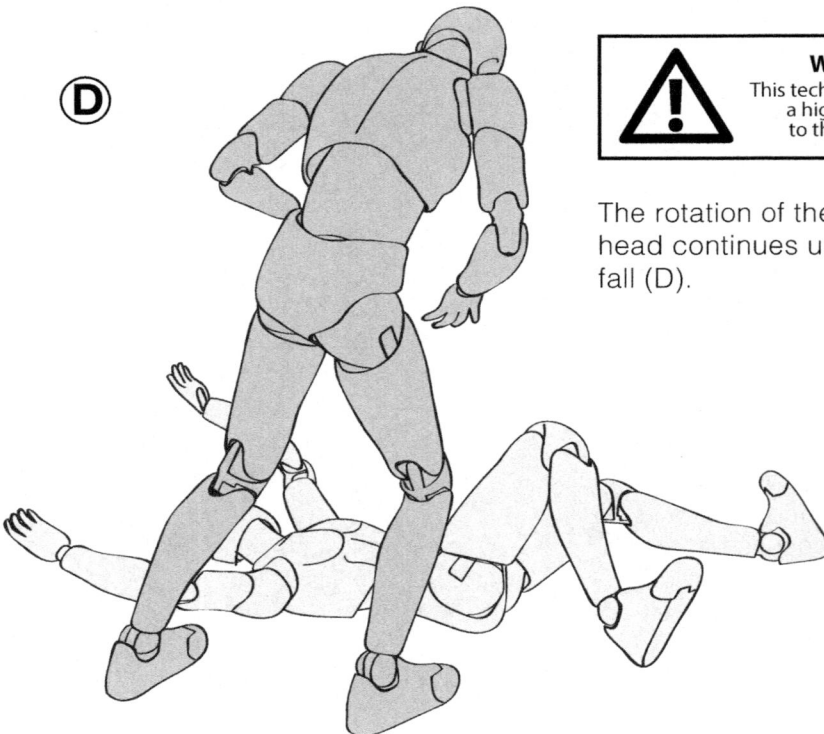

28 Defense Against a Front Grab

With hands free Nº2

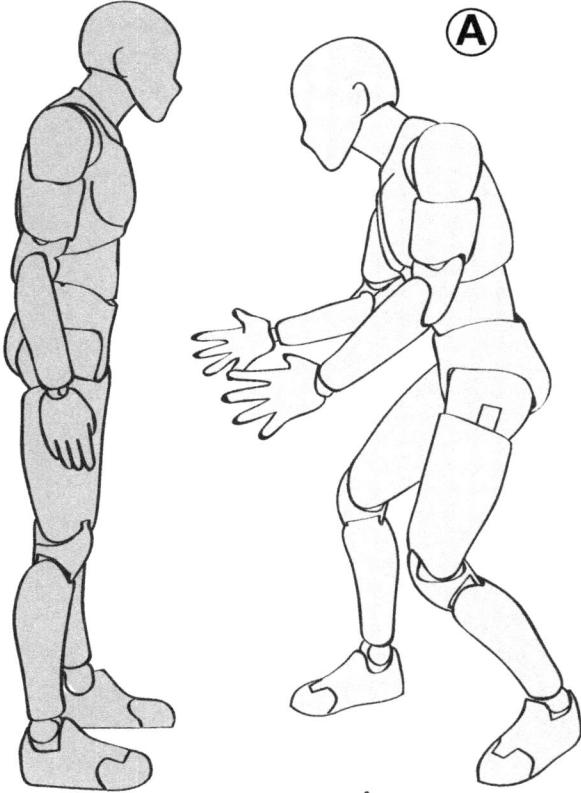

(A)

The opponent comes close to grab you at the trunk level (A), but now the defensive reaction occurs in advance when compared to that in the Release from a Front Grab Nº1.

The hands hold the opponent's head and both thumbs are pressed on his eyeballs to drive him away and to block completely any grabbing intention (B).

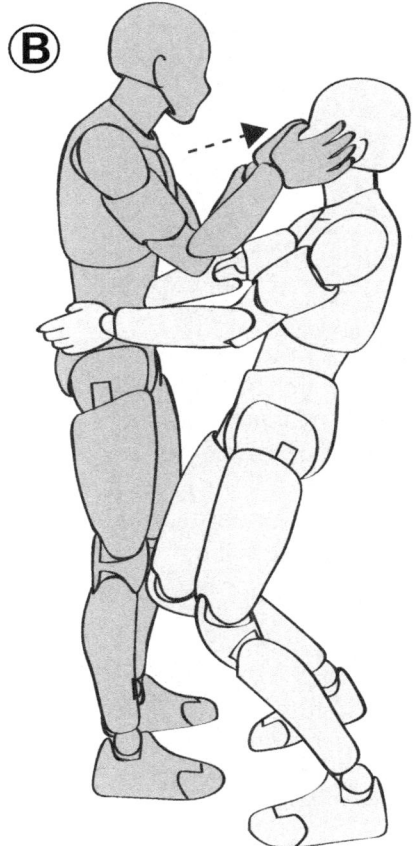

(B)

The tips of both thumbs make pressure on both eyeballs.

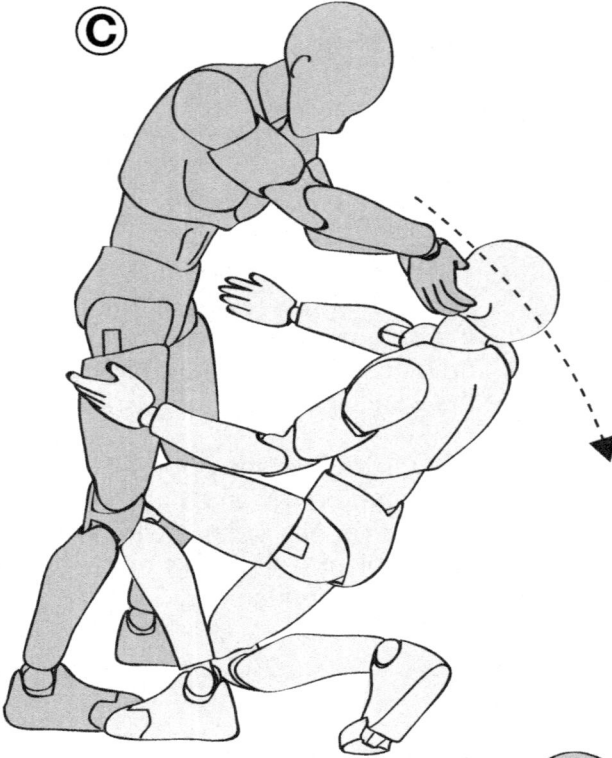

To make the opponent move away, the thumbs continue the press the eyeballs and the hands push the head toward the ground. This causes a strong pressure on the cervical spine (C).

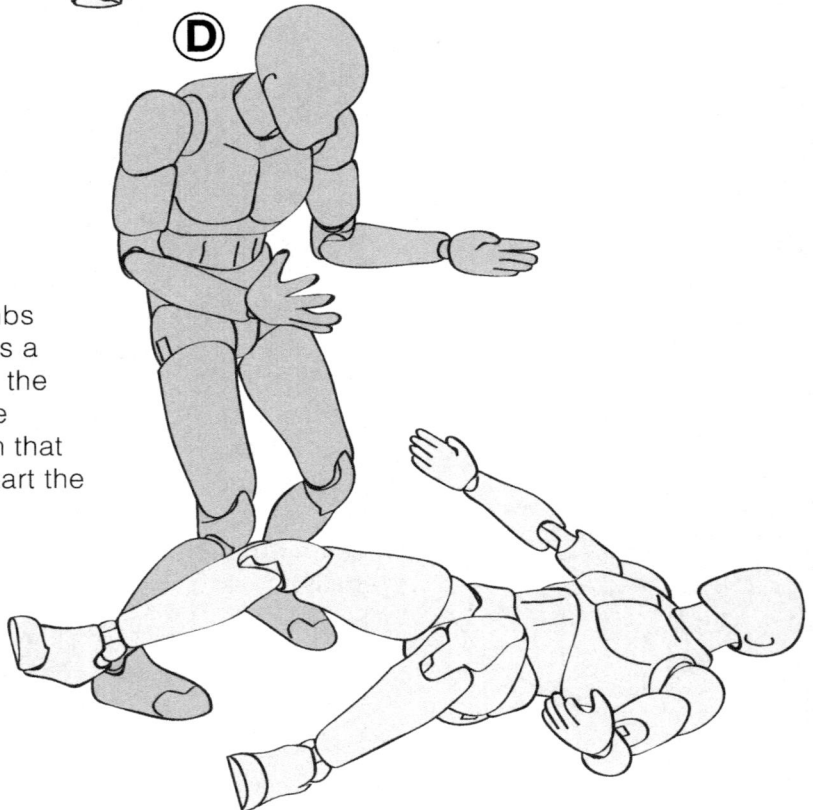

The set of the thumbs on the eyeballs plus a strong pressure on the spine can make the opponent fall. From that point on you can start the continuations (D).

29 Defense Against a Front Grab

With hands free N°3

Each defense against any Grab strongly depends on the position of the opponent's body and head. In this situation, the opponent comes close and is able to grab you, but his head is very close to the body (A).

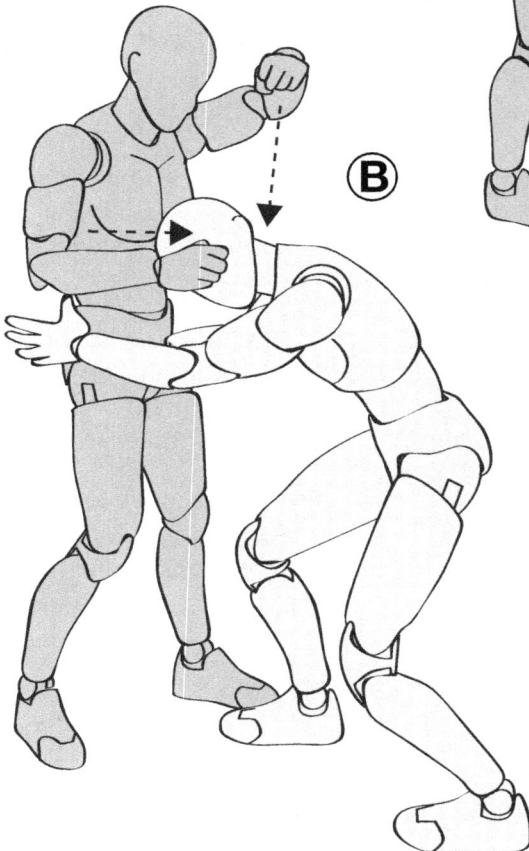

Ⓐ

Ⓑ

To make the opponent turn his head away, two moves are simultaneously made. The left hand hits the area of the opponent's nape and the right hand, the side of his head in an attempt to hit the temple (B).

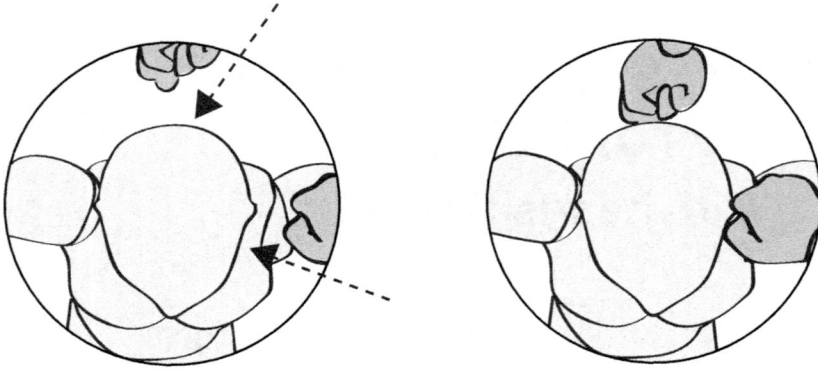

The left hand is locked and closed, and the middle finger hits the opponent's nape.

With the right hand locked and closed, the thumb is supported by the index finger, and it hits the sides of the temple.

Nape

Temple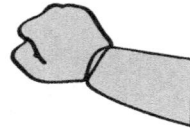

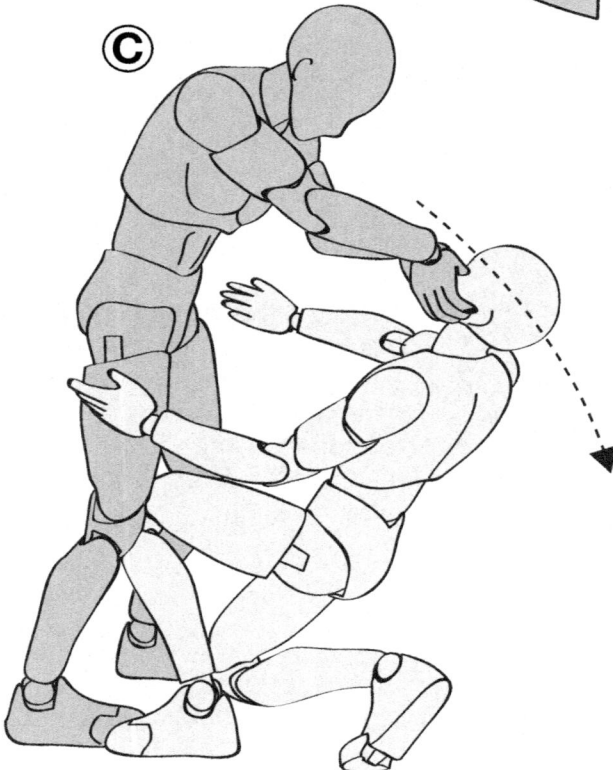

©

The hand moves on the nape and on the temple make the opponent turn away to gain space and, as in the previous defense, press your thumbs on the opponent's eyeballs to make the opponent go down (C).

30 Defense Against a Front Grab
With hands free Nº4

As much as in the Defense Against a Front Grab Nº2, the defensive reaction also occurs in advance to prevent the grab. To do that, a block is made with the left hand's thumb between the opponent's nose and upper lip (A).

Once that is an overly sensitive area, just pressing the thumb on that area is enough to turn the opponent's head away, but it is necessary to continue the defense to prevent a second reaction.

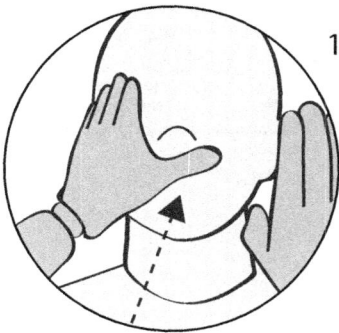

The block is made with a quick movement toward the opponent's nose. The thumb presses the area between nose and lip, and the right hand is prepared to reinforce the defense.

B

2

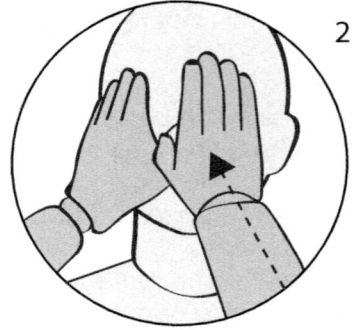

Deliver a move with the heel of the right hand on top of the thumb that is making the block (B).

WARNING

Hand moves here are delivered in a quite sensitive area.

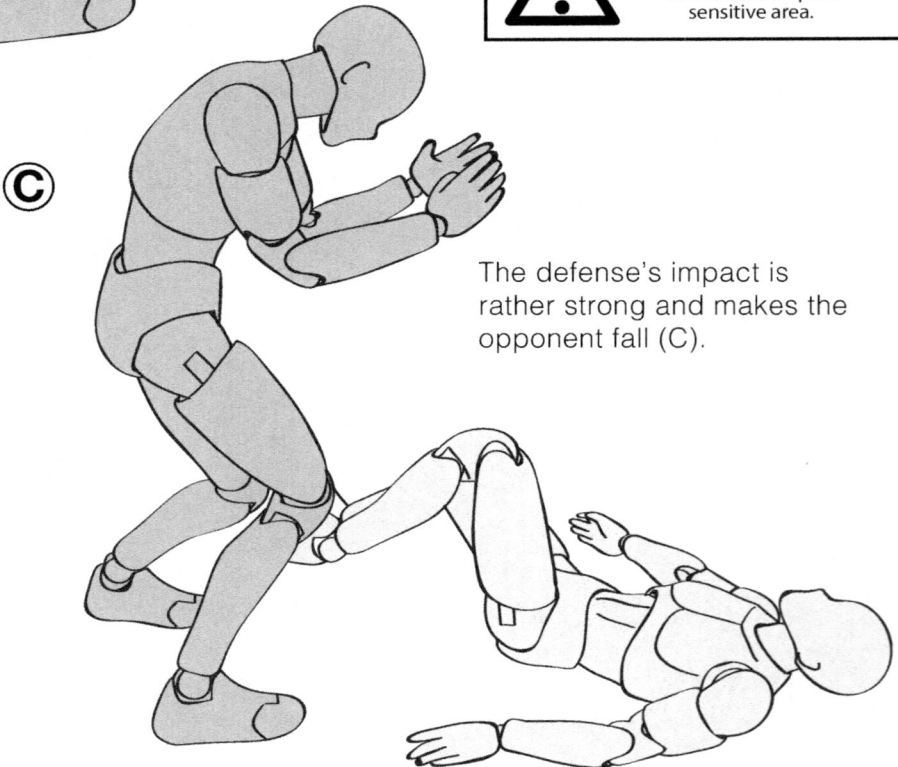

C

The defense's impact is rather strong and makes the opponent fall (C).

31 Defense Against a Front Grab

With hands free N°5

A

Like the Defense Against a Front Grab with hands free N°3, the opponent succeeds in grabbing you, but his head is too close to the body. To move his head away, two moves are simultaneously delivered in the area of nape and temple (A).

B

The left hand's thumb moves the opponent's head backward, and the heel of the right hand delivers a punch on the thumb positioned between the opponent's nose and upper lip, according to the previous Defense of a Front Grab (B).

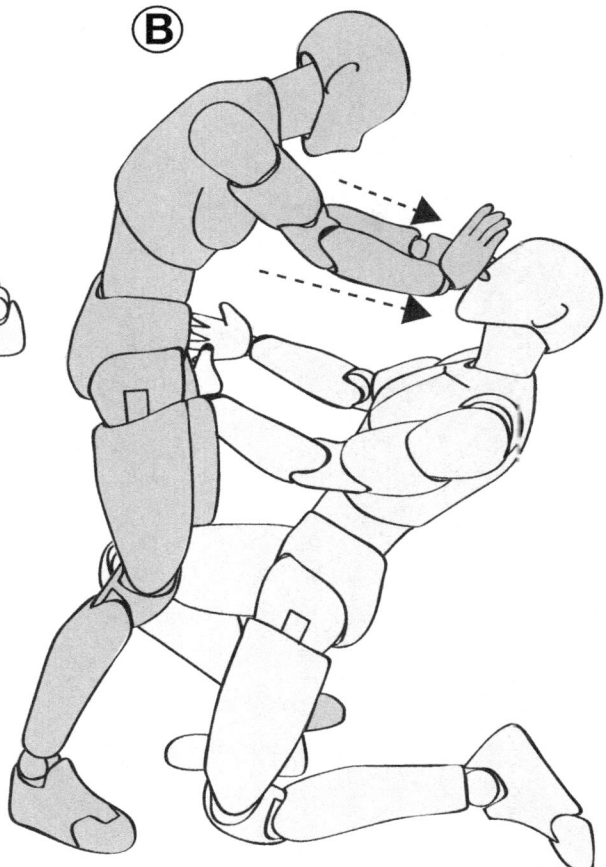

32 Defense Against a Front Grab

With hands free N°6

In the Defense Against a Front Grab with hands free N°6, the opponent ends up by positioning himself in a way that makes your initial movements difficult. To move his head away, as seen in the previous defense and in the Defense Against a Front Grab with hands free N°3, deliver hand moves on the nape and temple (A).

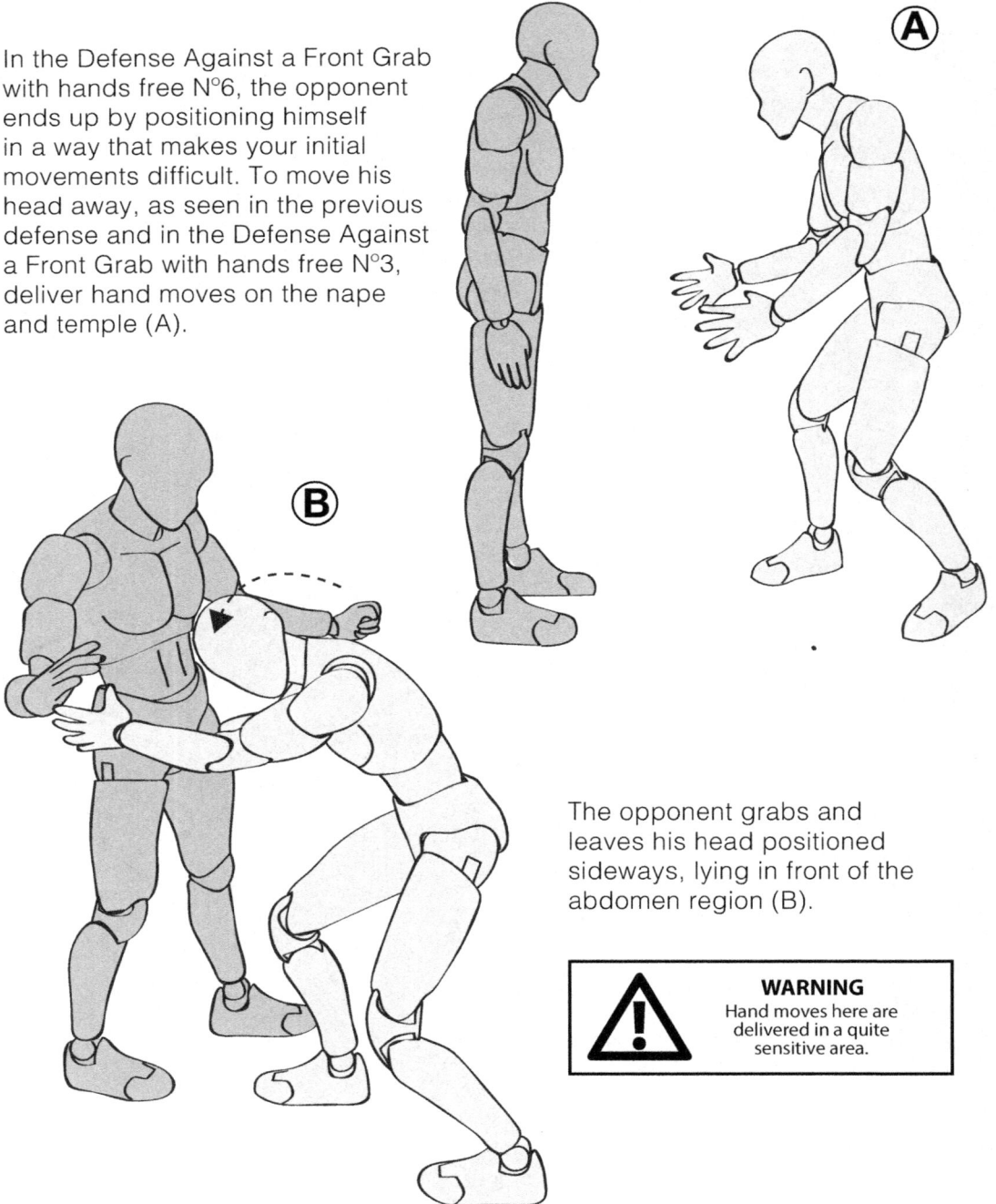

A

B

The opponent grabs and leaves his head positioned sideways, lying in front of the abdomen region (B).

⚠️ **WARNING**
Hand moves here are delivered in a quite sensitive area.

Ⓒ

The left hand grabs the opponent's hair, eyes, or nose, in order to pull his head back, while the right hand makes a hand attack in the neck area (C).

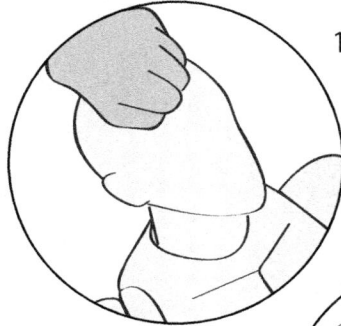

1

The head is pulled back by the hair.

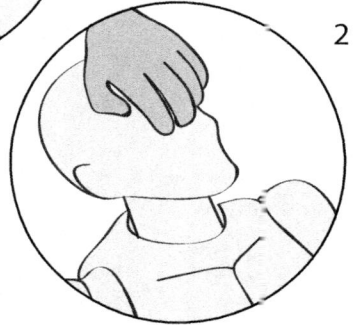

2

If the hair is too short, another alternative is to pull back the head by pressing the eyeballs or nose.

Ⓓ

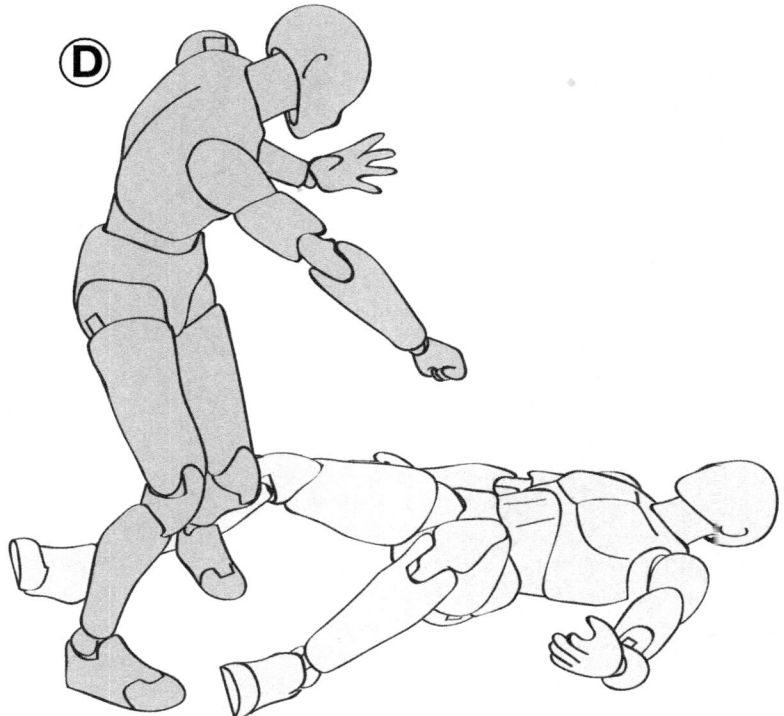

If necessary, continue with the sequences of attacks with kicks and hand moves (D).

Sergio Nisenbaum

33 Defense Against a Front Grab

With hands free N°7

In the Defense Against a Front Grab with hands free N°7, the opponent grabs faster and positions himself with the head farther back (A).

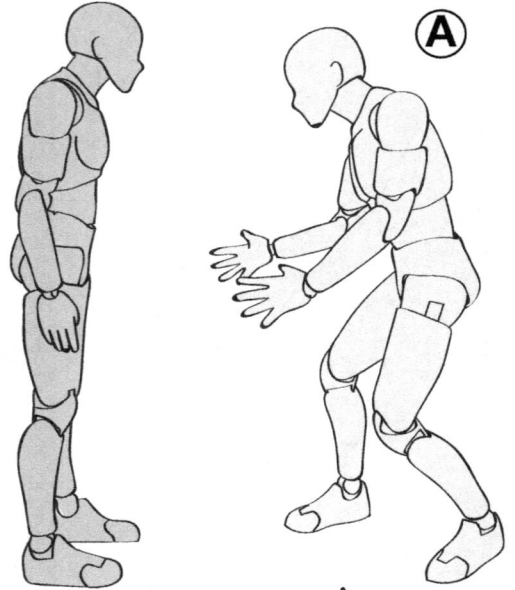

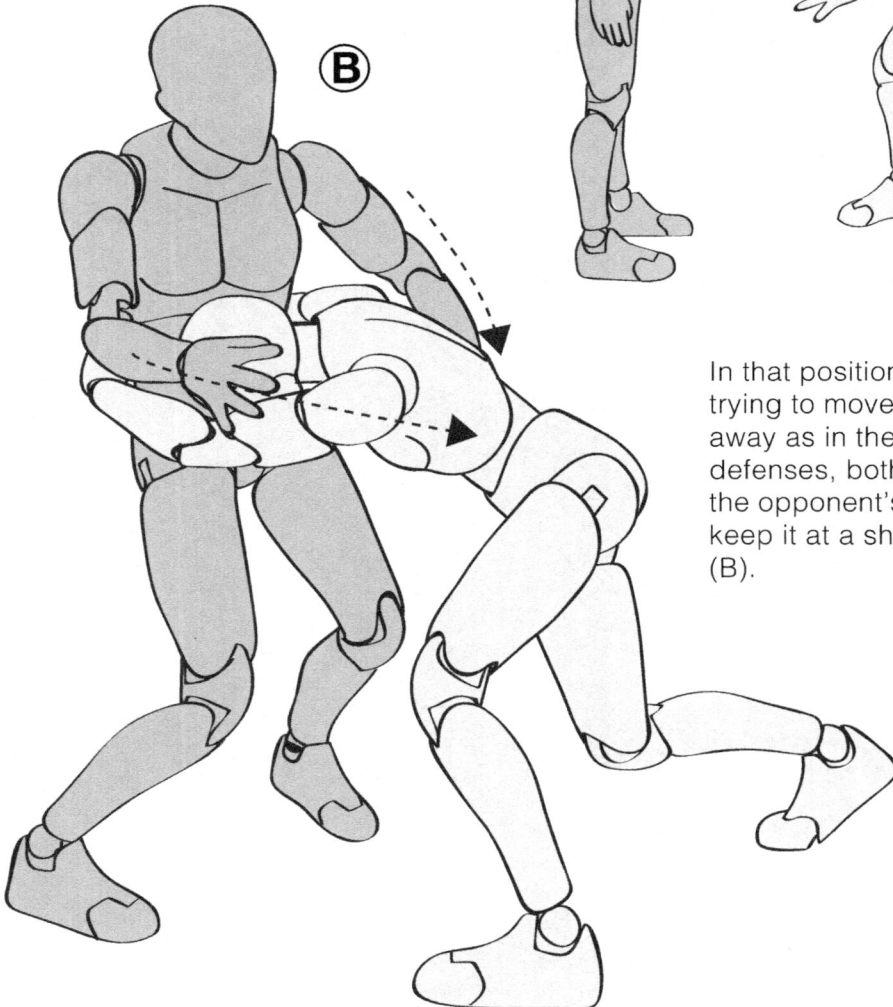

In that position, instead of trying to move his head away as in the previous defenses, both hands grab the opponent's body to keep it at a short distance (B).

C

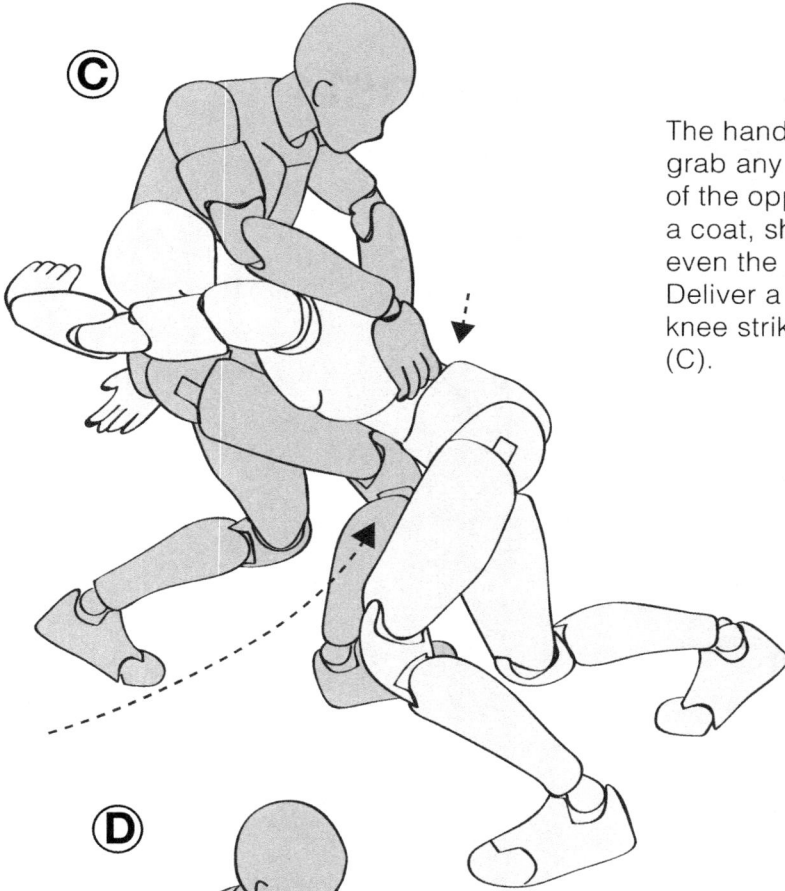

The hands can strongly grab any piece of clothing of the opponent, such as a coat, shirt, trousers, or even the body directly. Deliver a sequence of knee strikes on the groins (C).

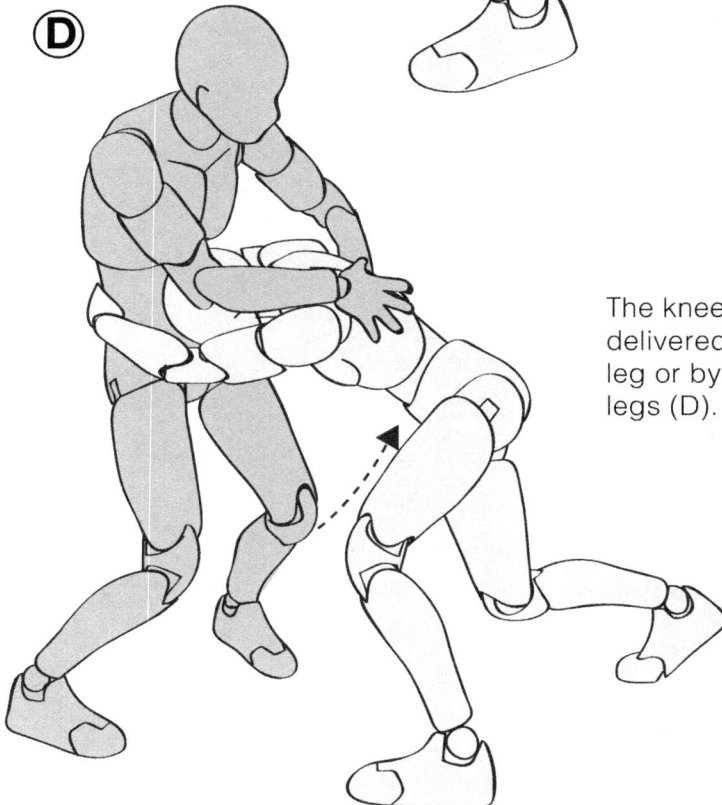

D

The knee strikes are delivered with the same leg or by alternating the legs (D).

34 Defense Against a Front Grab

At a lower level N°1

Ⓐ

As seen in the previous Defenses Against a Front Grab with hands free, it is hard to predict which the best defense would be. The reaction depends significantly on the opponent's position once he can come close in the same way (A) or change his body's inclination to grab at the level of the legs.

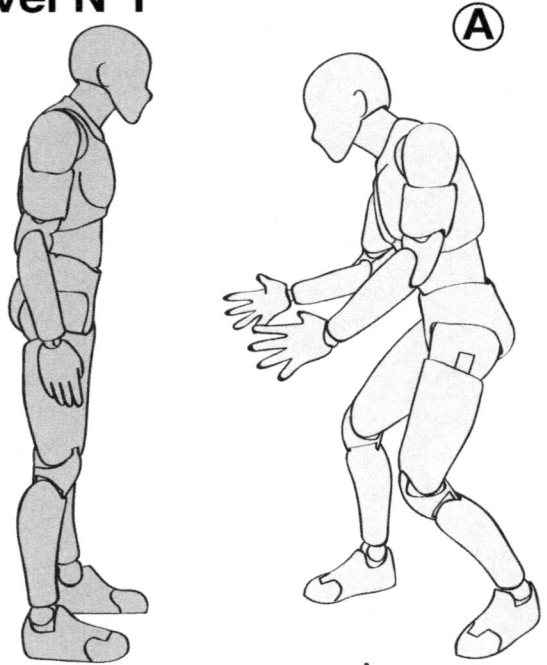

Ⓑ

When you realize that the opponent is going to grab at a lower level, two movements will be made simultaneously: both feet move quickly backward to move the legs away from the attack and the body tilts forward (B).

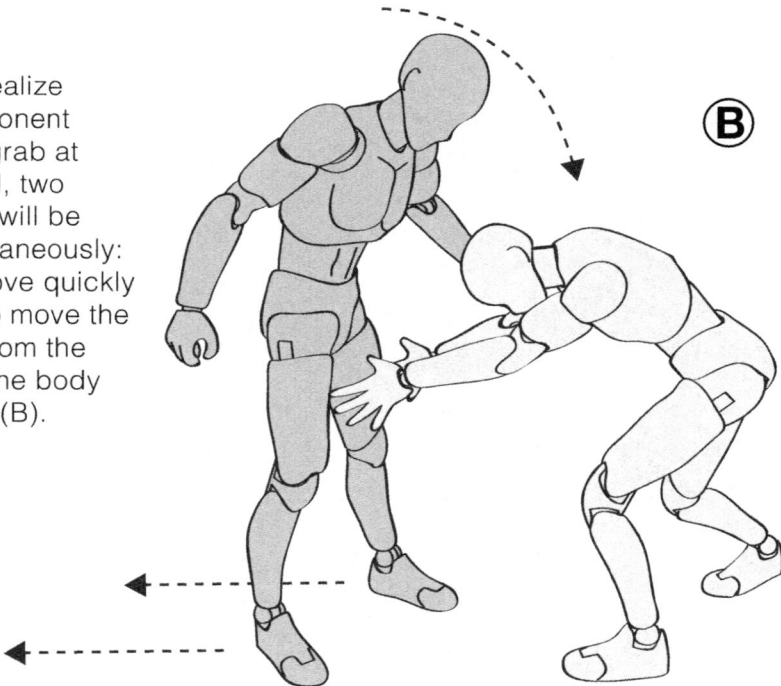

Ⓒ

The movements of moving the legs backward and tilting the body forward supported by the hands on the opponent's back will push him down to the ground (C).

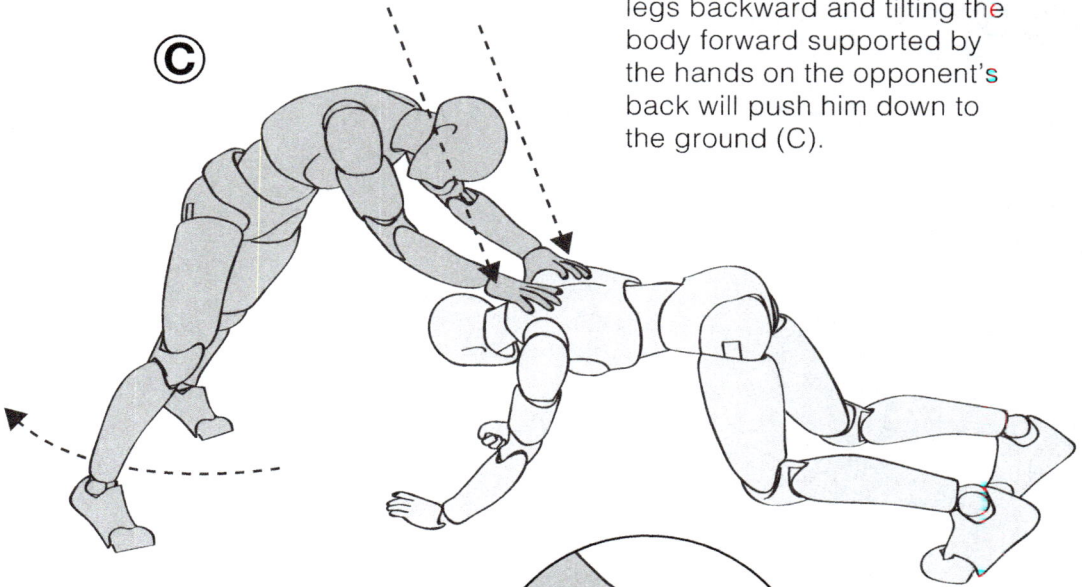

The hands do the support near the region of the shoulders.

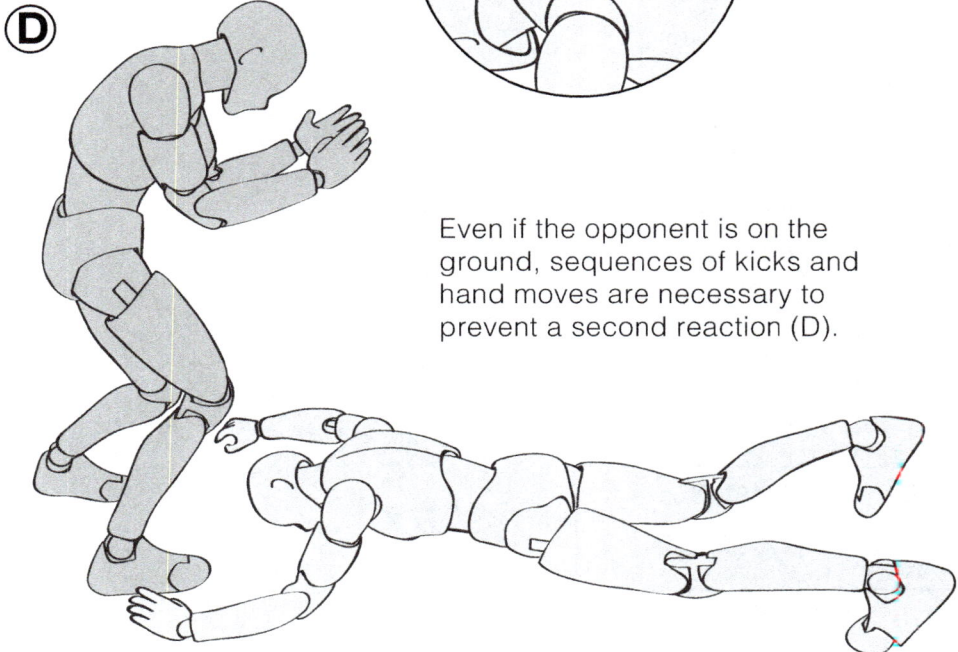

Ⓓ

Even if the opponent is on the ground, sequences of kicks and hand moves are necessary to prevent a second reaction (D).

Sergio Nisenbaum

35 Defense Against a Front Grab

At a lower level Nº2

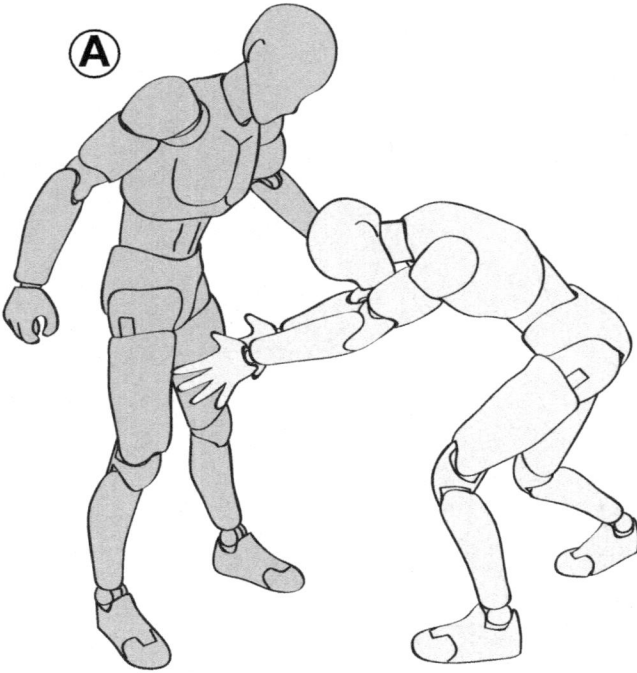

In the Defense Against Front Grab at a lower level Nº2, the opponent comes close faster, and he is able to grab your legs (A).

To defend yourself, tilt the trunk forward and, at the same time, deliver an elbow strike downward on the region of the opponent's nape (B).

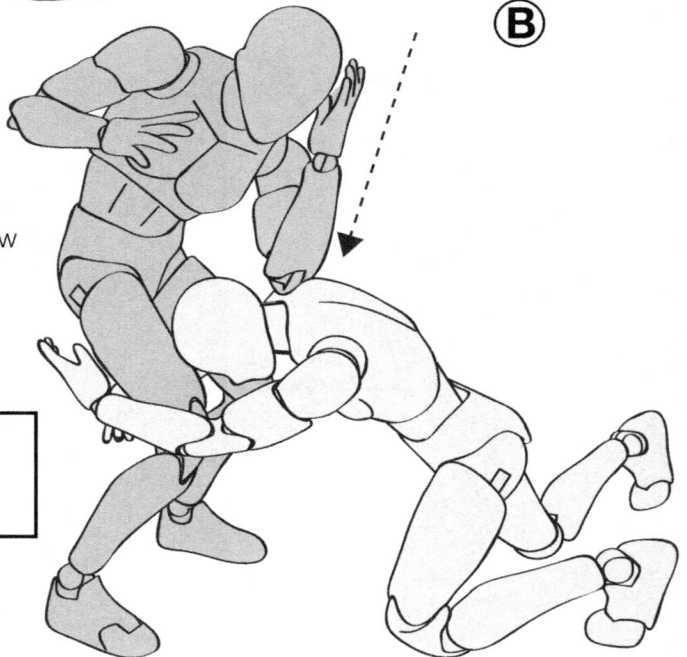

> **WARNING**
>
> Elbow strikes reach an overly sensitive area.

36 Defense Against a Front Grab

With hands pinned

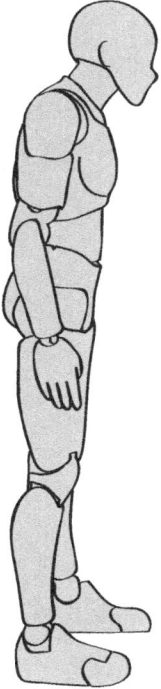

(A) The Defense Against a Front Grab with hands pinned is more dangerous and requires a much faster reaction.
Here, the opponent intends to grab by pinning your arms to your body or to try to overthrow you (A).

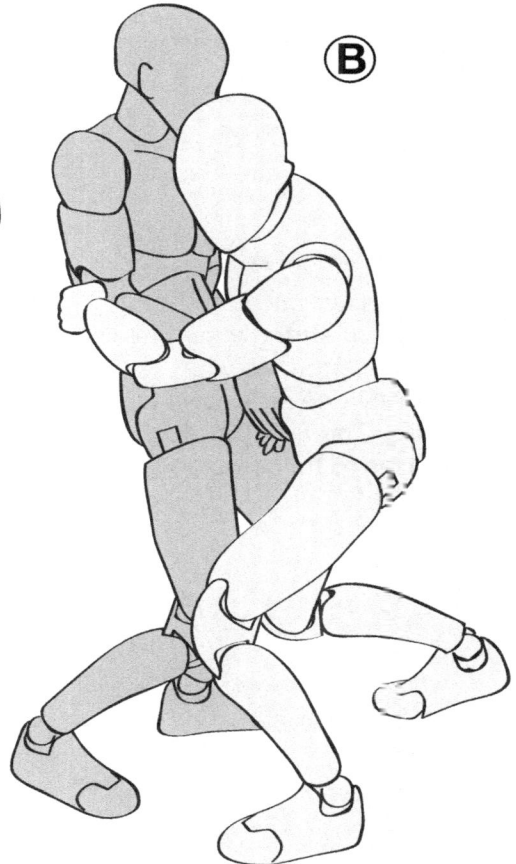

(B)

The defensive reaction must be instantaneous to be able to move the opponent away, and it can be done with a set of reactions. The first option is to hit the opponent's groins with both hands together and, at the same time, to bite the side of his neck (B).

Ⓒ

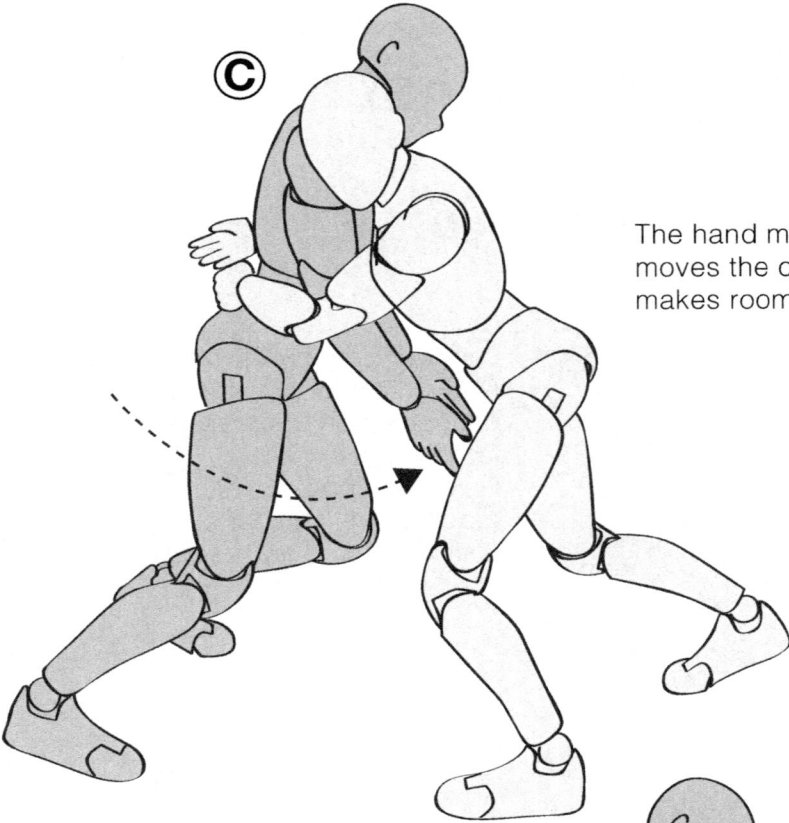

The hand move on the groins moves the opponent away and makes room to knee strikes (C).

Your hands will hold the opponent strongly so that you can continue with several knee strikes on his groins. Then, the left foot crosses to the left side (D).

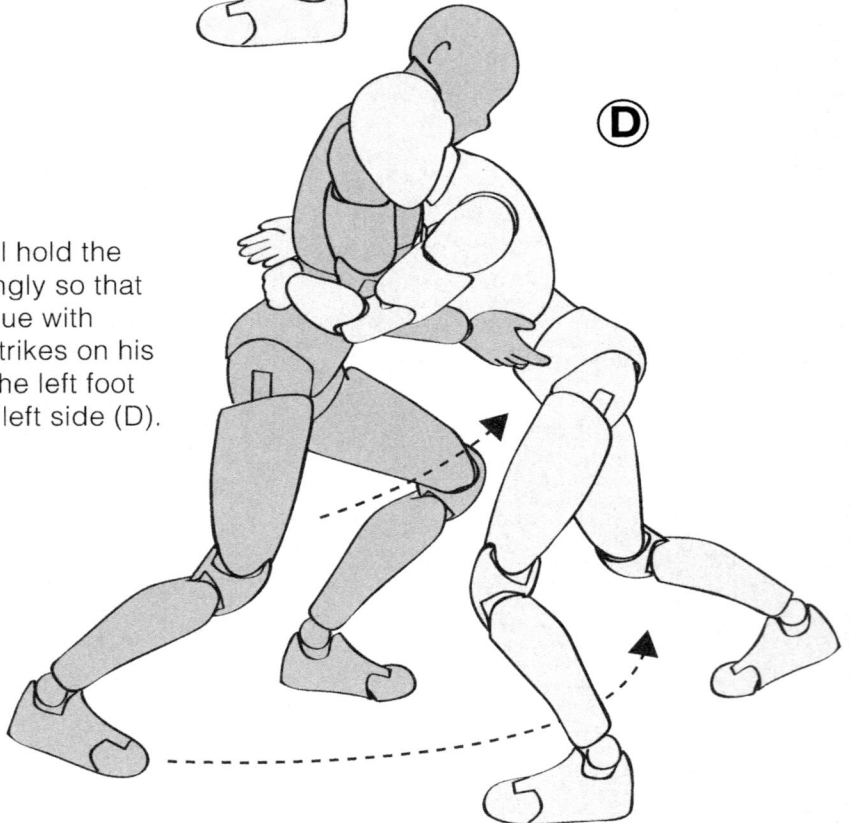

Ⓓ

(E)

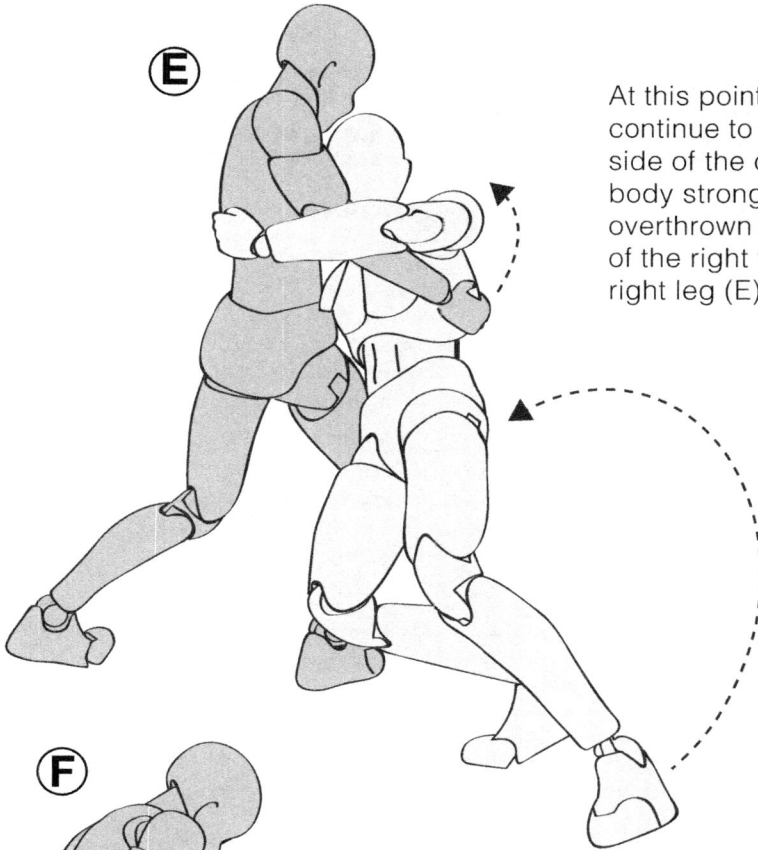

At this point, the hands
continue to hold the
side of the opponent's
body strongly, and he is
overthrown with the support
of the right foot behind his
right leg (E).

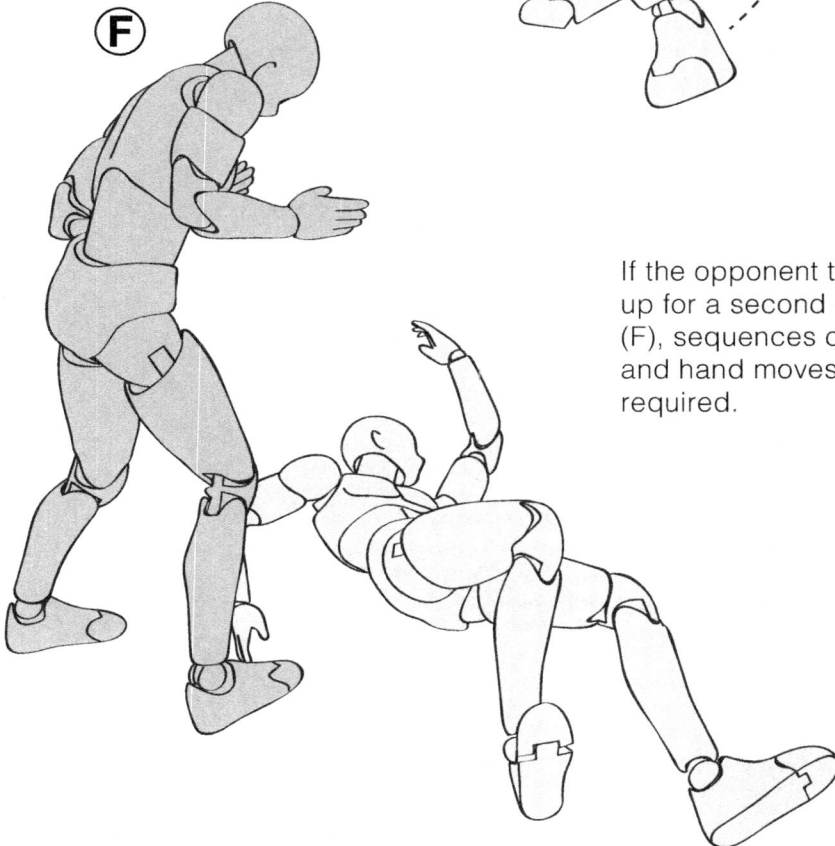

(F)

If the opponent tries to get
up for a second reaction
(F), sequences of kicks
and hand moves will be
required.

Sergio Nisenbaum

37 Defense Against a Grab from Behind

With hands free N°1

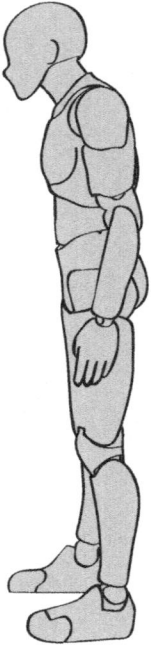

The Grab from Behind is more complicated than the front one simply because it comes as a surprise. You may be standing or inattentive with someone in front of you when the aggression occurs. The reaction must be immediate, and it can be done in two moments: first, when you feel the opponent's hands coming closer; and second, when he is already grabbing you.

The Defense Against a Grab from Behind with hands free N°1 is fully instinctive. The moment you feel the opponent's hands, tilt your body forward (B).

C

At the same time, while your body tilts forward, deliver sequences of elbow strikes alternating your arms, both on the opponent's right and left sides until he releases you (C).

D

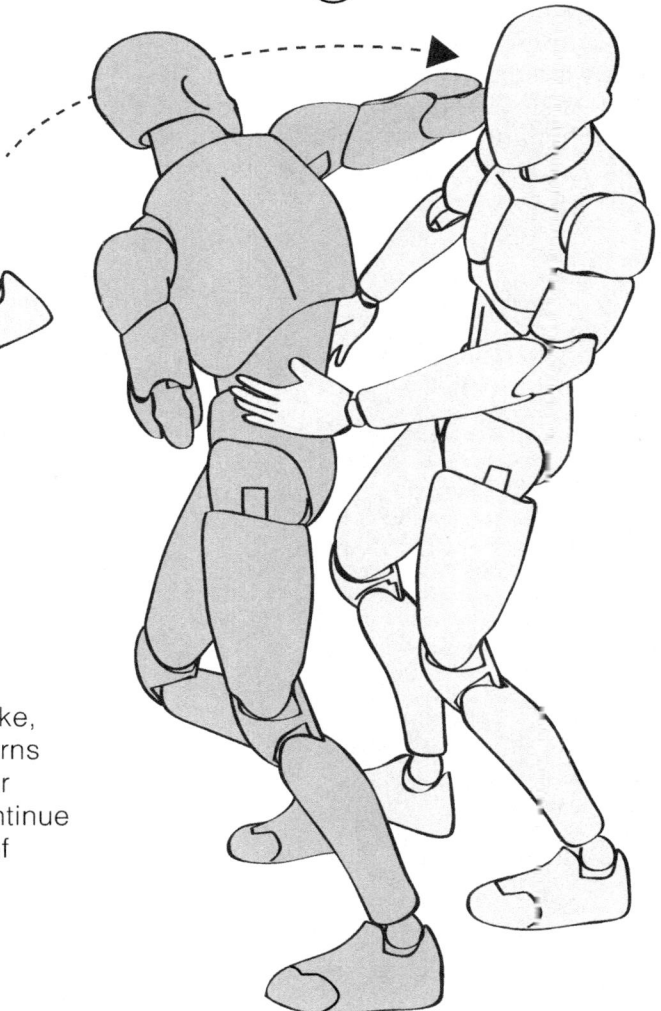

After the last elbow strike, even if the opponent turns away, you can turn your body to face him to continue with more sequences of attacks (D).

38 Defense Against a Grab from Behind

With hands free N°2

Ⓐ

In this situation, the opponent has been able to grab you. The first reaction is to tilt the body strongly forward to make it difficult for him to try to get you off the ground. It is also important to take advantage of the moment and see which hand the opponent is lying on the other hand (A). Here, his right hand is on his left hand. At the same time, the right hand grabs the opponent's forearm near his right wrist, your left hand hits the back of his right hand with the middle finger so that his hand opens because of the impact (B).

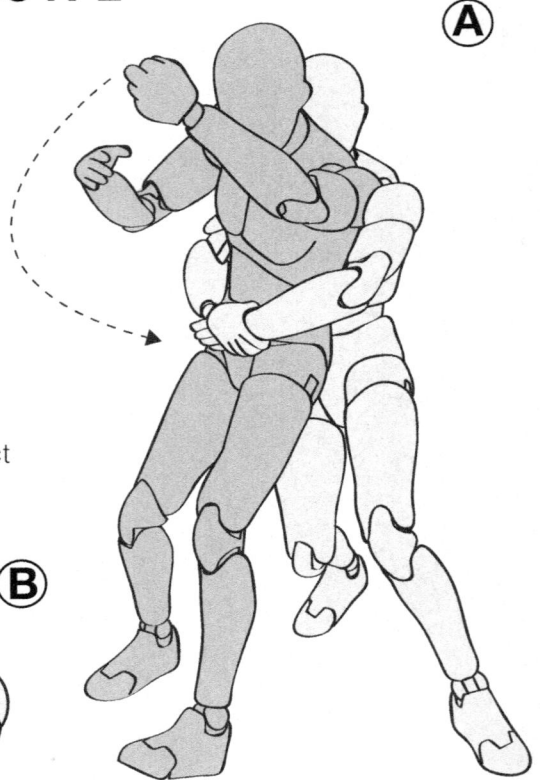

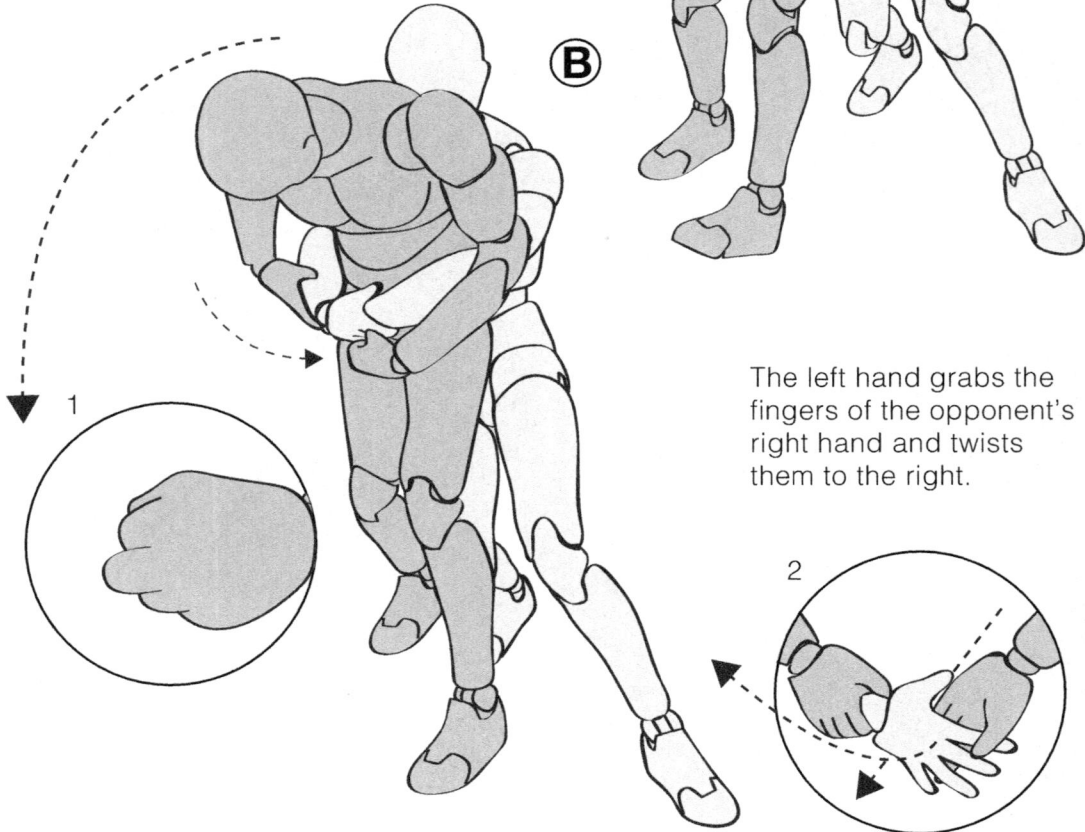

Ⓑ

1

The left hand grabs the fingers of the opponent's right hand and twists them to the right.

2

©

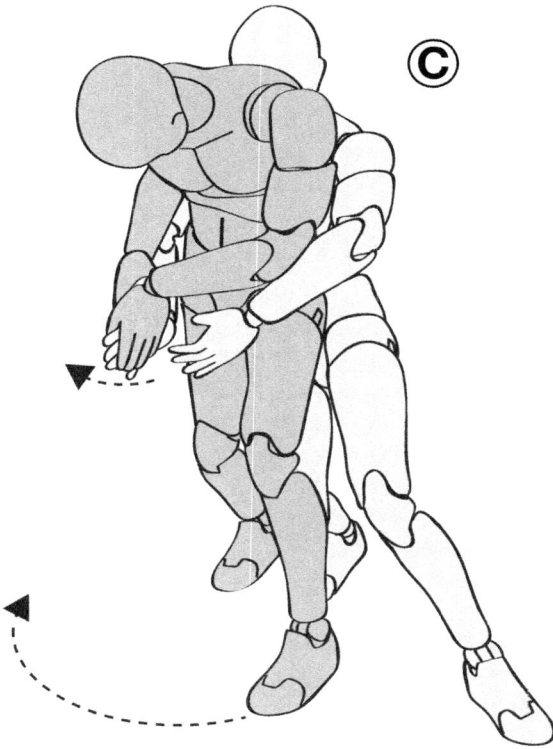

The same hand that hit, in this case, the left hand, now grabs the opponent's fingers and twists them to the right. At the same time, to move yourself away to the side, the left foot rotates virtually 180 degrees (C).

With the right hand holding the opponent's forearm and the left hand, his fingers, strike a sickle kick on the groins (D).

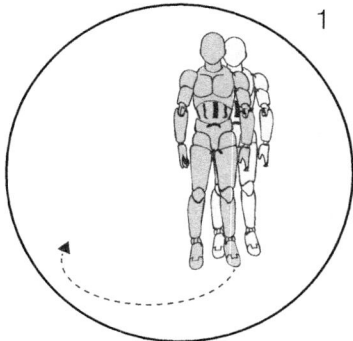

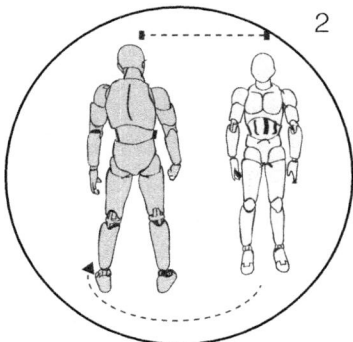

1

2

After rotating, the final position is side by side, or facing the opponent at an ideal distance to strike the sickle kick.

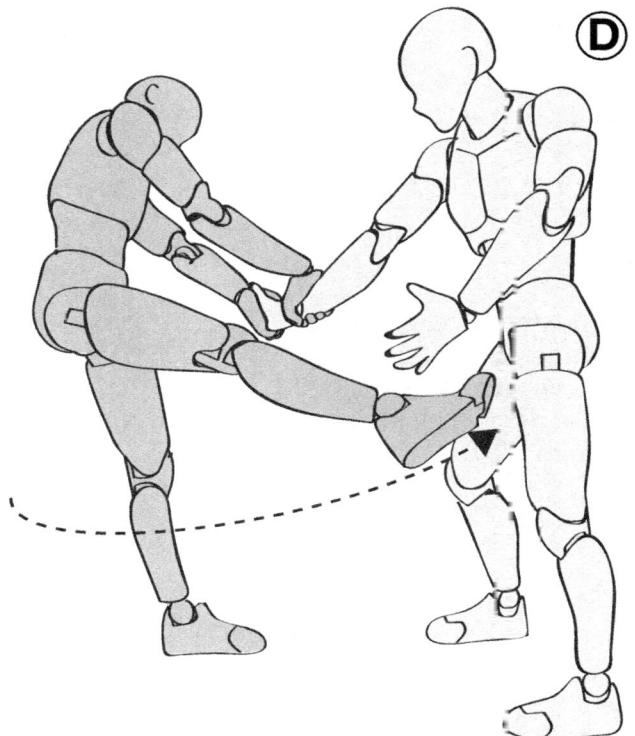

(D)

(E)

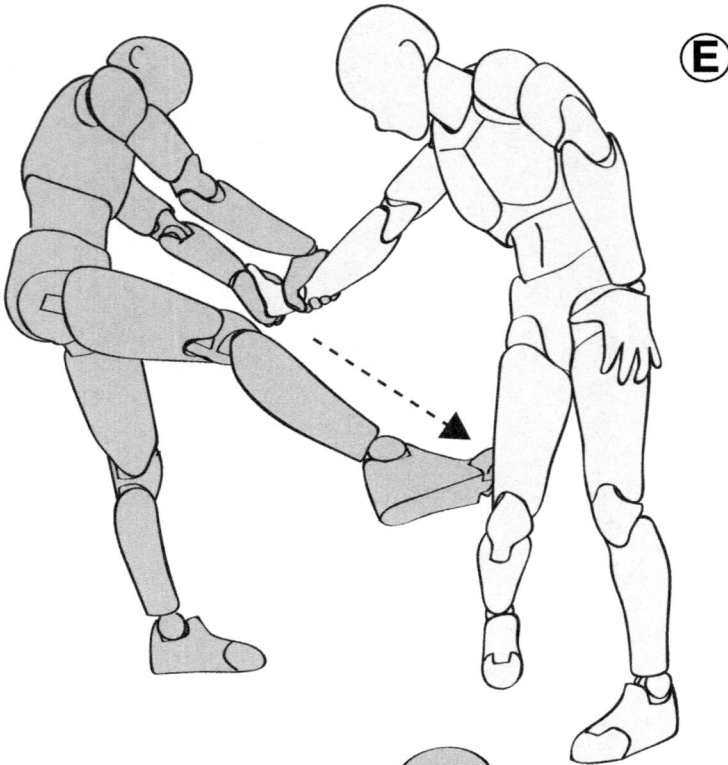

After the right-leg sickle kick and before you put your foot back on the ground, use the movement and the body weight to deliver a heel kick on his knee (E).

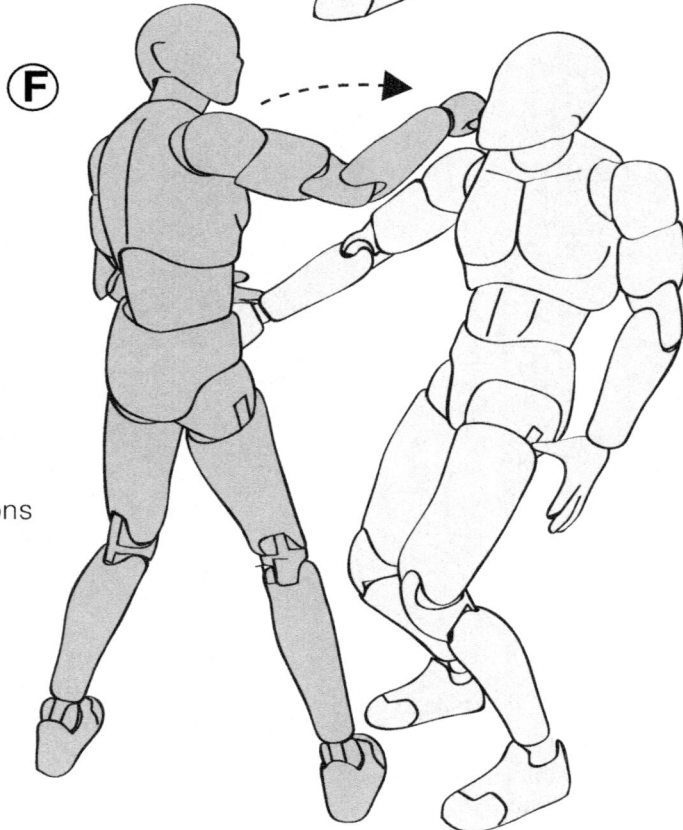

(F)

To complete, after the heel kick, deliver hammer fists and make the continuations required (F).

39 Defense Against a Grab from Behind

With hands free N°3

Ⓐ

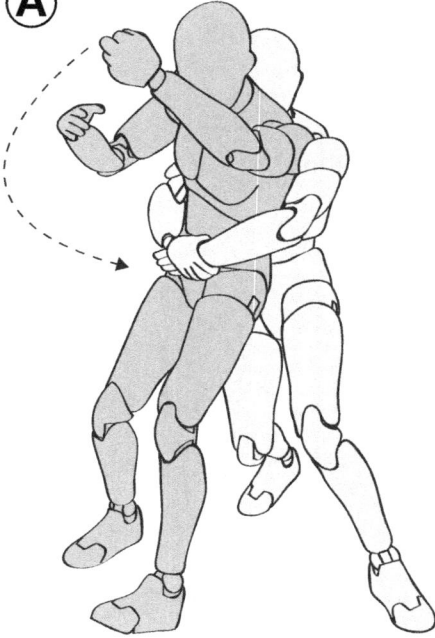

The Defense Against a Grab from Behind with hands free N°3 starts the same way than the previous defense (A). The right hand is also on the left hand and, while the right hand grabs the opponent's forearm close to his right wrist, the left hand hits the back of the right hand with the middle finger so that the opponent's hand opens because of the impact (B).

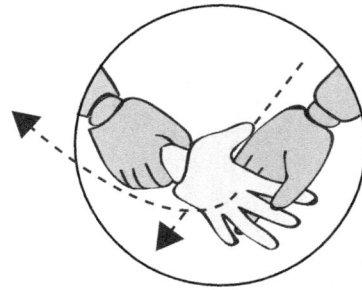

Ⓑ

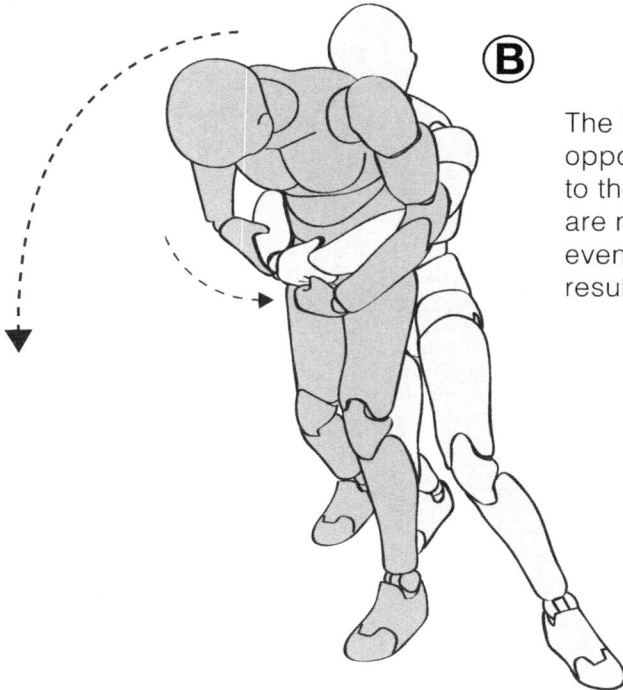

The left hand grabs the fingers of the opponent's right hand and twists them to the right. There is no problem if you are not able to grab all fingers because even if you grab just one finger, the result will be the same (C).

Ⓒ

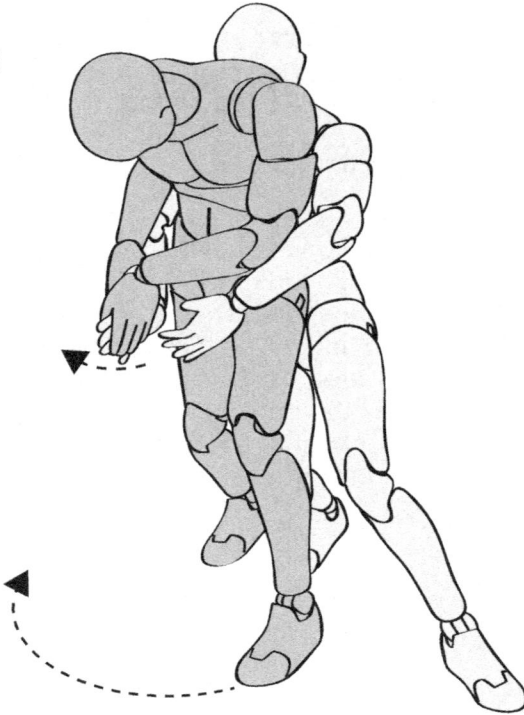

The difference between the previous defense and this one starts with the 180 degree rotation. To move yourself to the side, the left foot makes a shorter rotation and comes nearer the opponent.
Compare the images below with those of the previous defense.

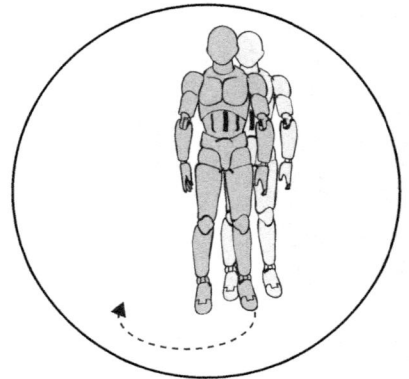

Ⓓ

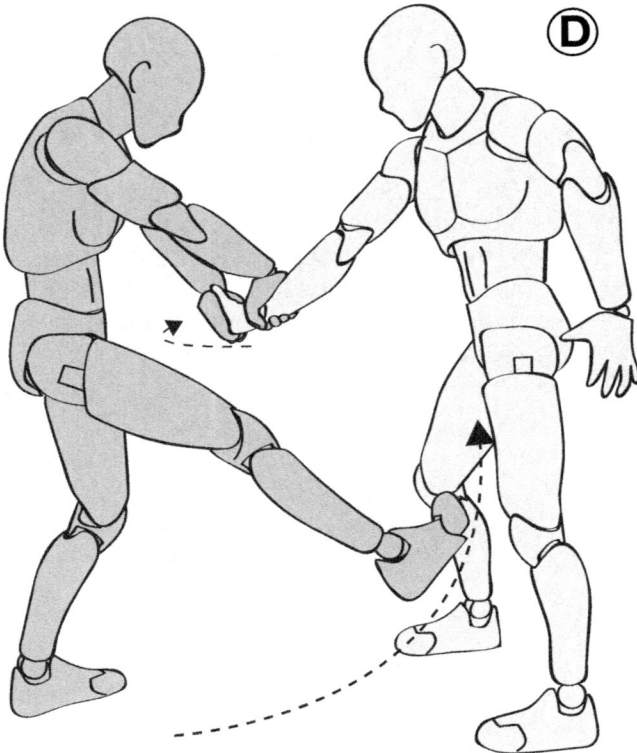

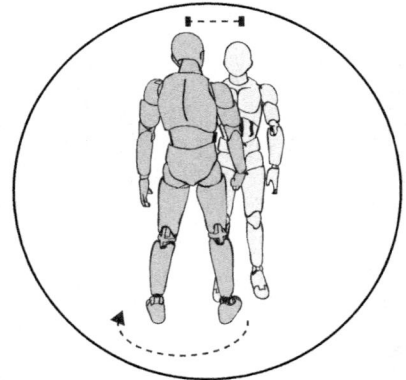

After rotating, the final position is side by side and facing the opponent in an ideal distance to strike a regular kick.
After the regular kick, you can start random sequences (D).

40 Defense Against a Grab from Behind
With hands pinned N°1

The Defense Against a Grab from Behind with hands pinned can be done with simple movements to release yourself from the opponent, or with a set of those movements. The opponent holds your arms strongly (A) and he can even press them against your own body, which may make breathing difficult.

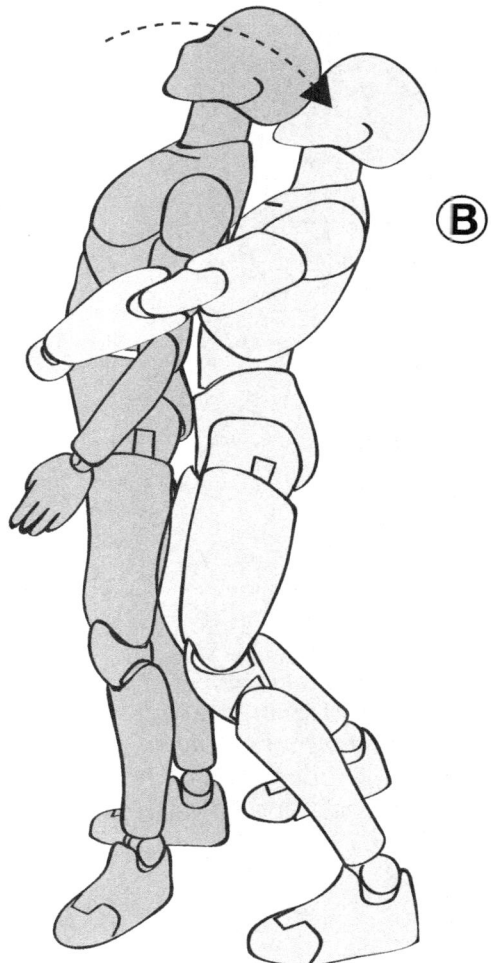

When feeling your hand pinned, tilt your head backward to hit the opponent's face.
The movement can be repeated several times until he releases you (B).

Sergio Nisenbaum

41 Defense Against a Grab from Behind
With hands pinned Nº2

(A)

When the opponent grabs you from behind with your hands pinned (A), he can try to lift you up or to overthrow you.

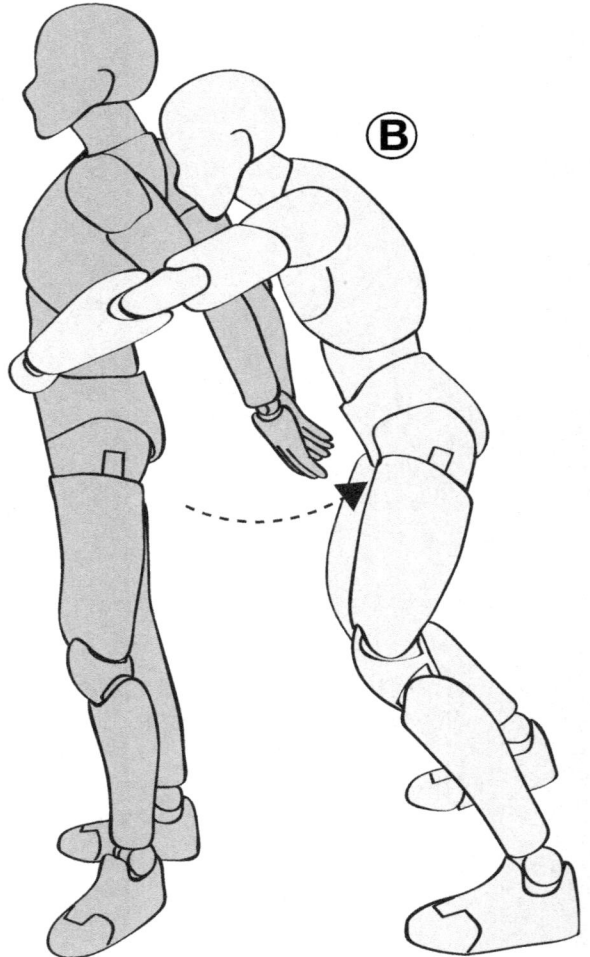

(B)

When you feel your hands pinned, to move the opponent away, hit your hands on his groins and hold tightly (B).

42 Defense Against a Grab from Behind
With hands pinned N°3

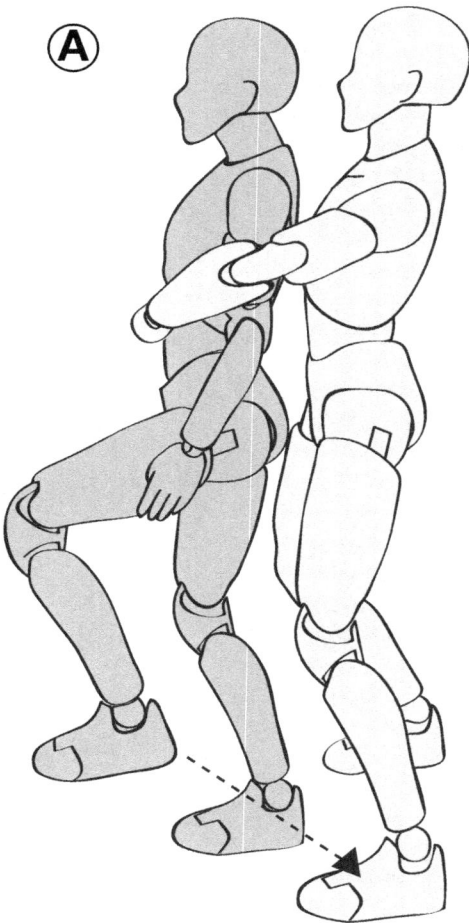

In the Defense Against a Grab from Behind with hands pinned N°3, the reaction is to step strongly on the opponent's instep with the heels of your foot.

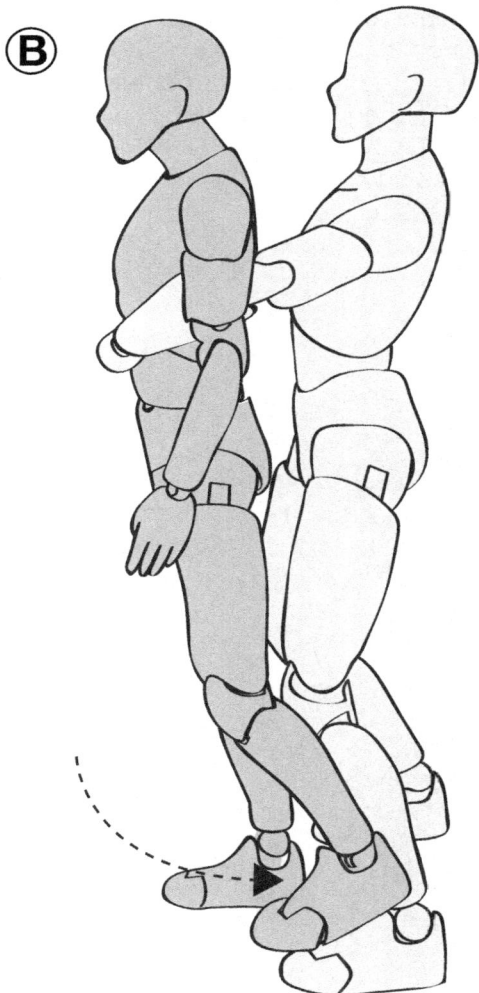

The movement of stepping on the opponent's instep can be made by alternating on both of his feet, or you can also hit the region of the opponent's shins with your heels (B).

Sergio Nisenbaum

43 Defense Against a Grab from Behind
With hands pinned N°4

The Defense Against a Grab from Behind with hands pinned N°4 is a set of all the previous defenses. When you feel the grab (A), all defensive movements are launched randomly until the opponent releases your arms. In this case, the defensive reaction starts with stepping on the opponent's instep (B). Next, the head is tilted to hit the opponent's face (C), then both hands hit his groins (D) and, as soon as he releases you, deliver elbow strikes outward.

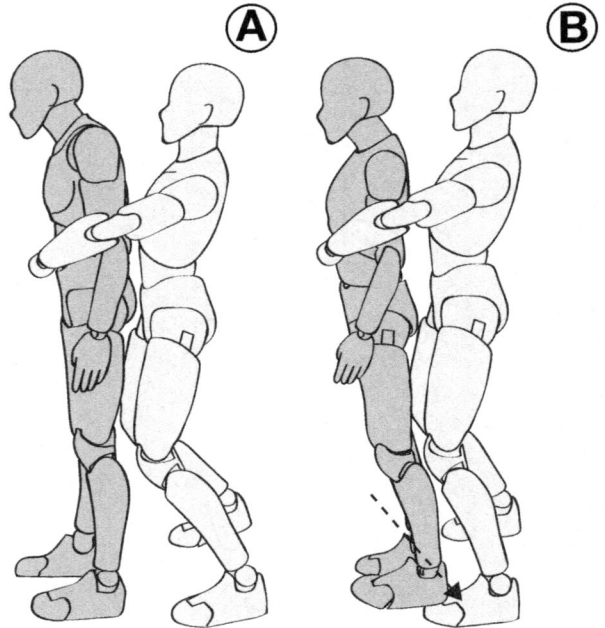

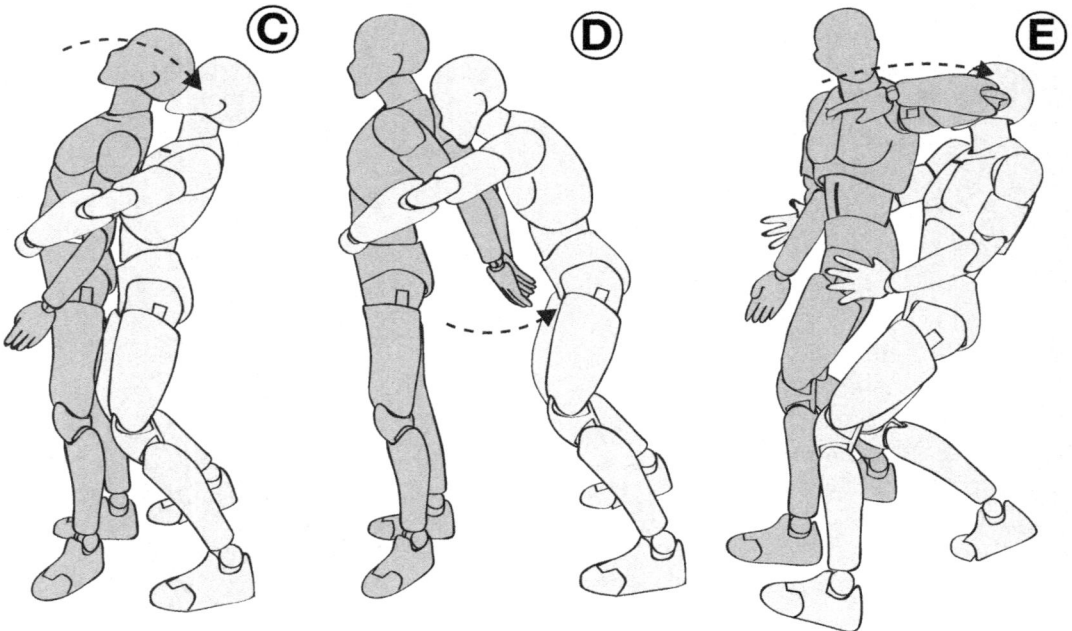

44 Defense Against a Grab from Behind

With hands pinned N°5

(A)

Observing the complete sequence since the beginning of the attack (A), in the Defense Against a Grab from Behind with hands pinned N°5, when the opponent starts to grab you (B), the body makes a sudden, quick, and strong movement sideways (C).

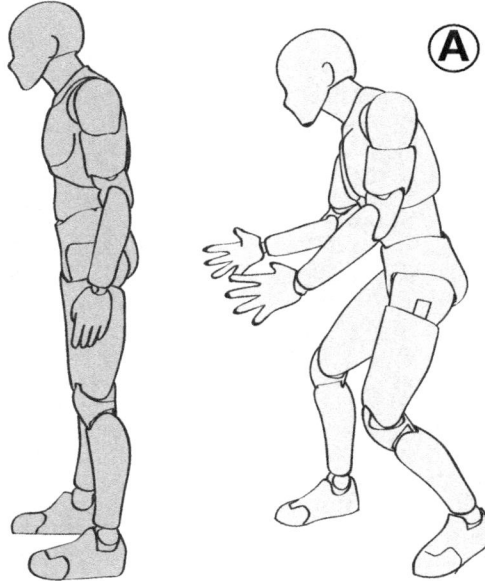

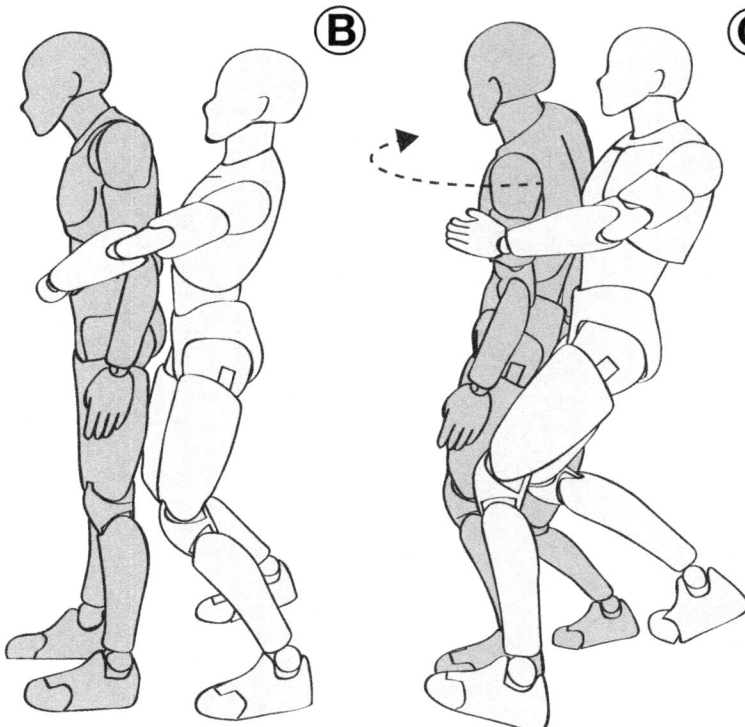

(B)

(C)

Swaying your body's weight helps making room to start to have your arms released. During the movement sideways you can try to tilt the head backward to hit the opponent's face, or you can hit his shin with your heels.

D

Even if the opponent continues to grab, the movement is repeated a few times to both sides until you feel that one of your arms is starting to be released (D).

The first arm released strikes a hand move in the opponent's groins (E) and does not let go. The body starts to tilt forward in a way that the other arm can also be released, and an elbow strike forward is delivered (F).

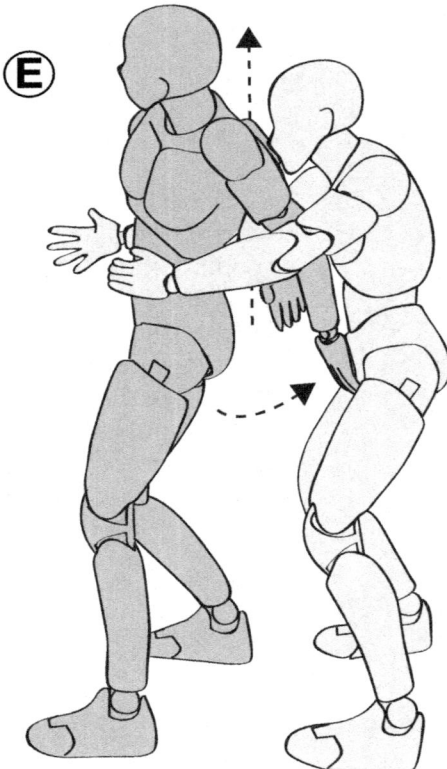

E

F

45 Defense Against a Grab from Behind when Lifted
With hands free

In the Defense Against a Grab from Behind when Lifted with hands free, the opponent comes from behind with the intention of grabbing and lifting you (A). As seen in the previous defenses, a simple movement tilting the body forward can make this task difficult.

If the opponent succeeds in lifting you up, the first reaction, which must be immediate and instinctive, is to hit the opponent's shins with your heels (B).

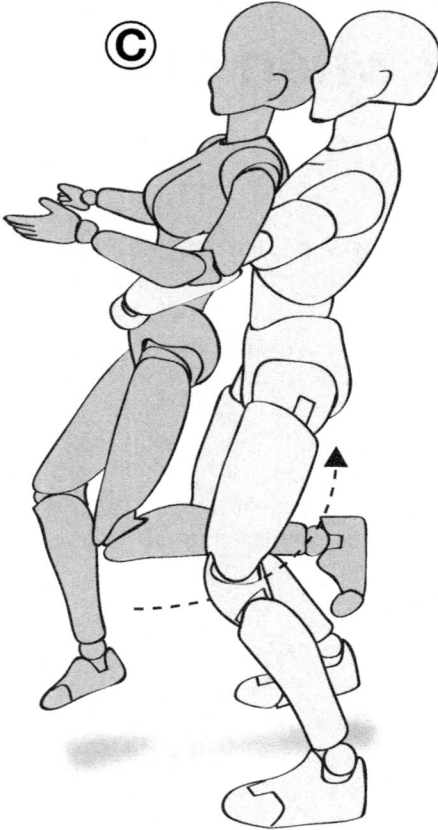

Another alternative is to raise your heels to hit the opponent's groins (C). Both movements can be used in combination: while one side hits the shin, the other hits the groins.

Now a lock is done with the foot behind the opponent's leg to deliver elbow strikes outward (D). Once the arms are free, the sequences of kicks and elbow strikes happen virtually at the same time, and they can be done in random order. For instance, the choice of locking the foot and launching an elbow strike can be the first reaction with several moves and, next, with other moves.

46 Defense Against a Grab from Behind when Lifted

With hands pinned

In the Defense of a Grab from Behind when lifted with hands pinned, the first reaction can also be, as in the previous defense, to hit the opponent's shin with your heels (A) and, at the same time, to raise the heels to hit the opponent's groins (B).

At the same time, the head makes movements backward to hit the opponent's face. The three movements happen simultaneously and randomly (B).

47

Defense Against a Front Grab when Lifted

With hands free N°1

(A)

In the Defense Against a Front Grab when lifted with hands free N°1 (A), both hands' thumbs go into the opponent's eyeball (B), as seen in exercise 28. When the opponent releases your arms, you make the continuations and the sequences required.

(B)

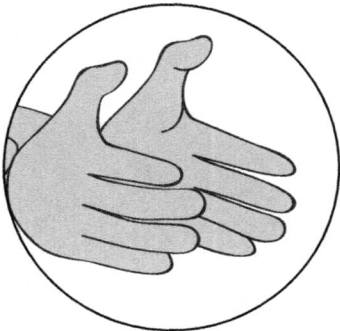

The tips of both thumbs press the opponent's eyeballs.

48 Defense Against a Front Grab when Lifted

With hands free N°2

(A)

In the Defense Against a Front Grab when lifted with hands free N°2 (A), the option here is to deliver a Hammer Fist forward to hit the upper part of the opponent's nose (B).

(B)

After the hammer fist forward, pressuring the thumbs on the eyeballs can be done before the sequences, if it is still necessary.

49 Defense Against a Front Grab when Lifted

With hands pinned

In the case of Front Grab but with the hands pinned (B), deliver knee strikes on the opponent's groins (B).

The knee strikes must be very quick and delivered at the beginning of the attack when the opponent is starting to lift you (B). Other options are biting the neck region or, depending on the hands' position, even with the arms pinned, to hit the opponent's groins.

50 Defense Against a Grab from Behind

With hands pinned, against two opponents

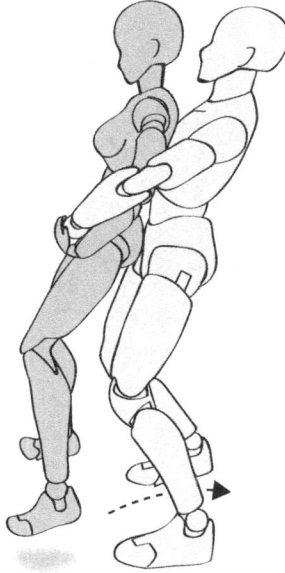

Any of the exercises previously seen can be used as a defensive reaction when the opponent grabs you from behind, regardless if the grab happens on the ground or when you have been lifted (A). The situation now is quite dangerous because it involves 2 opponents. The one who is behind you aims at grabbing you for the other one to come closer and attack.

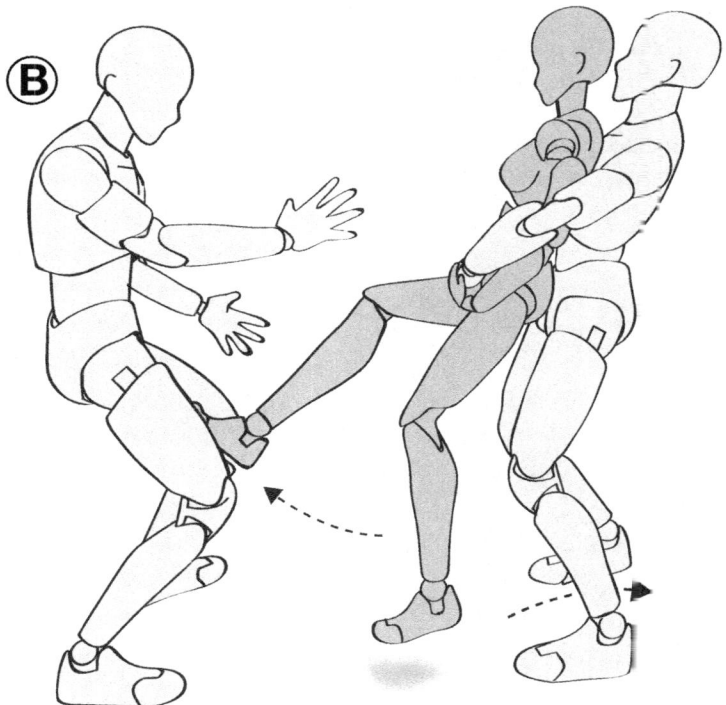

Deliver a regular kick on the groins as soon as the second opponent comes closer (B). Other kicks can also be delivered, such as with your heels on his knee or a sickle kick.

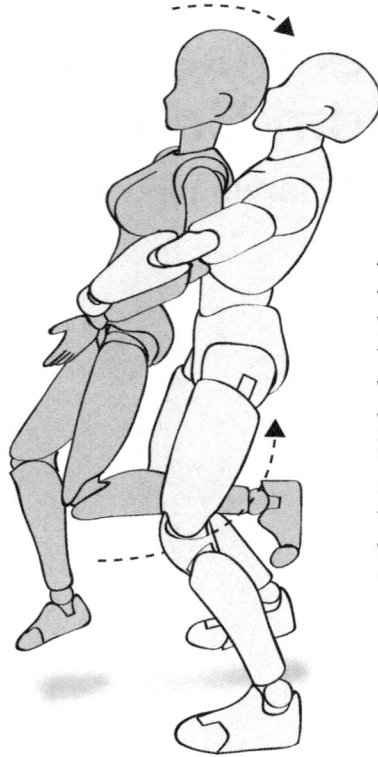

©

As seen in exercise 46, to release yourself from the opponent who is grabbing you, your head makes movements backward to reach the opponent's face while the heel hits his groins (C).

Ⓓ

If necessary, after locking with your foot from behind the opponent's leg, deliver elbow moves outward (D). When you are free, the continuations can be done against the opponent who was grabbing you and against the one who came closer.

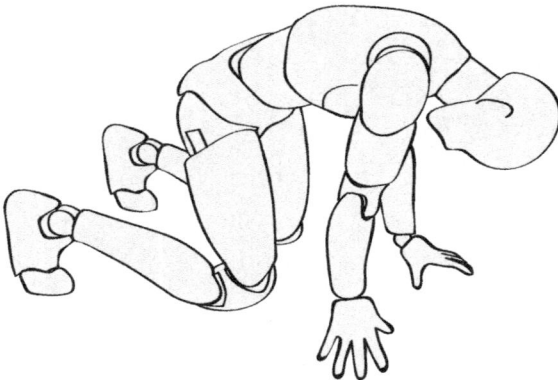

Defenses Against Attacks on the Ground

Two situations can lead to this type of attack, which is rather dangerous. The first one, when you are already lying on the ground when you are attacked; the second, when the opponent has overthrown you. Next, you will see two types of attacks on the ground with you in different positions: one, where the opponent is holding your arms to immobilize you, and the other when he is choking you. Regardless if the opponent is jus holding your arms or choking you, the lying position is a disadvantage, and it needs to be immediately changed with an extremely quick reaction.

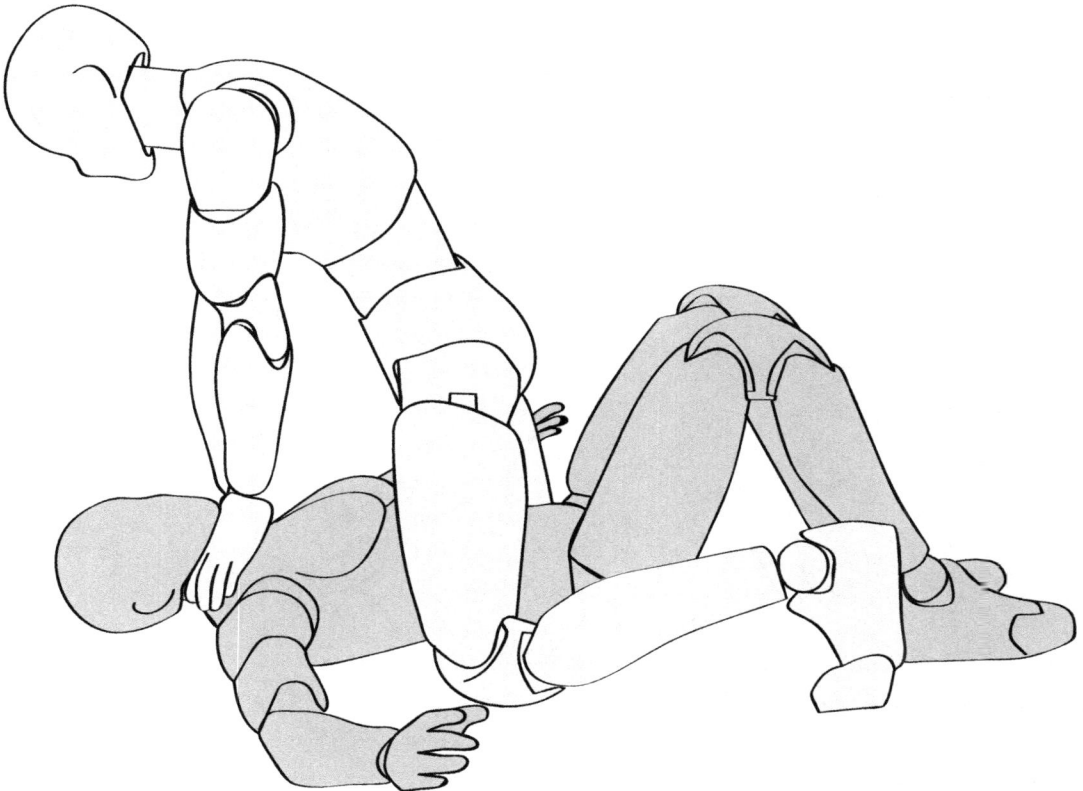

Sergio Nisenbaum

51 Defense Against an Attack on the Ground
With hands pinned

In this situation, the opponent is sitting on top of you and pinning your arms (A). To start the defense, the arms pinned move until they are positioned downward, the hands are locked and closed to simultaneously make a rotation inward supported by the elbows.

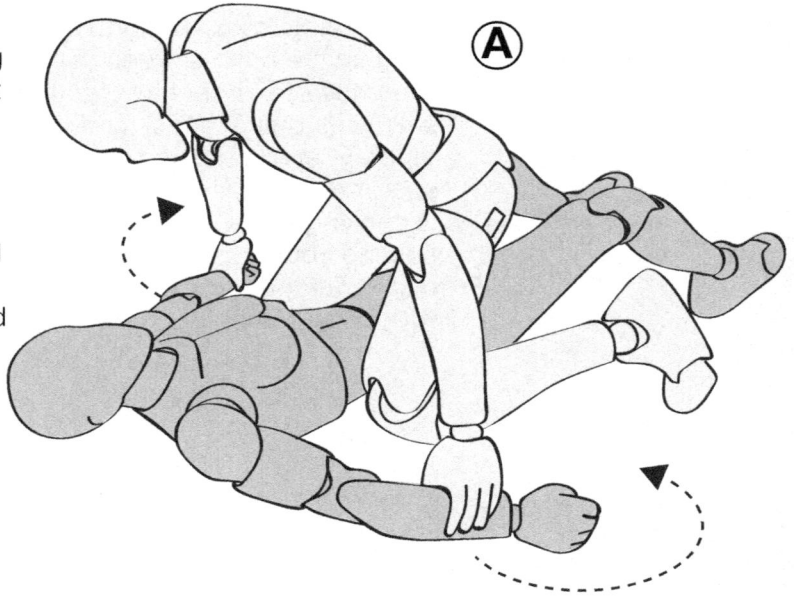

(A)

The closed hands deliver a boxing strike on the abdomen or ribs. At the same time, the right foot offers support on the ground to help lifting the hips up (B).

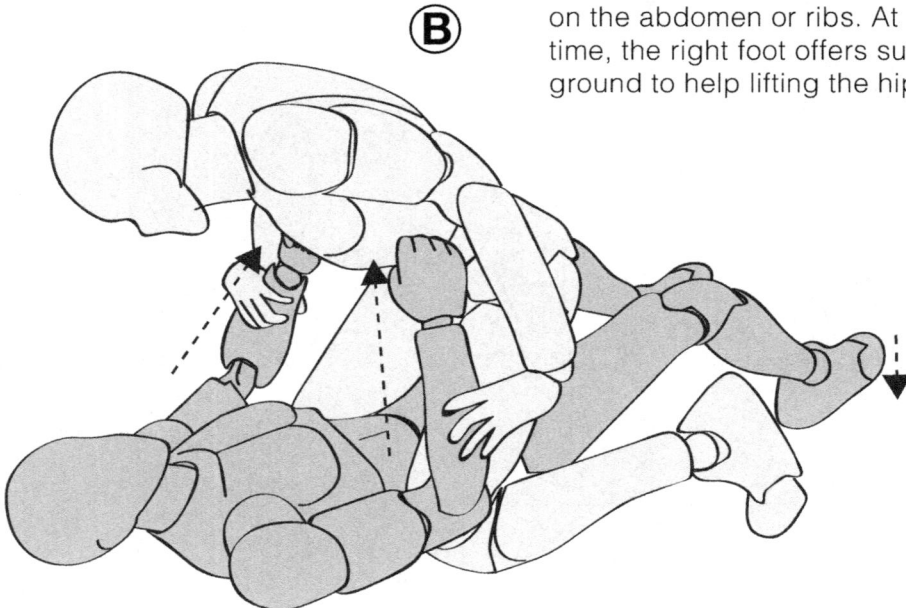

(B)

Supported by the right foot, the hips are raised from the ground and turn the body sideways. All movements will be made virtually at the same time: the boxing strike, foot support, and rotation. The result makes the opponent lose his balance and fall sideways (C).

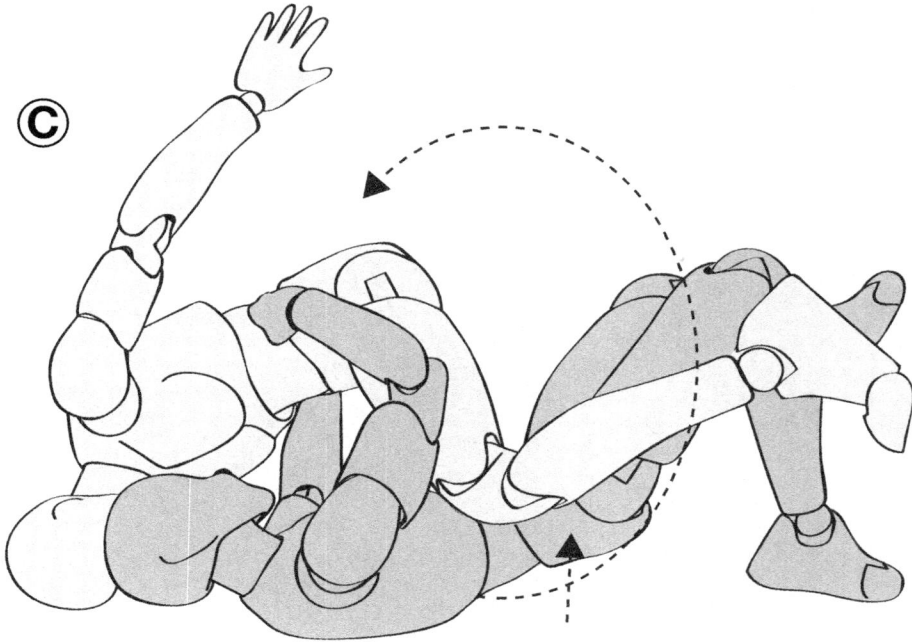

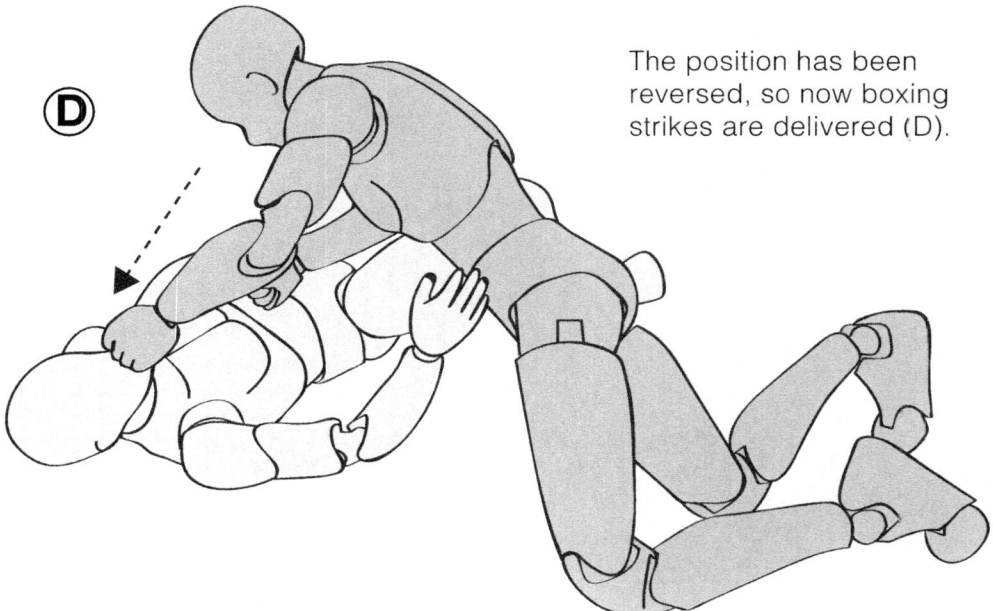

Ⓒ

Ⓓ

The position has been reversed, so now boxing strikes are delivered (D).

52 Defense Against a Choke on the Ground Nº1

In a choke on the ground, the opponent may be positioned in several different ways. Here he is kneeling at your side (A).

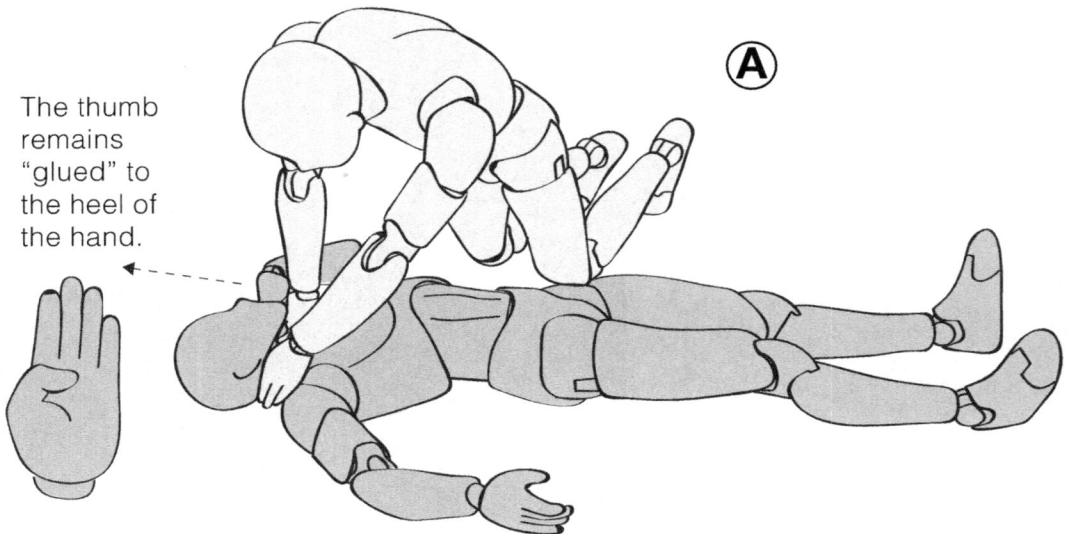

The thumb remains "glued" to the heel of the hand.

(A)

The fingers jointly make a hook position (1) and pull the opponent's thumb thus making his hand move away. At the same time, the right hand's fingertips strike the opponent's trachea (2). This movement can be made between the opponent's arms or from the outside (B).

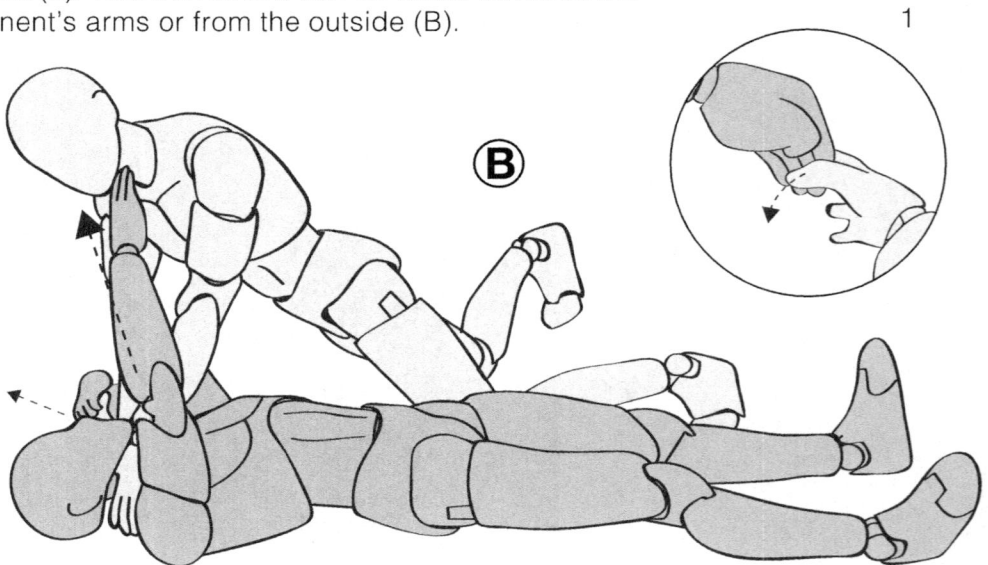

(B)

1

The move of the fingertips on the trachea makes the opponent's veer away. In this moment, the left knee is placed on the opponent's body, thus preventing him from coming closer (C). The higher the area where the knee is placed, the fewer are the chances of having the opponent come closer again.

2

C

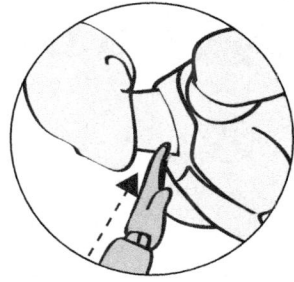

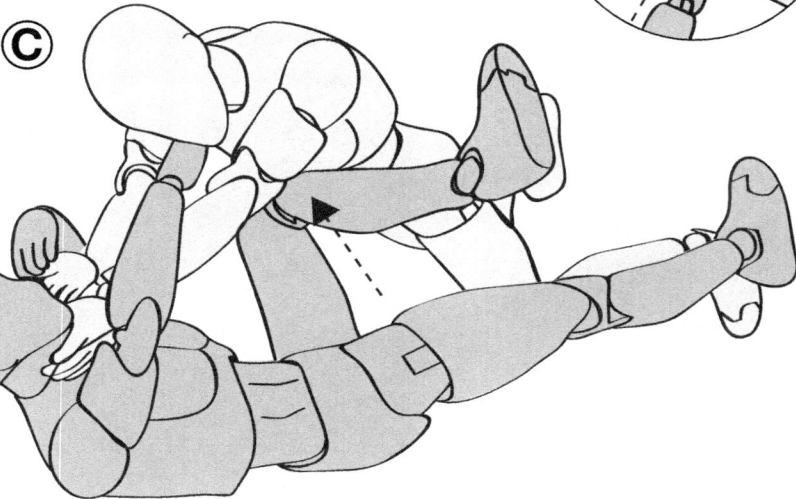

With both hands holding the opponent's right hand and supported by the knee, deliver heel strikes with your right foot on the opponent's face (D).

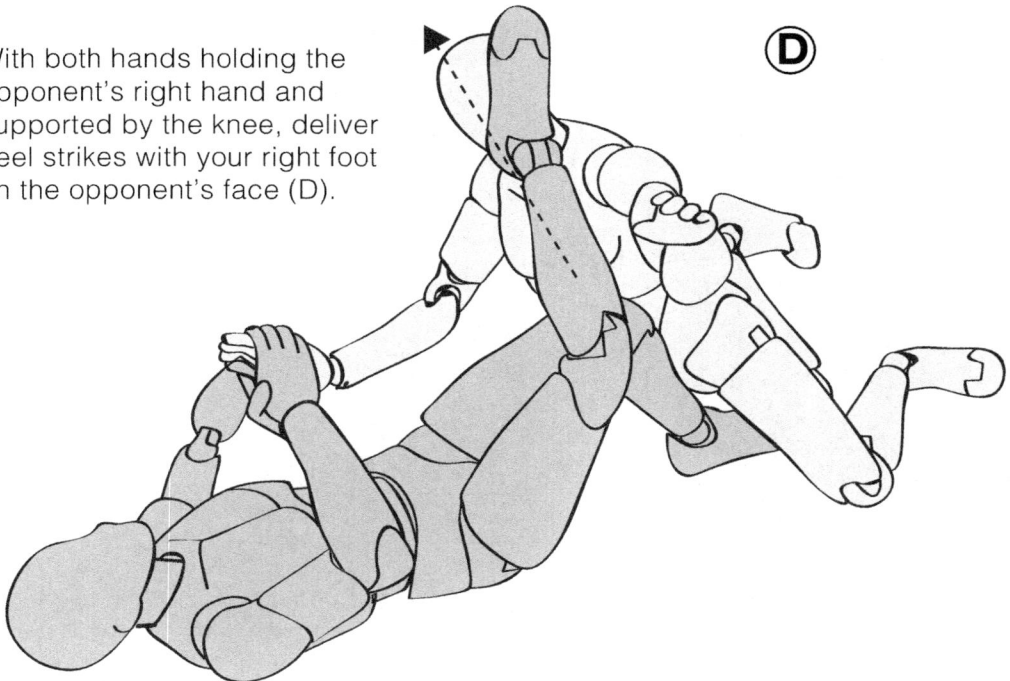

D

Sergio Nisenbaum

53 Defense Against a Choke on the Ground Nº2

A

In this defense, the opponent is also choking you kneeling at your side (A). The defense is done with a set of simultaneous quick movements of hands and legs.

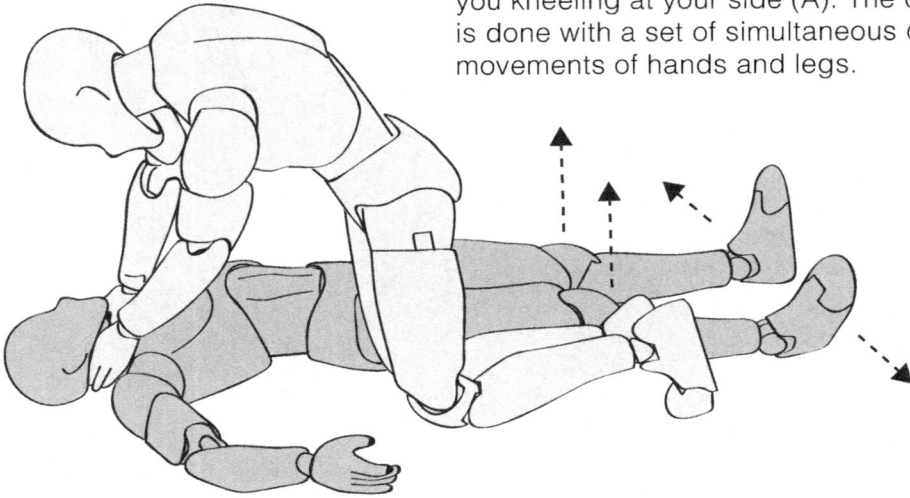

B

The left hand pulls the opponent's thumb, thus making his hand veer away, the right hand strikes with a move of the fingertips on the side of the opponent's neck, the legs move sideways stretched or with the knees flexed, and the trunk gets off the ground (B).

The fingers strike the side of the neck to move it away and to have the opponent fall between the legs.

With the set of all movements made at the same time and the impact of the hand move on the neck, the opponent loses his balance and falls between the legs (C).

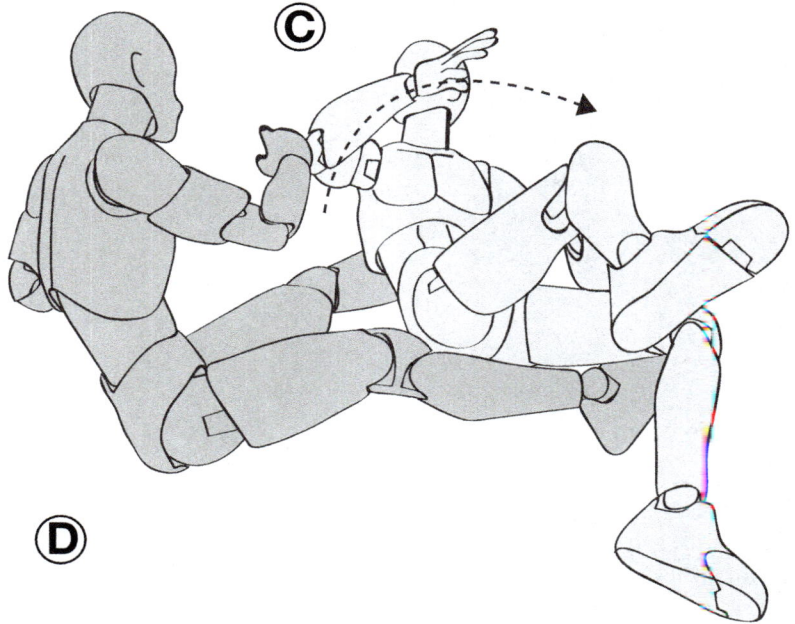

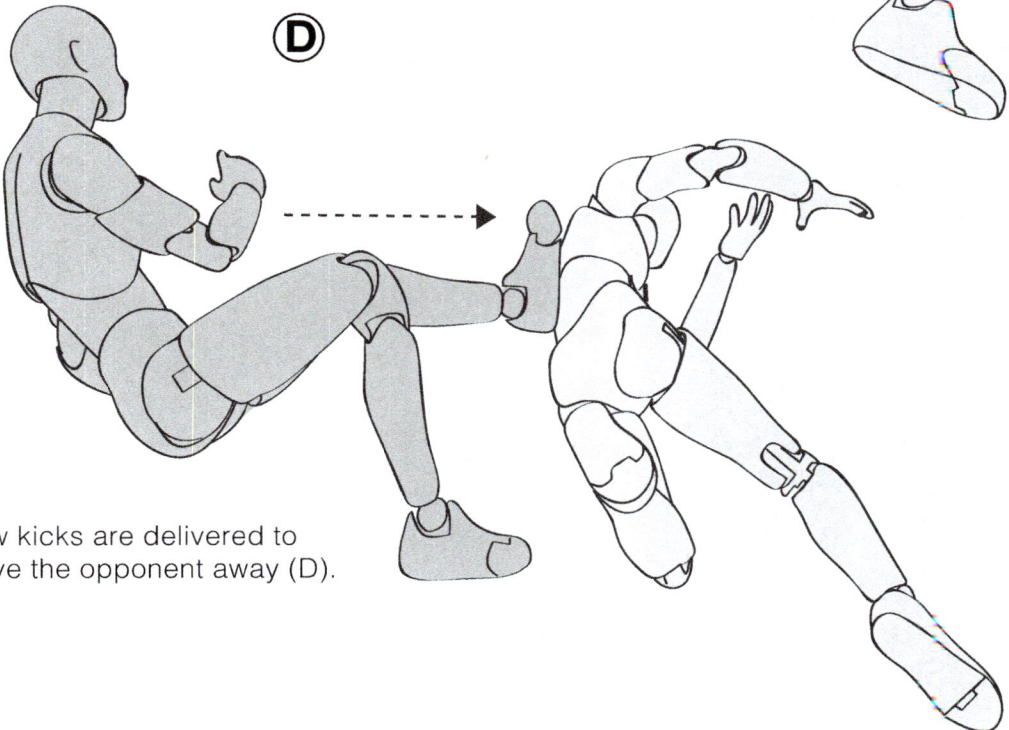

Ⓒ

Ⓓ

Now kicks are delivered to move the opponent away (D).

54 Defense Against a Choke on the Ground N°3

In the Defense Against a Choke on the Ground N°3, the opponent is sitting on top of you to choke you (A). The defensive reaction is extremely quick, and its movements are rather like those in the previous defenses.

Both hands pull the opponent's thumbs making his hands move away from the neck (B).

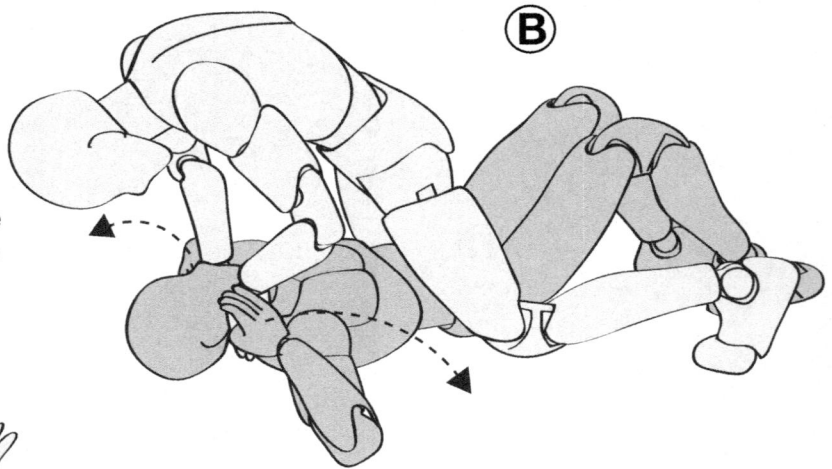

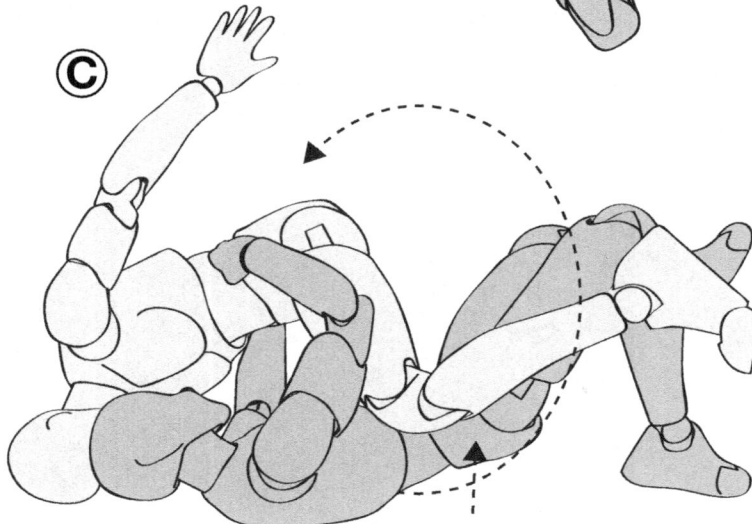

The hands closed launch a boxing strike on the abdomen or ribs. At the same time, the right foot offers support on the ground to help raise the hips and to overthrow the opponent to the side (C).

55 Defense Against a Choke on the Ground N°4

Like in the previous defense, the opponent is also sitting on top of you to choke you, but now with a small difference: his head is closer (A).

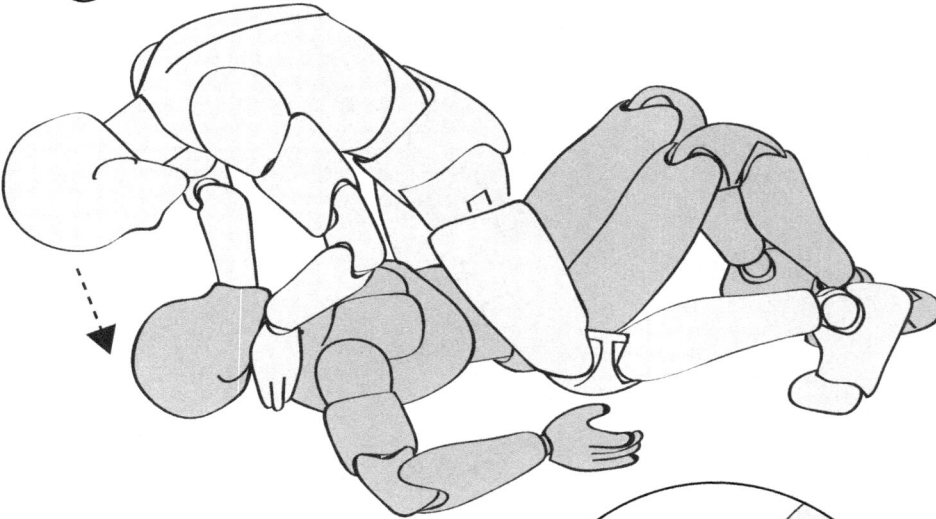

As the opponent's head is at a shorter distance or getting closer, use the thumbs of both hands to press his eyeballs (B).

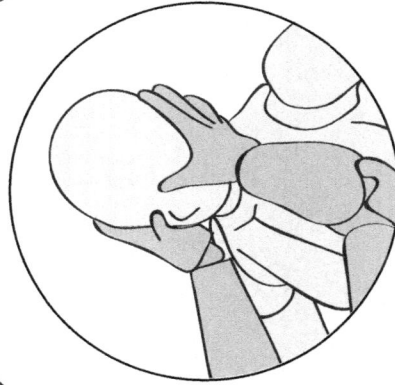

The tips of the thumbs press the eyeballs inward.

The thumbs' tips continue to press the eyeballs, and, at the same time, they push the opponent's head to the side. Supported by the right foot, the hips come off the ground and help to turn the body sideways (C).

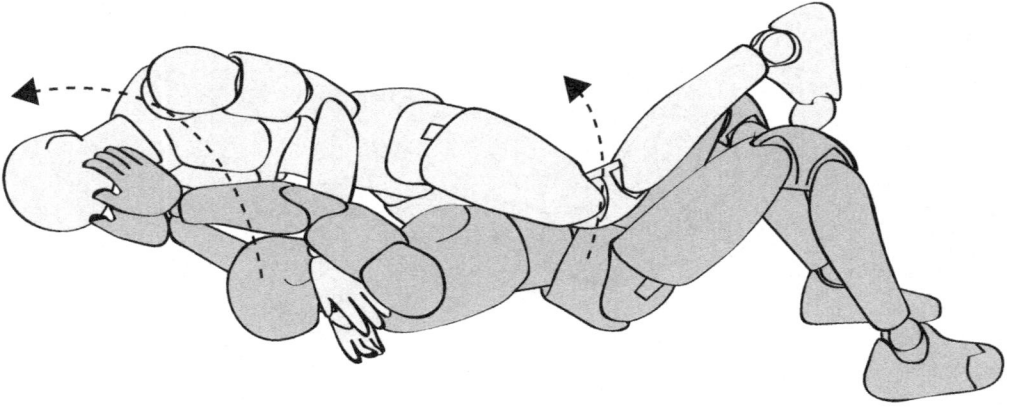

The position is reversed, and the thumbs keep on pressing the opponent's eyeballs until you can control the situation and, if necessary, continue delivering boxing and elbow strikes (D).

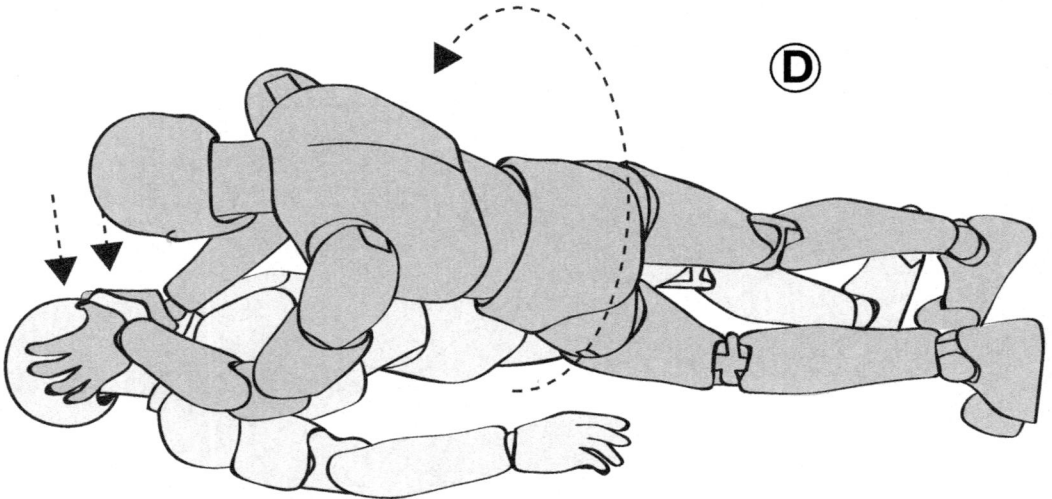

Defenses Against Hair Grabs

The attacks involving hair grabbing result from a lack of control caused by the opponent's movements and they can occur in many different directions. The opponent may try to lead you elsewhere, to overthrow you on the ground, or to try another attack. When you feel your hair has been grabbed, the first instinctive reaction should be delivering sequences of kicks and hand moves, which will be delivered at sensitive and vital points, or to grab the opponent's hand to control and do the defenses shown next.

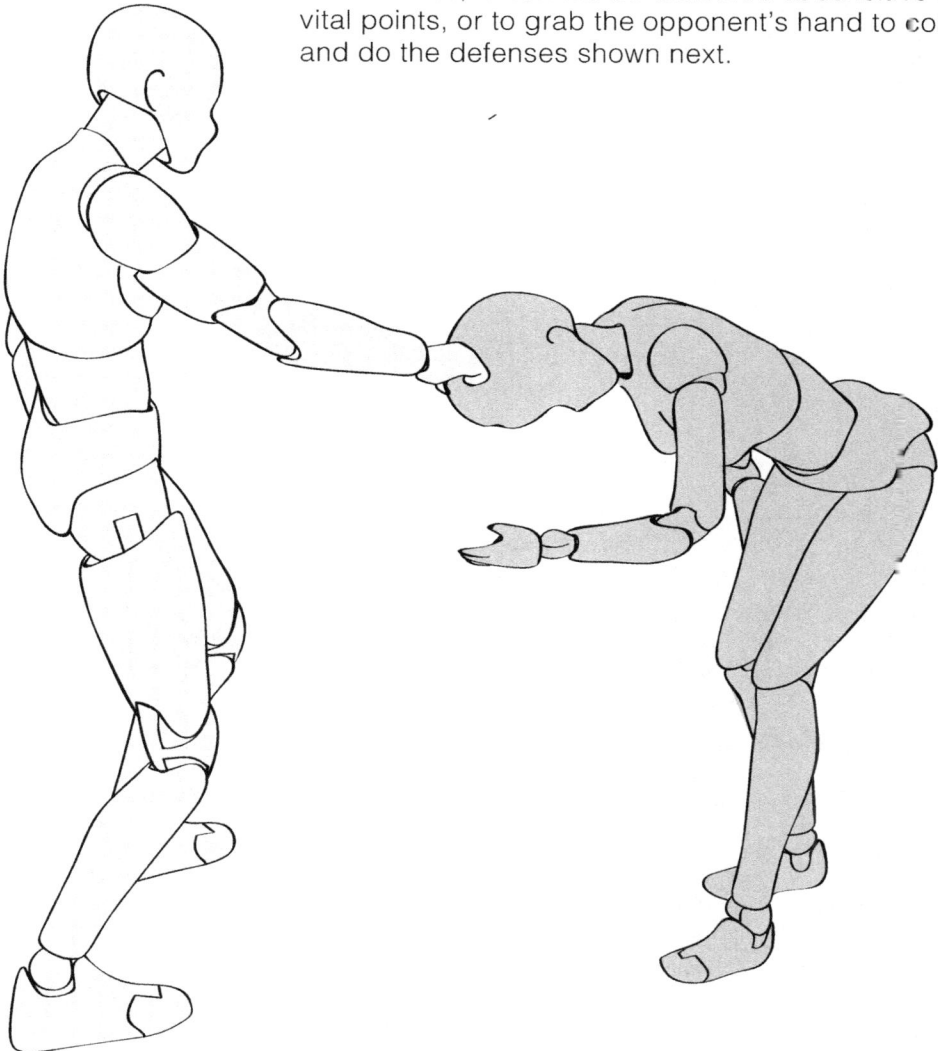

56 Defense Against a Front Hair Grab

Here, the opponent is holding your hair positioned in front of you to try to overthrow you (A). The first defensive reaction is to have the control of the situation back.

Both hands press the hand grabbing the hair against your own head. At the same time, deliver a regular kick on the opponent's groins (B). Tilt your body downward and keep the opponent's hand pressed against your head up to the end of this movement, which will make a strong pressure on his wrist (C).

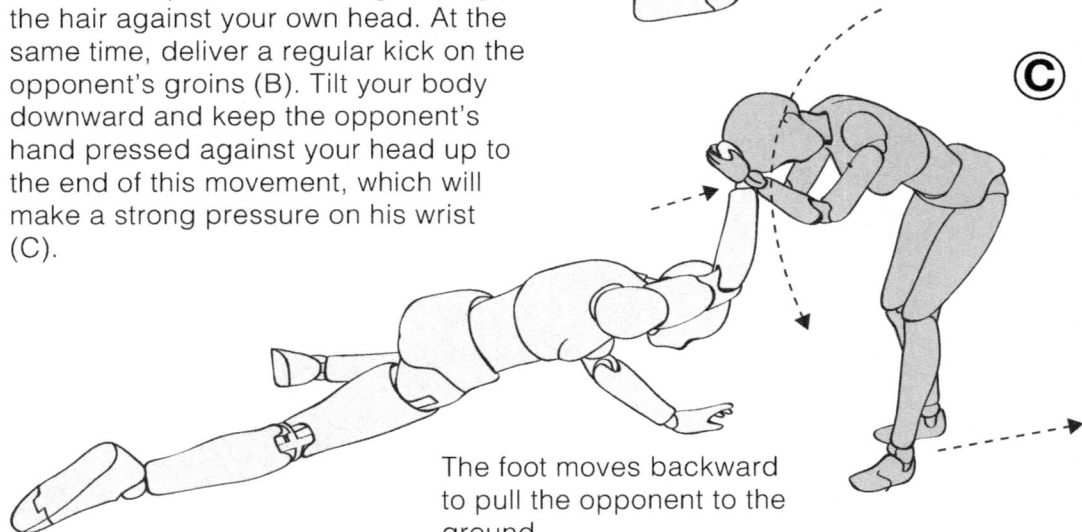

The foot moves backward to pull the opponent to the ground.

57 Defense Against a Hair Grab from Behind

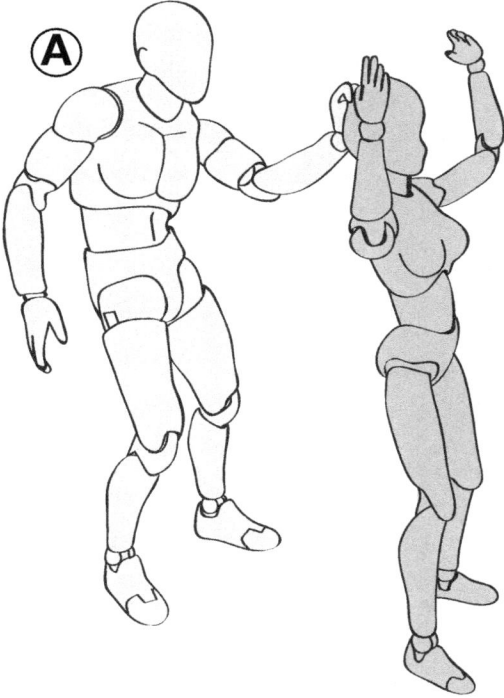

(A)

Now, the opponent is grabbing your hair backward to try to drag you, to overthrow you, or to make strong movements sideways (A).

As in this situation, the hair is being grabbed from behind, this position causes more lack of control and loss of balance when compared to the previous one, which happens in front of you.

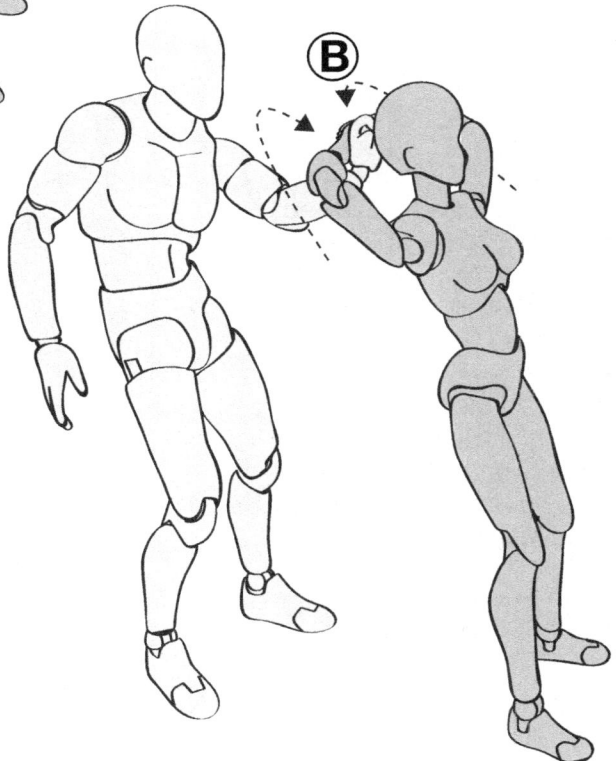

(B)

To regain control, one hand, or both, grab the hand of the opponent that is grabbing your hair (B). If you are not able to grab the hand, you can also grab your hair quite close to the head.

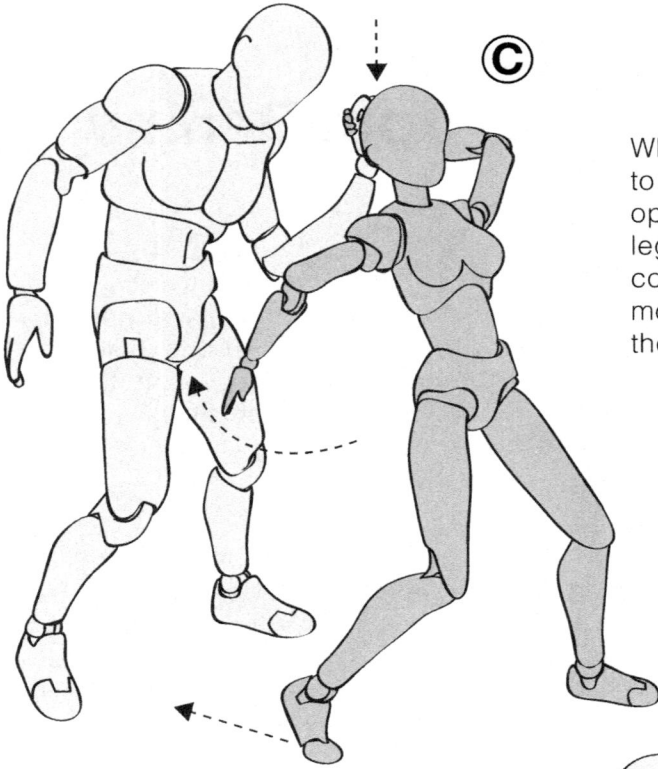

While one hand continues to hold and control the opponent's hand, the right leg takes a step back to come closer and deliver a move with the hand open on the opponent's groins (C).

You can deliver repeated moves on the opponent's groins until you feel his hand starts to release your hair.

After the moves on the groins, and still holding the opponent's hand, your elbow raises to hit the opponent's chin (D).

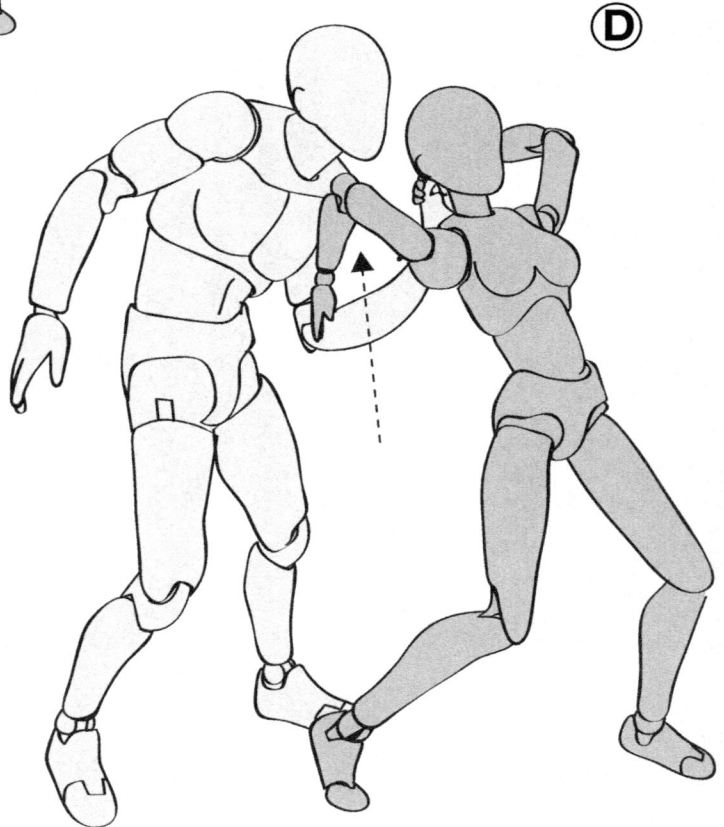

58 Defense Against a Hair Grab from the Side

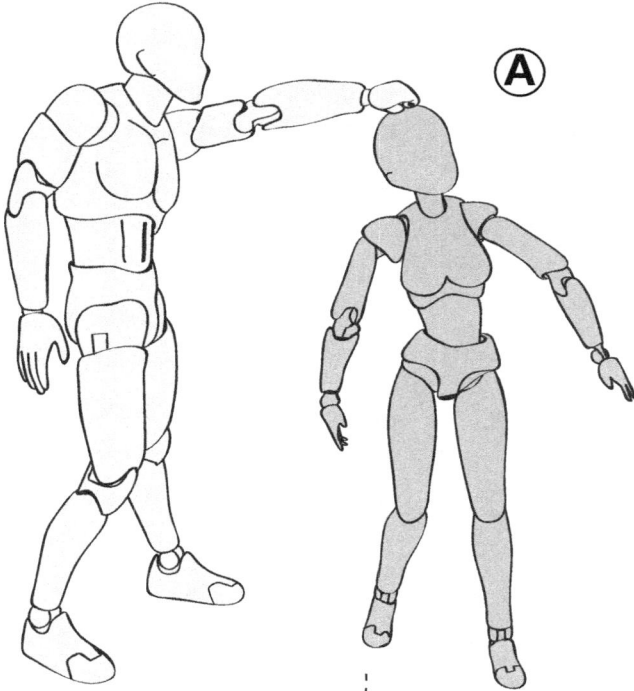

Ⓐ

The opponent is positioned by your side and is grabbing your hair from above (A). To try to regain control, the hand that is farther, in this case, the left hand, grabs from above the opponent's hand. The right leg takes a sidestep to come closer and, at the same time, delivers moves with the right hand on the opponent's groins (B). Like in the previous defense, after the moves on the groins, and still holding the hand, you raise the elbow toward the opponent's chin (C).

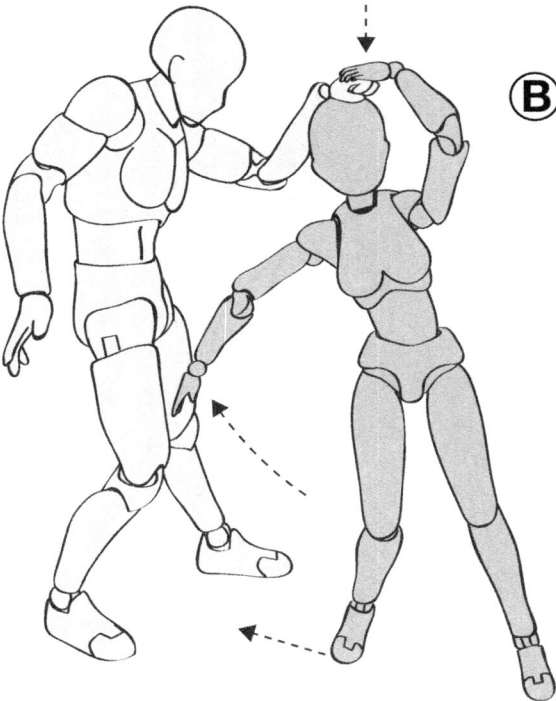

Ⓑ

Ⓒ

Defenses Against Arm Pulls

This is a situation where both opponents simultaneously grab each arm to take it elsewhere, or even for a third person to come close and attack you. Like in the previous attack of hair grab, quick movements of arm pull to each side also can result in a lack of control and a difficult reaction. For that purpose, the defense combines movements of the arms and kicks, which must happen immediately.

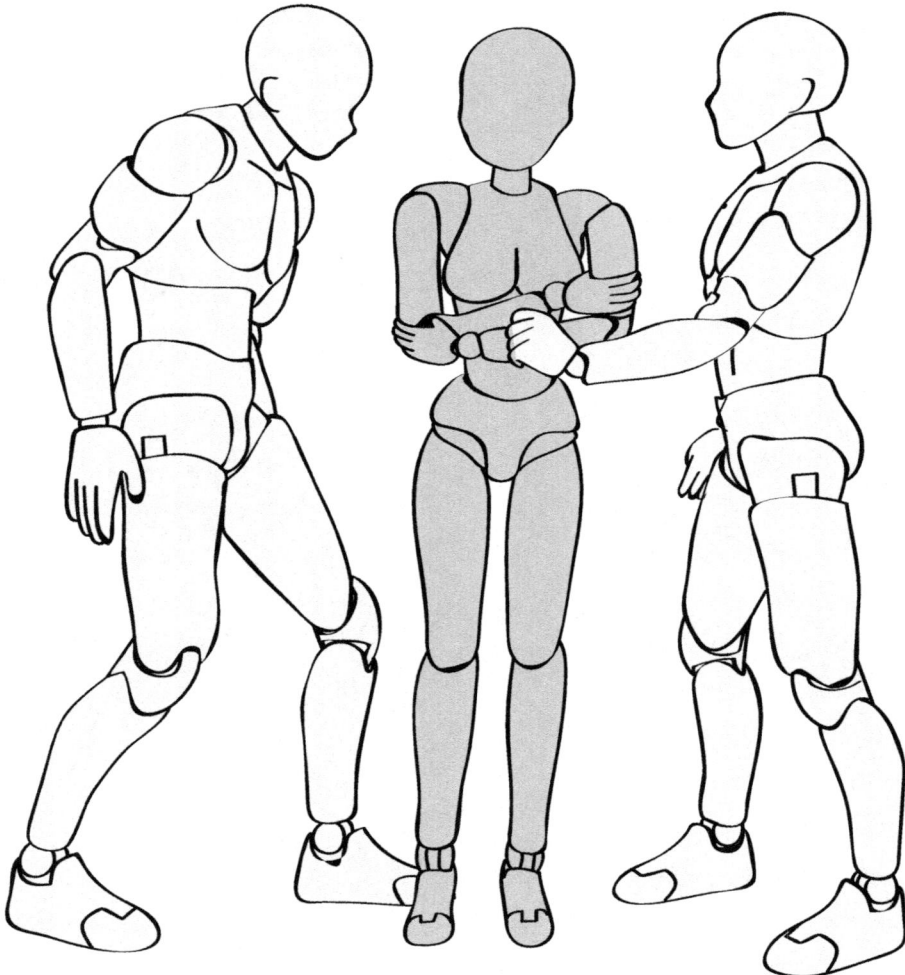

59 Defense Against an Arm Pull N°1

Against 2 opponents

An attack involving more than one opponent always stands for more danger. In this case, each one is holding one arm and pulling it to each side (A).

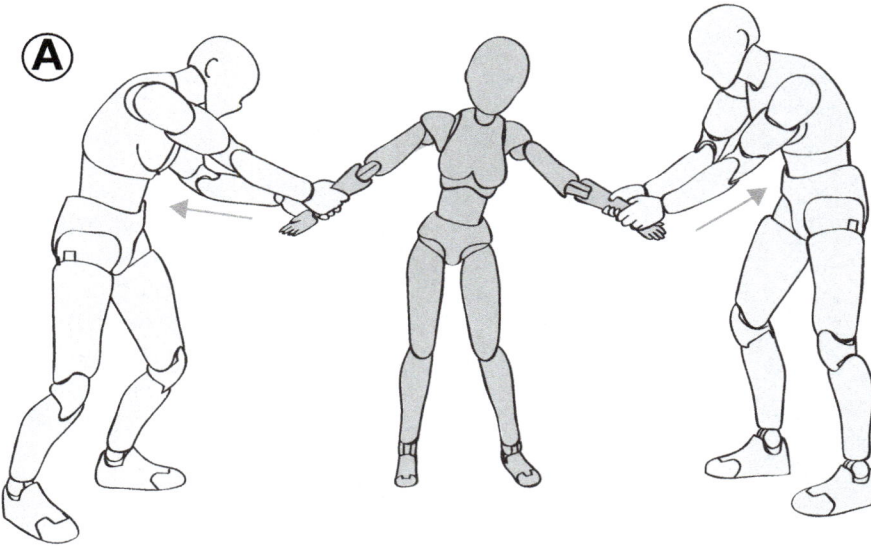

To prevent the arms from stretching and allowing the opponents to take control of the situation, the elbows must be flexed and come closer to the body to be positioned and stay at an adequate distance for the reaction (B).

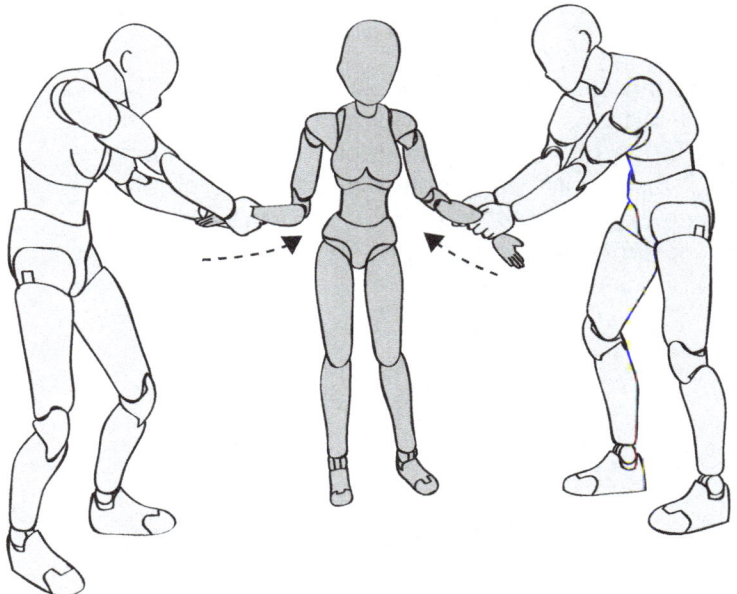

Ⓒ

At the proper distance and position, deliver a right-leg regular kick (1) on the opponent's groins who is at your right side (C).

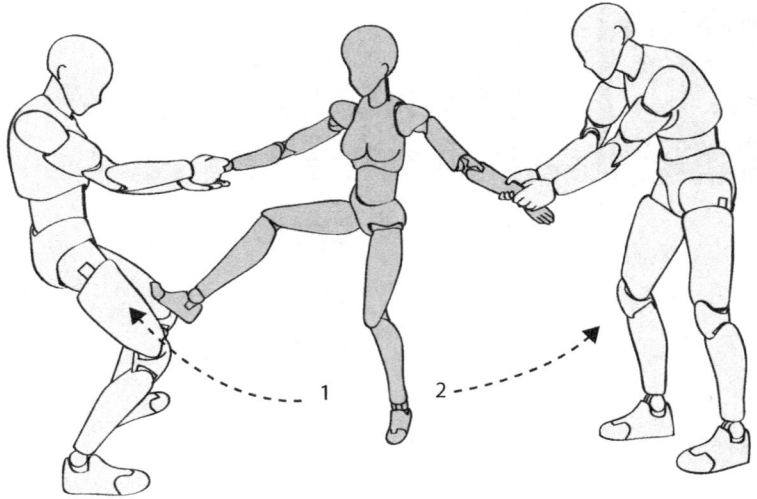

Ⓓ

The right foot goes back to the ground, and, at the same time, you change legs and deliver a left-leg regular kick (2) aimed at the second opponent (D).

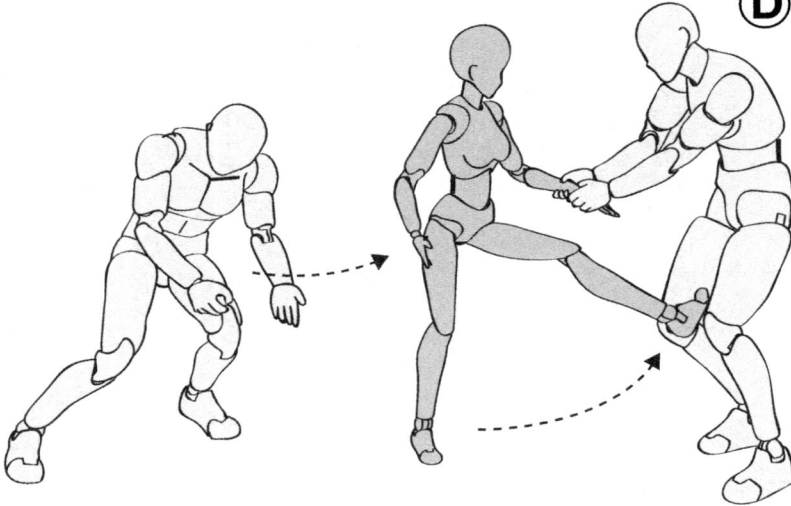

Ⓔ

After the second regular kick, quickly do the continuations with the sequences of boxing strikes and other movements of attack. Once there are two opponents, the reaction must be extremely quick to avoid that you remain too long with your back turned to the first opponent who has been hit (E).

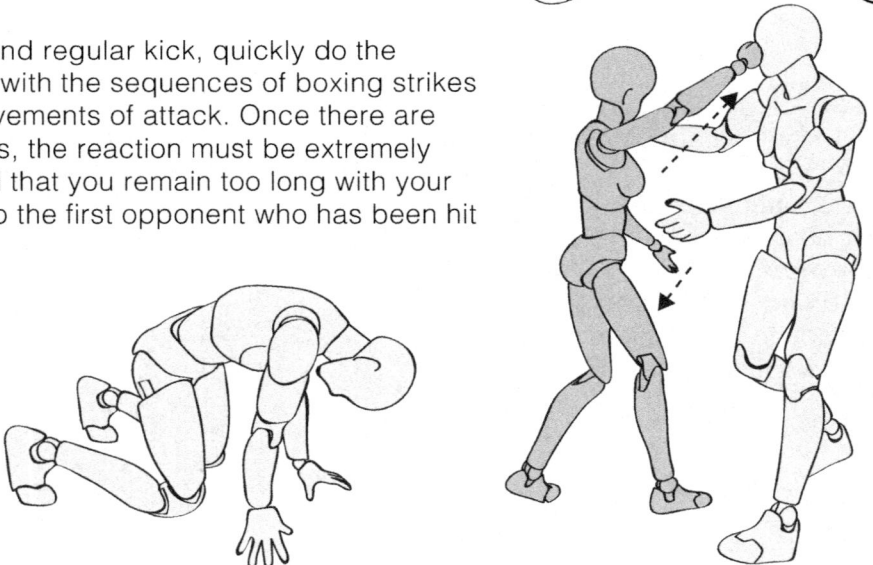

60 Defense Against an Arm Pull N°2

Against 2 opponents

The situation here is the same as the previous one, with two opponents pulling your arms. Now you deliver two regular kicks with the right leg. The first kick (1) reaches the opponent's groins, which is at the right side (A).

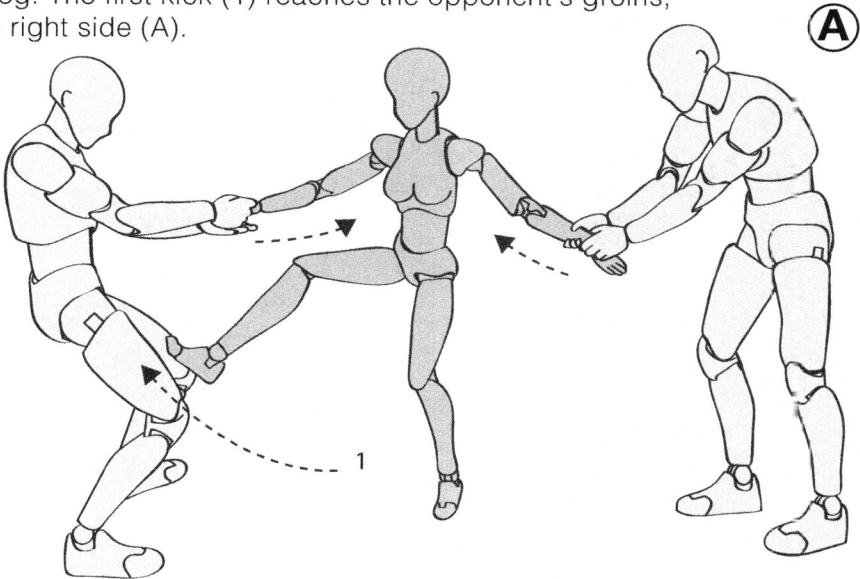

Ⓐ

Your right hand (2) is pulled to be released from the first opponent and then, the foot that kicked does not go back to the ground, it goes straight to another kick (3) aiming at the second opponent's groins (B). If the opponents continue to hold your arms, with the elbows still flexed you deliver more kicks until the opponents release them.

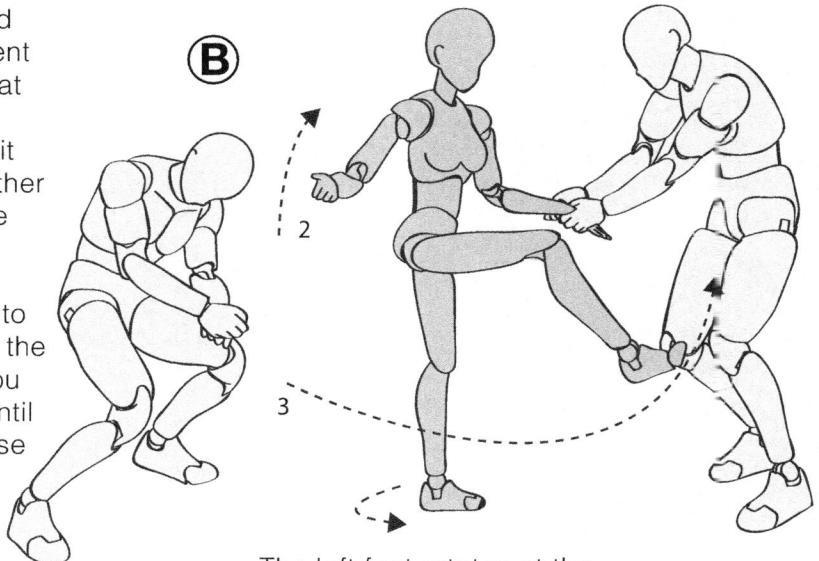

Ⓑ

The left foot rotates at the moment of the second kick.

61

Defense Against an Arm Pull N°3

Against 2 opponents

Another option for the same defense is first to deliver a heel kick on the knee (1) of one opponent and to pull the right hand to release it (A).

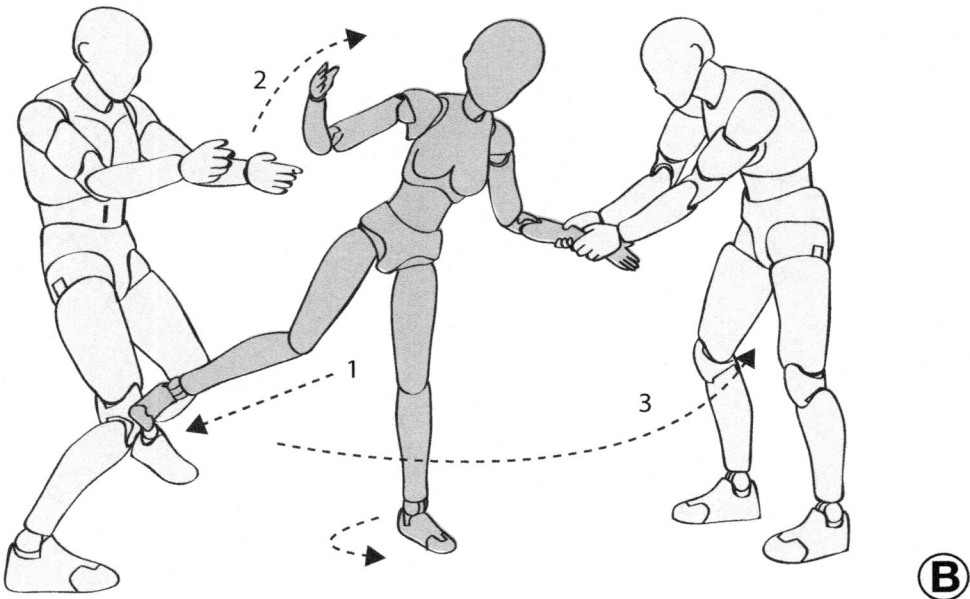

After the heel kick, the same right foot does not go back to the ground, it straight delivers a regular kick (3) aiming at the second opponent's groins (B).

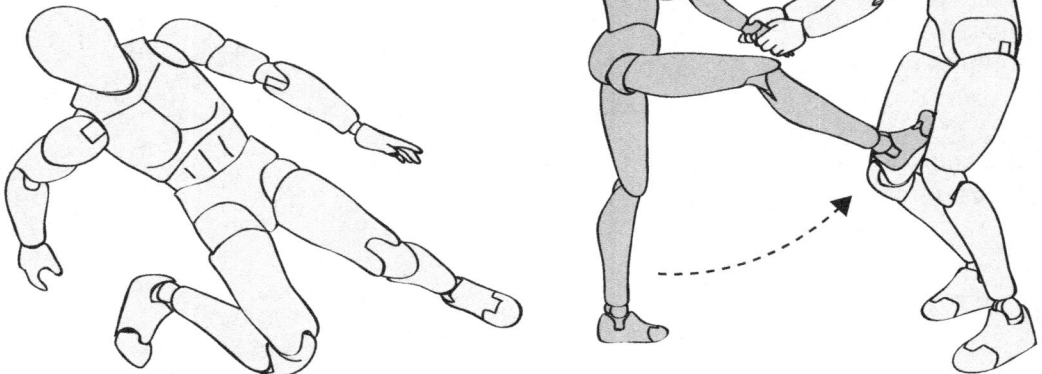

Defenses Against Boxing Strikes

An attack with boxing strikes is quite common. The defenses are done by deflecting from the attack, and they continue with sequences of simultaneous movements such as boxing strikes, kicks, and other movements to prevent the attack from going on. Next, you will see some options of defense.

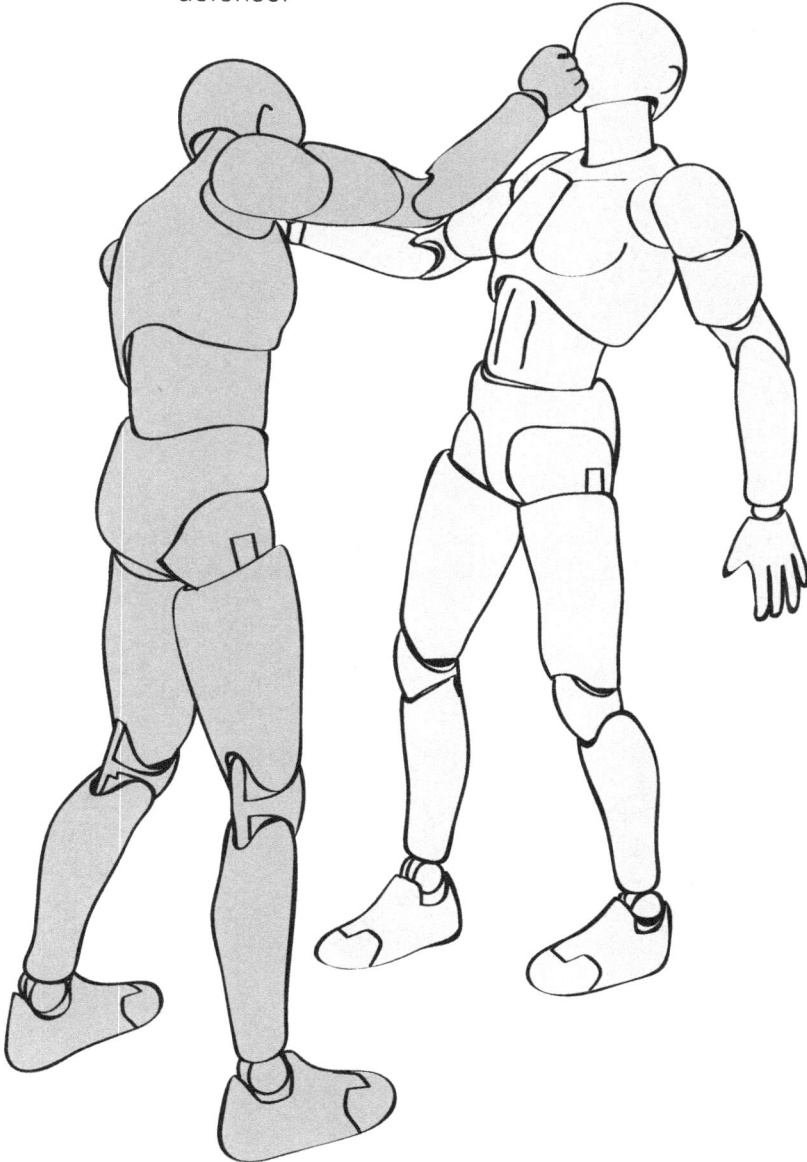

Sergio Nisenbaum

62 Defense Against a Boxing Strike with the Wrist

The Defense Against a Boxing Strike with the Wrist can be used to defend attacks of boxing strikes delivered in front of you (A), and attacks coming from the sides.

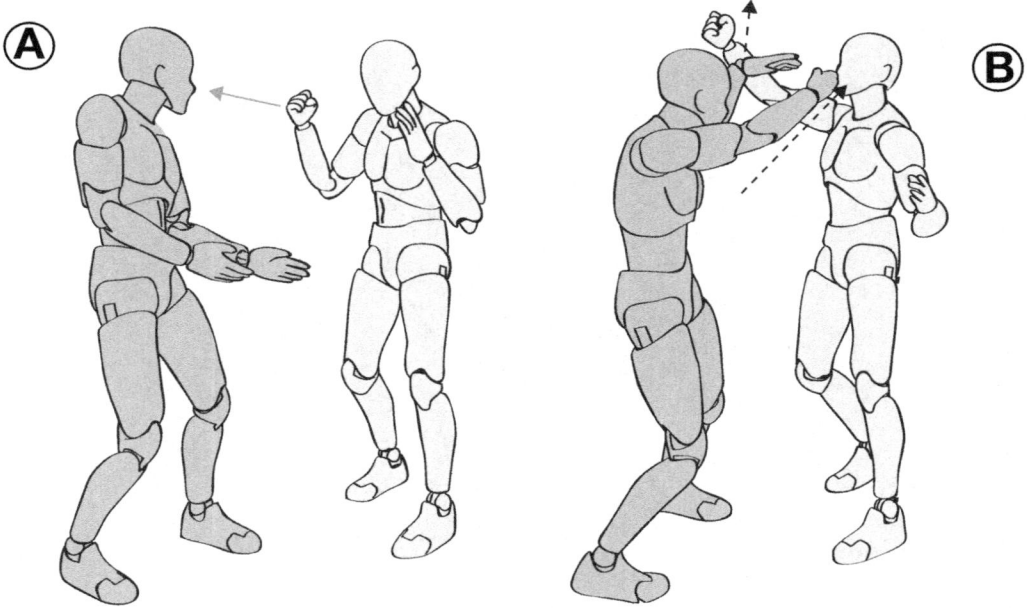

To defend yourself from a right-hand boxing strike, make a fast movement by raising your left arm to deflect the attack. At the same time, deliver a boxing strike on the opponent's face (B). As from then, use the continuations with hand moves and kicks.

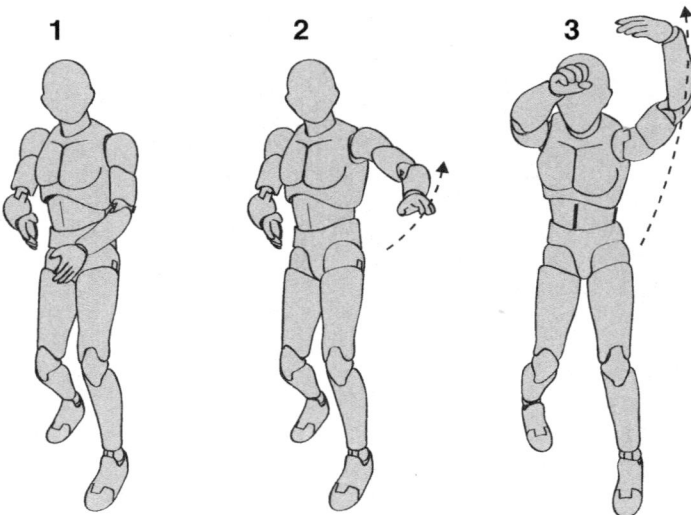

The defense stance is with the two hands pointing forward and at the line of the waist (1).

The defensive hand raises quickly to deflect the attack (2).

The speed of raising the hand deflects the attack with the wrist (3).

63 Defense Against a Boxing Strike with a Knife-Hand

The Defense of a Boxing Strike with a knife-hand is another option for the same defense, and it can also be used to defend against attacks of front boxing strikes (A) and those coming from the sides.

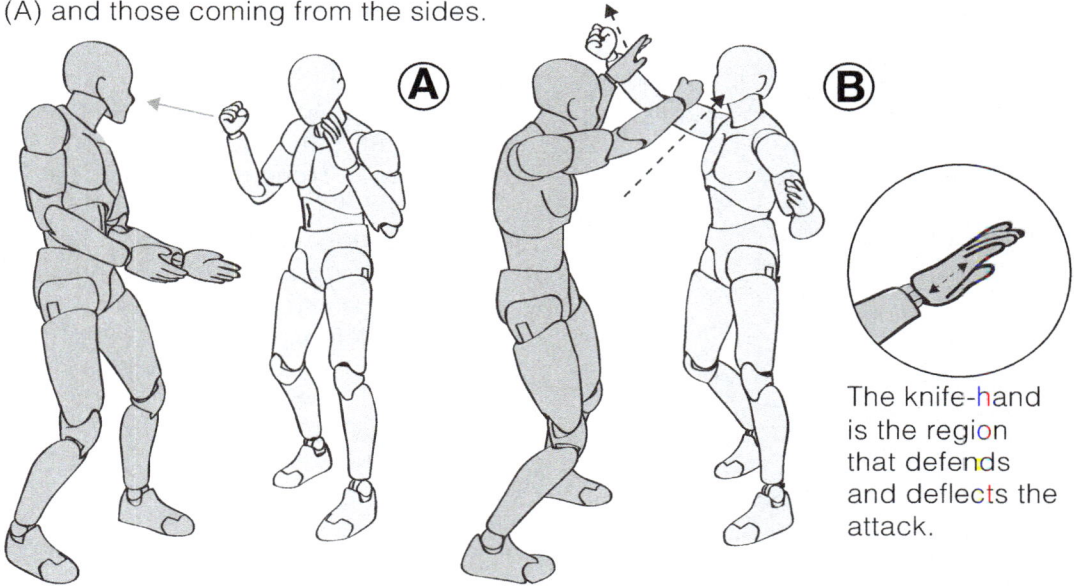

The knife-hand is the region that defends and deflects the attack.

To defend yourself from a right-hand boxing strike, make a quick lifting movement with the left arm to deflect the attack with a knife-hand at an angle slightly more open compared to the same defense with the wrist. At the same time, deliver a boxing strike on the opponent's face (B) and the continuations must follow to prevent a second reaction from the opponent.

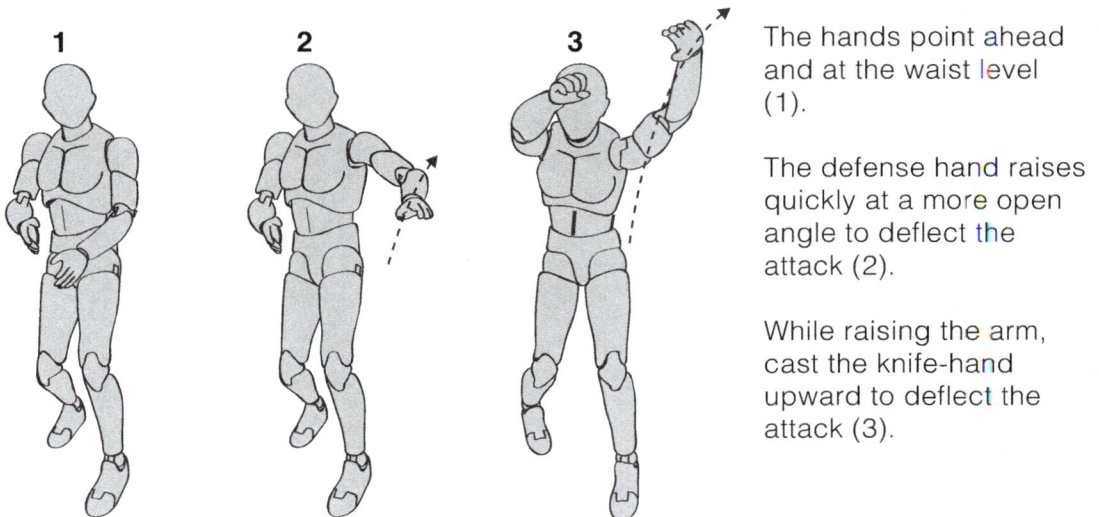

1

2

3

The hands point ahead and at the waist level (1).

The defense hand raises quickly at a more open angle to deflect the attack (2).

While raising the arm, cast the knife-hand upward to deflect the attack (3).

64 Controlled Defense Against a Boxing Strike Nº1

(A)

In controlled defenses, the objective is to deflect the attack with a boxing strike and immediately grab the opponent's arm during the whole defensive reaction. In this defense, the left forearm defends against a right-hand boxing strike (A). Together with the deflection of the attack, deliver a right-hand boxing strike and immediately grab the opponent's arm close to his wrist with your left hand (B). The defense is done for the "live" side and, after the attack with a right-hand boxing strike, continue with the sequences of attacks with regular kicks and hand moves (C).

(B)

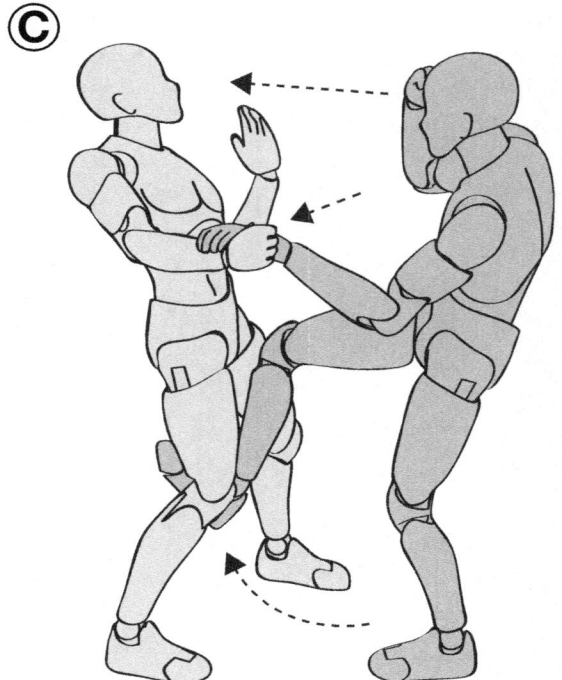
(C)

65 Controlled Defense Against a Boxing Strike N°2

(A)

In a Controlled Defense Against a Boxing Strike N°2, the defense is done from the "dead" side. The left forearm defends against a left-hand boxing strike (A).

The forearm deflects the attack, and the left hand turns immediately to grab and control the opponent's arm. At the same time, the right hand launches attacks (B).

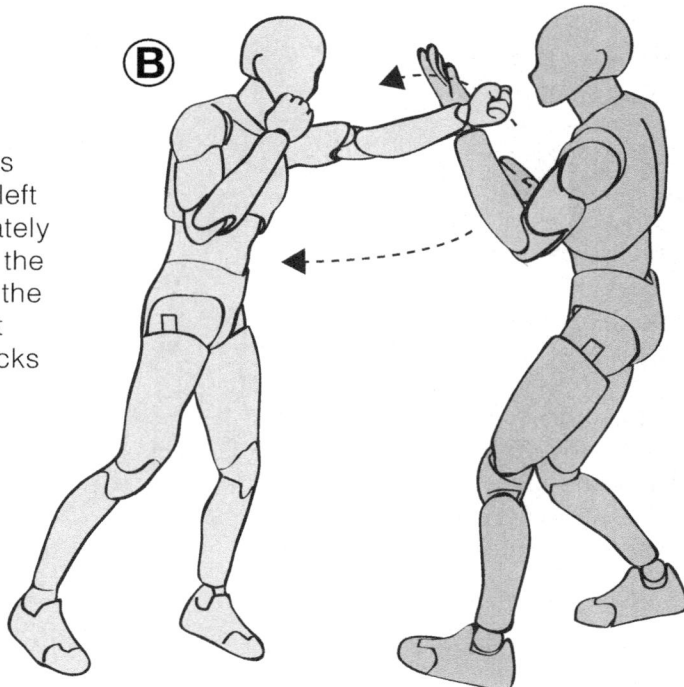

(B)

C

Once the defense was done for the "dead" side, the sequences start with side moves. The first attack that happens together with the defense is a sickle kick on the ribs (C).

D

The second attack is a sickle kick on the temple. After the second attack, and still controlling the opponent, move ahead with the sequences of kicks and hand moves (D). The defenses can be done in the same stance with the right forearm defending right-hand boxing strikes and moving to the "dead" side, or defending left-hand boxing strikes and moving to the "live" side.

66 Defense Against a Boxing Strike N°1

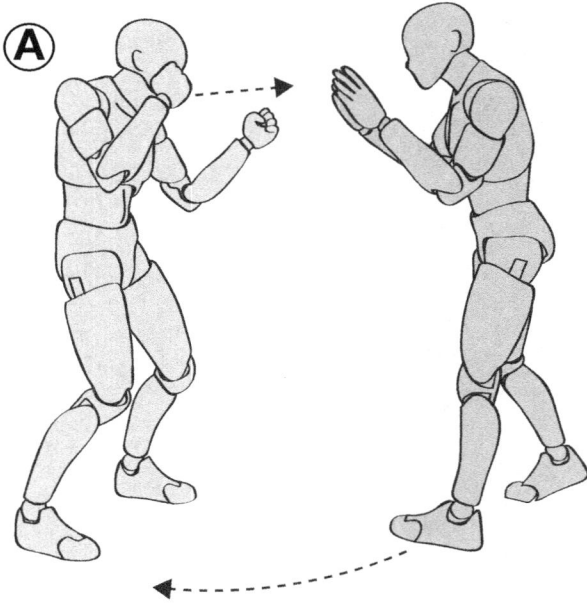

In this defense, the left forearm deflects the attack of right-hand boxing strike. The left foot advances to come closer to the opponent and to move away from the "dead" side (A). The same arm that deflects the attack, counterattacks with a left-hand boxing strike to hit the opponent's face (B).
Next, deliver another right-hand boxing strike (C), moving then to the necessary continuations.

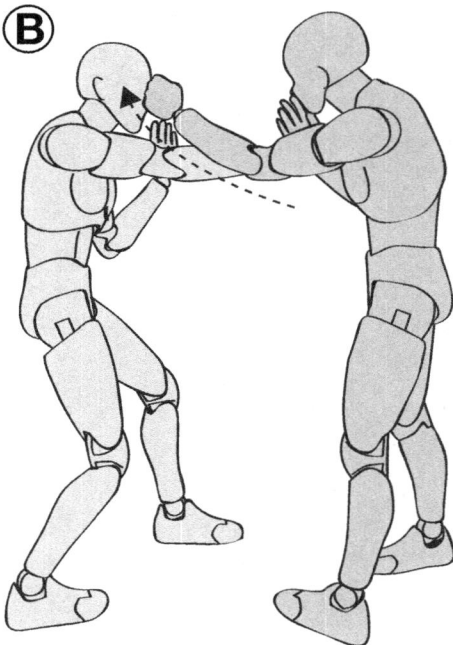

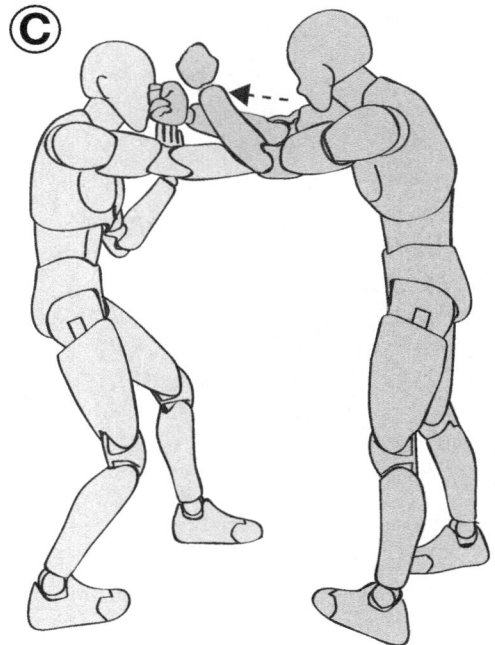

Sergio Nisenbaum

67 Defense Against a Boxing Strike N°2

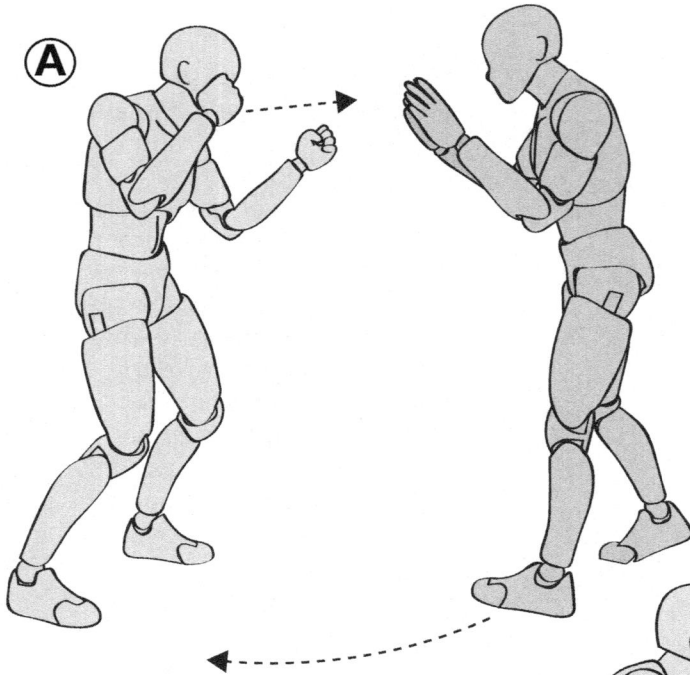

In the Defense Against a Boxing Strike N°2, the opponent attacks with a right-hand boxing strike. The defense requires a large movement of the legs to come closer to the opponent from the "dead" side. The defense starts with the left foot advancing diagonally (A).

The moment the opponent attacks, the left foot advances, and the left hand deflects the boxing strike moving inside and downward. The right hand hits the opponent's groins, the right leg passes behind the opponent's left leg (1) and is taken to the left at an angle of almost 180 degrees (2).

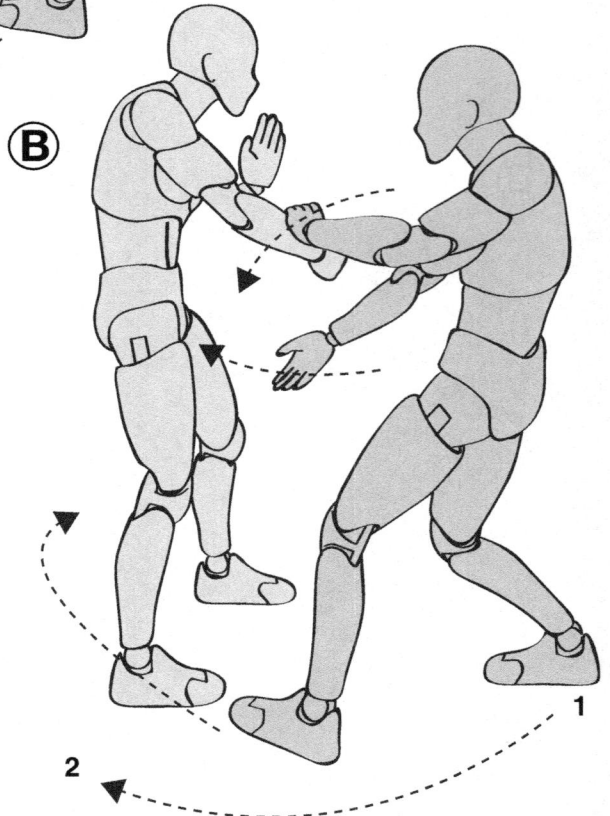

As soon as the right foot passes behind the left leg, the hands move upward and grab the opponent from behind his head on the eyes level (C).

The left foot delivers a heel kick on the opponent's knee fold and supported by the foot, the hands pull the opponent backward and down (D).

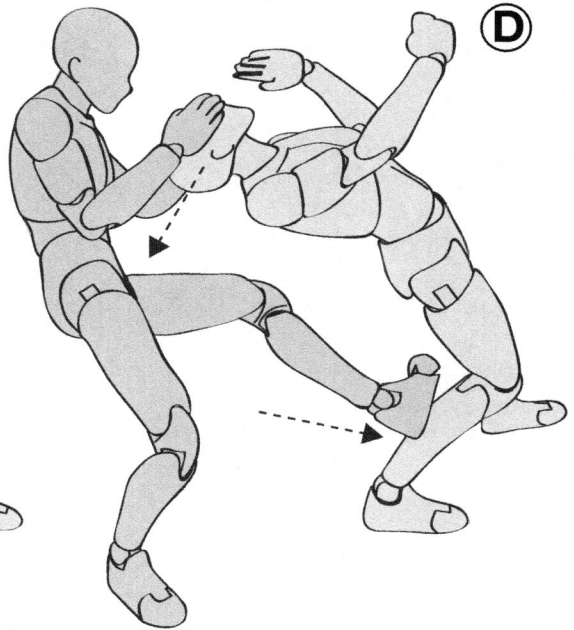

The sequences of the defense, the strong pressure on the region of the cervical spine, and the kick on the knee fold make the opponent go down to the floor (E).

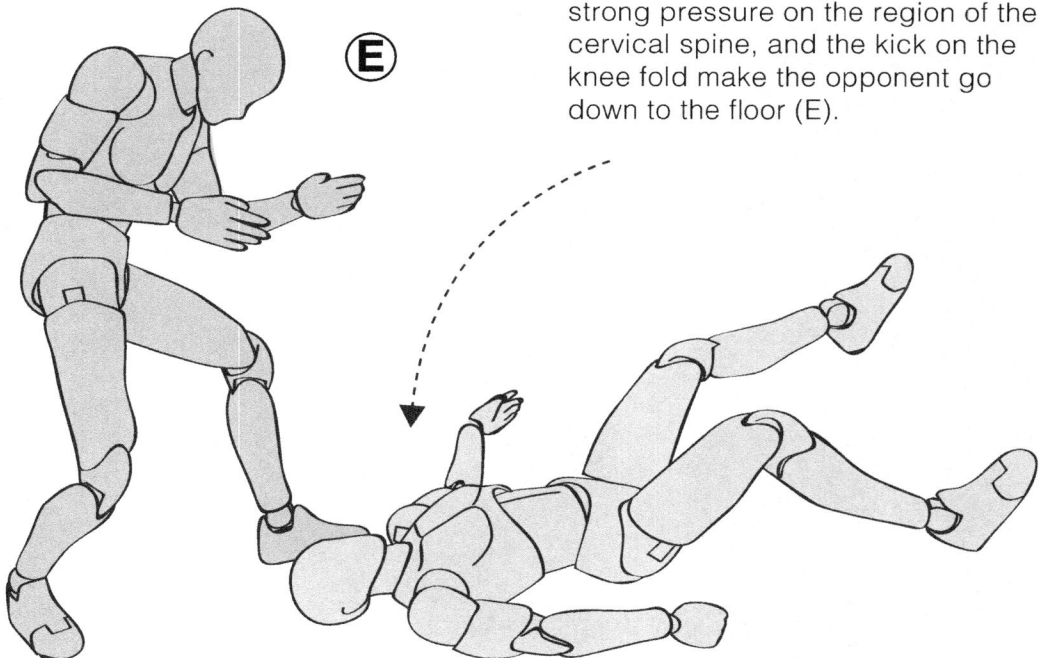

Sergio Nisenbaum

68 Defense Against a Boxing Strike Nº3

A

In the Defense Against a Boxing Strike Nº3, the opponent is attacking with a right-hand boxing strike. As much as in the previous defenses, this one requires significant movements of the legs to come closer to the opponent from the "dead" side (A).

B

When the opponent attacks, the left hand deflects the boxing strike to inside and to the side. The right hand delivers a sickle boxing strike on sensitive areas, such as the bladder or the sternum (B).

© C

Then, the same hand goes up to attack with another sickle boxing strike on the opponent's neck or face. At the same time, both feet move forward and to the "dead" side (C).

© D

While deflecting to the "dead" side, the right arm goes up and the forearm offers support on the neck, pulling from behind and to the ground. At the same time, the hips move to the right to offer support from behind to overthrow the opponent (D).

WARNING
Be careful when pressuring the trachea area.

Sergio Nisenbaum

69 Defense Against a Boxing Strike N°4

A

Another option when the opponent attacks with a right-hand boxing strike (A). Like in the previous defense, while deflecting from the attack, the feet quickly change positions.

B

The palm of the left hand deflects the attack to the side and, at the same time, there is a change of stance. The right foot crosses and advances to the left side (B).

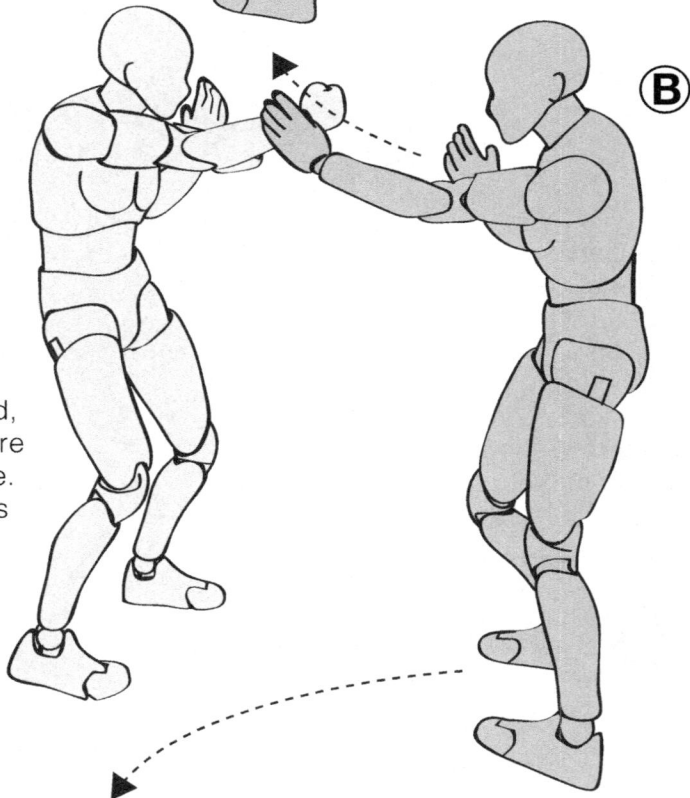

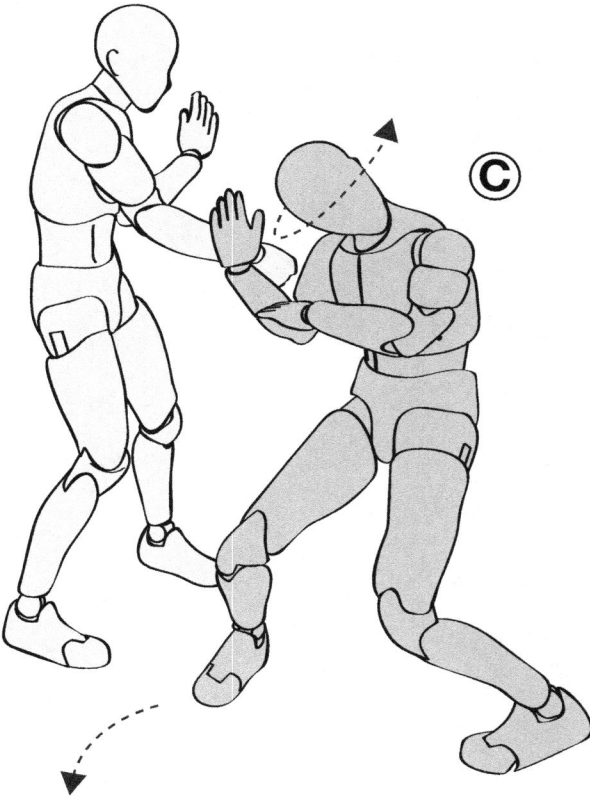

With the advance of the right foot, the stance changes completely, and now a spinning movement is made to kick the opponent with the heel of the left foot (C).

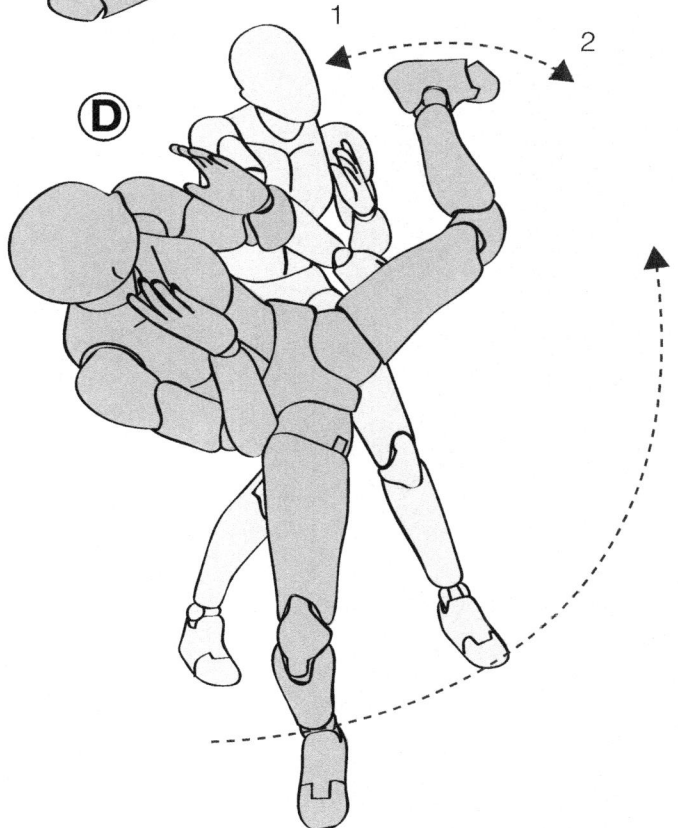

The speed of the spin raises the leg for you to deliver a spinning back-kick to hit the opponent's face (D). The movement of the kick reaches the opponent's face with the back of the heel (1) and comes back to the front (2) to go back to the ground.

70 Defense Against a Boxing Strike Nº5

The objective of a Defense Against a Boxing Strike Nº5 is to deflect an attack with the forearm and, at the same time, to come closer to the opponent. In this situation, he is attacking you with a right-hand boxing strike (A).

The left forearm deflects the attack and, at the same time, launches an attack with a right-hand boxing strike (B). Quickly, both hands grab the opponent's right shoulder and, together with a step ahead, knee strikes are delivered on the groins (C), continuations are made with hammer fists and other sequences.

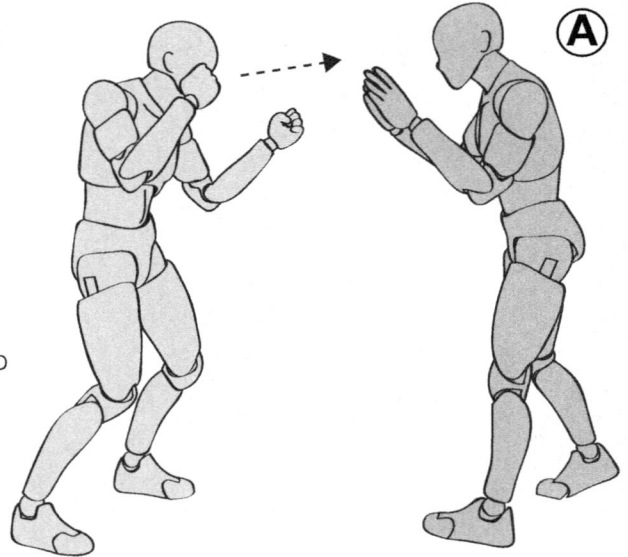

Regardless of the side the opponent attacks, the defense can be the same by just changing sides.

71 Defense Against a Boxing Strike N°6

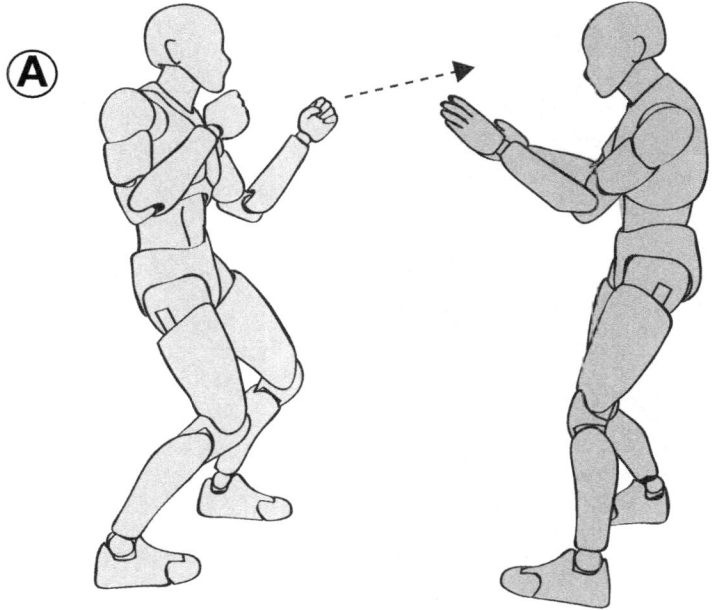

This defense is virtually the same as the previous one, with the same objective of deflecting and coming closer.
The difference is that the opponent is attacking with two boxing strikes, starting with the left hand (A).

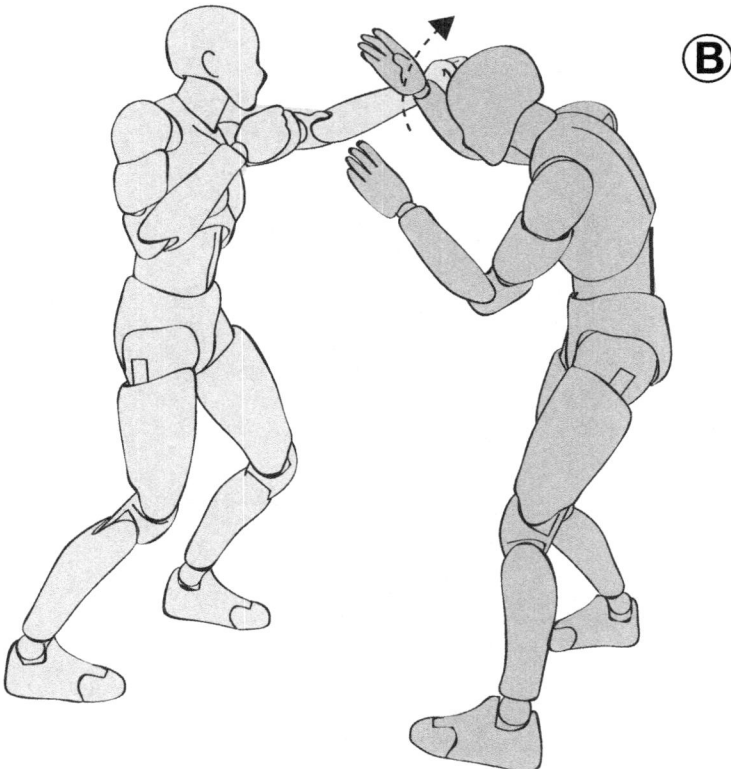

The right forearm deflects the attack of the left-hand boxing strike (B).

Quickly, the left forearm defends with the other boxing strike the opponent is delivering with his right hand (C).

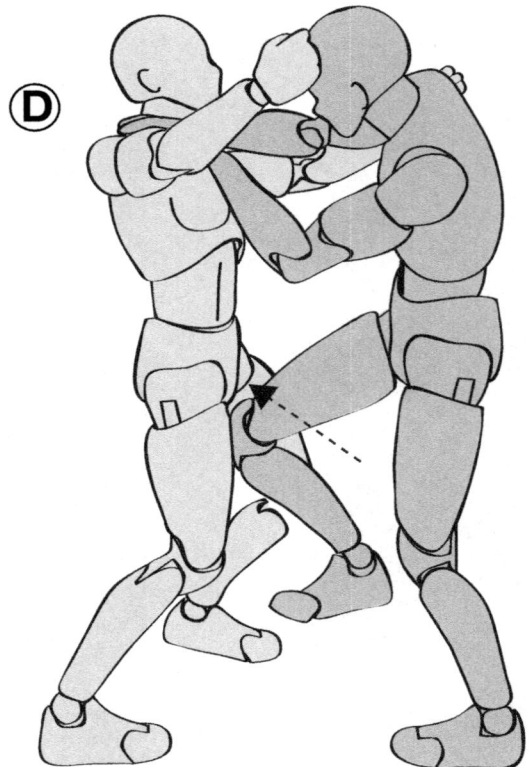

In the end, both hands can grab the opponent's shoulder, like in the previous defense, or you can also grab each shoulder separately and thus deliver knee strikes on his groins (D).

72 Defense Against a Boxing Strike N°7

Here, the opponent is attacking with two boxing strikes, starting with the left hand. Another option is to defend with the left forearm to deflect the first attack (A). Then, the same forearm deflects the right-hand boxing strike like in exercise 70. At the same time, deliver a right-hand boxing strike on the opponent's face (B). Both hands grab his shoulder and deliver knee strikes on the groins (C).

Sergio Nisenbaum

Defenses Against Backward Pulls

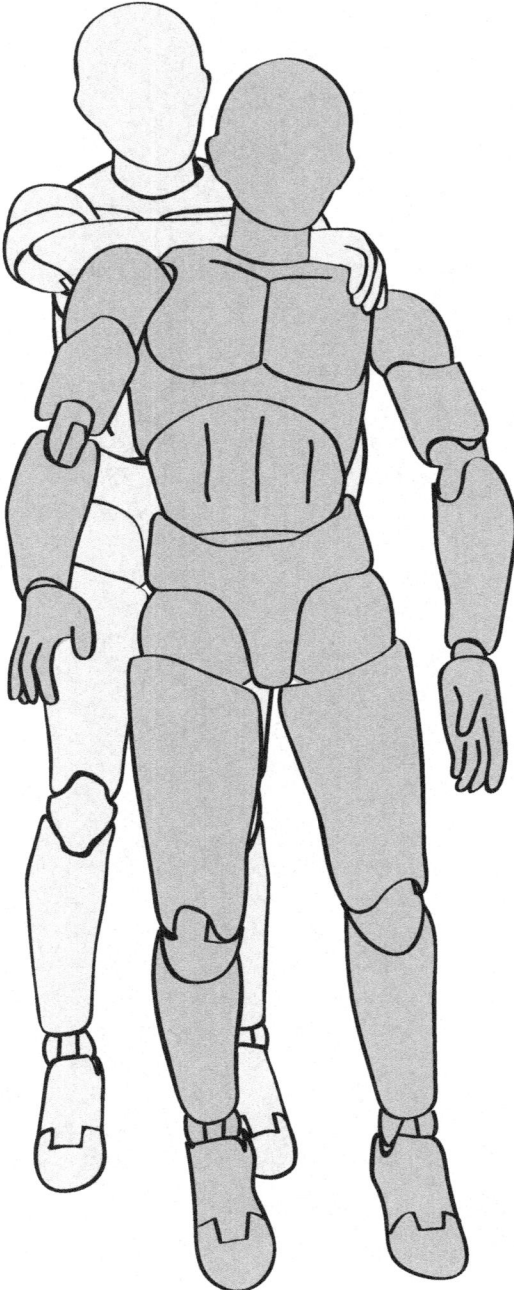

As seen in some defenses against immobilizations or grabs, many types of aggression can happen from behind. In the next exercises, you will see another type of situation where the opponent grabs your shoulder and pulls it backward to try to make you lose your balance and to overthrow you, or to attack with the other hand. The defense follows the pattern of movements able to resolve both cases, regardless of the side the opponent is pulling, also including when he is holding an object to attack you.

73 Defense Against a Backward Pull N°1

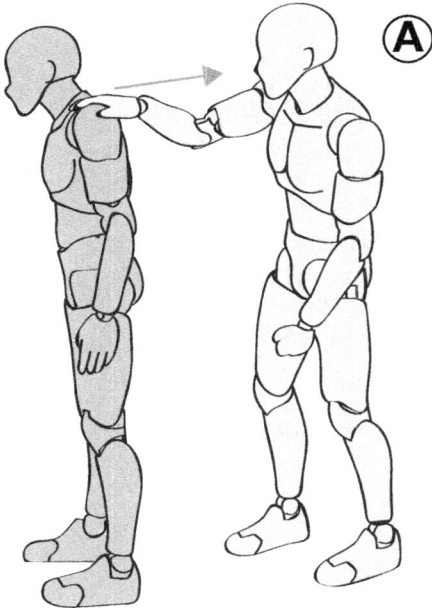

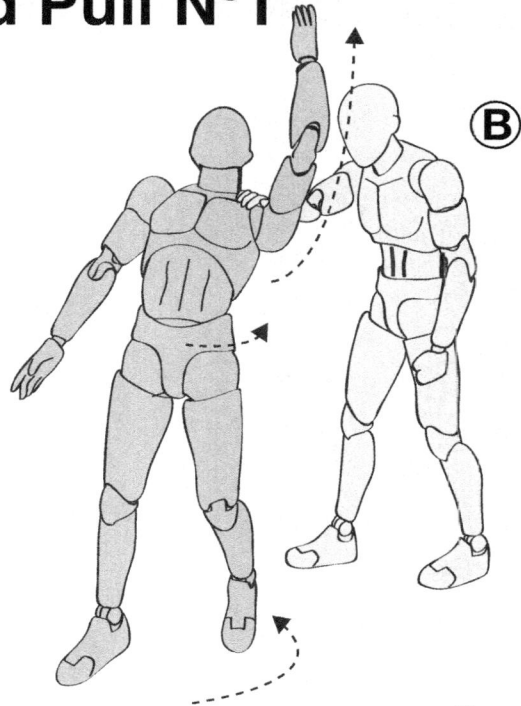

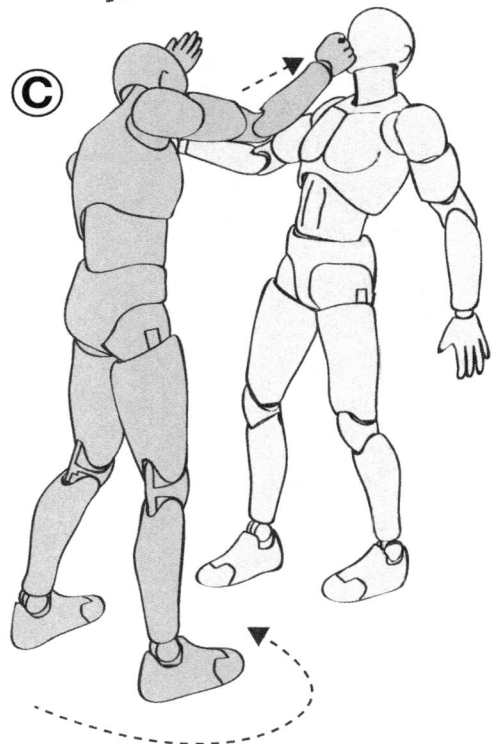

Ⓐ

Ⓑ

Ⓒ

The opponent is holding your left shoulder with his right hand (A). When he pulls the shoulder, naturally the body tilts backward. The left arm goes up fully stretched and, at the same time, the left foot moves backward and offers support for you not to lose your balance (B). The hips rotate together with the foot that moved backward, and the left arm still stretched, deflects the opponent's right arm. Simultaneously, deliver a right-hand boxing strike on the opponent's face (C). As from then, do the continuations.

74 Defense Against a Backward Pull N°2

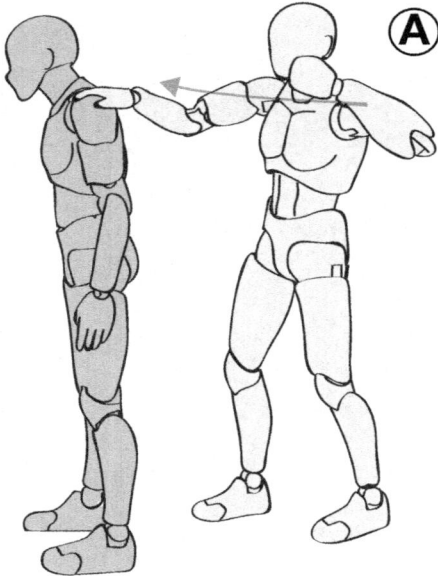

(A)

In this situation, the opponent is also holding your left shoulder with his right hand, but now he is preparing an attack of a left-hand boxing strike to hit your face when he pulls (A). When you feel the pull on your shoulder, raise your left arm fully stretched upward and, at the same time, move your left foot backward (B). The left arm, which is stretched, like in the previous defense, deflects the opponent's right arm and counterattacks with a right-hand boxing strike to hit the opponent's face (C), as seen in exercise 66. Next, do the necessary continuations.

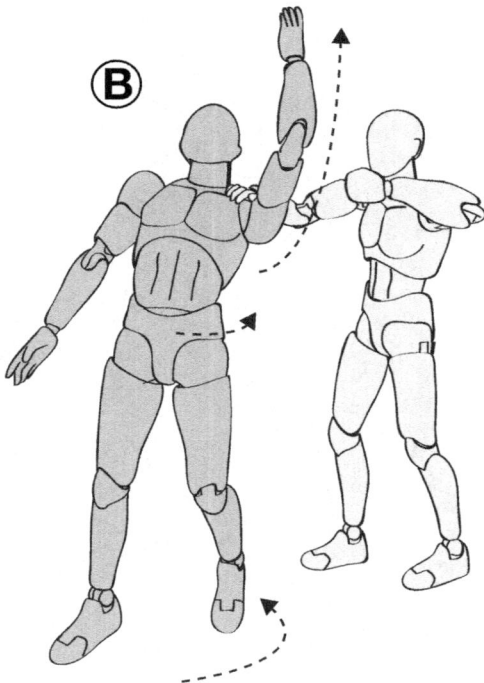

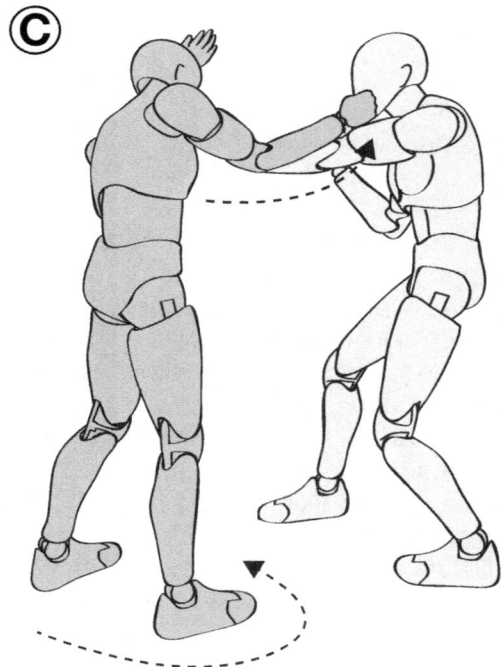

(B)

(C)

75 Defense Against a Backward Pull N°3

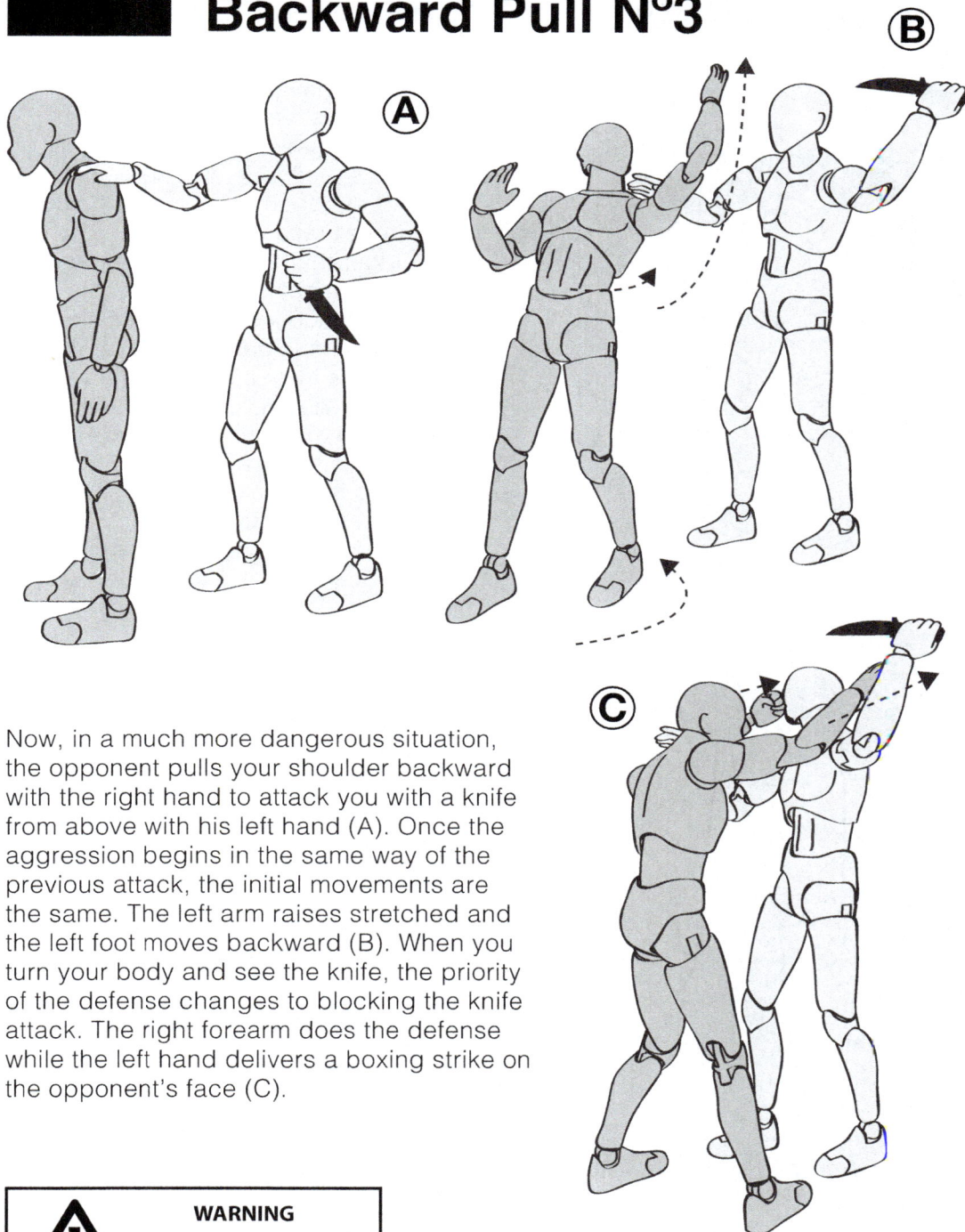

Ⓐ

Ⓑ

Ⓒ

Now, in a much more dangerous situation, the opponent pulls your shoulder backward with the right hand to attack you with a knife from above with his left hand (A). Once the aggression begins in the same way of the previous attack, the initial movements are the same. The left arm raises stretched and the left foot moves backward (B). When you turn your body and see the knife, the priority of the defense changes to blocking the knife attack. The right forearm does the defense while the left hand delivers a boxing strike on the opponent's face (C).

WARNING
Never use a real knife when practicing this exercise.

See in Volume 1 the complete didactics of the Defense Against a Knife Attack from Above.

Defenses Against Razor Attacks

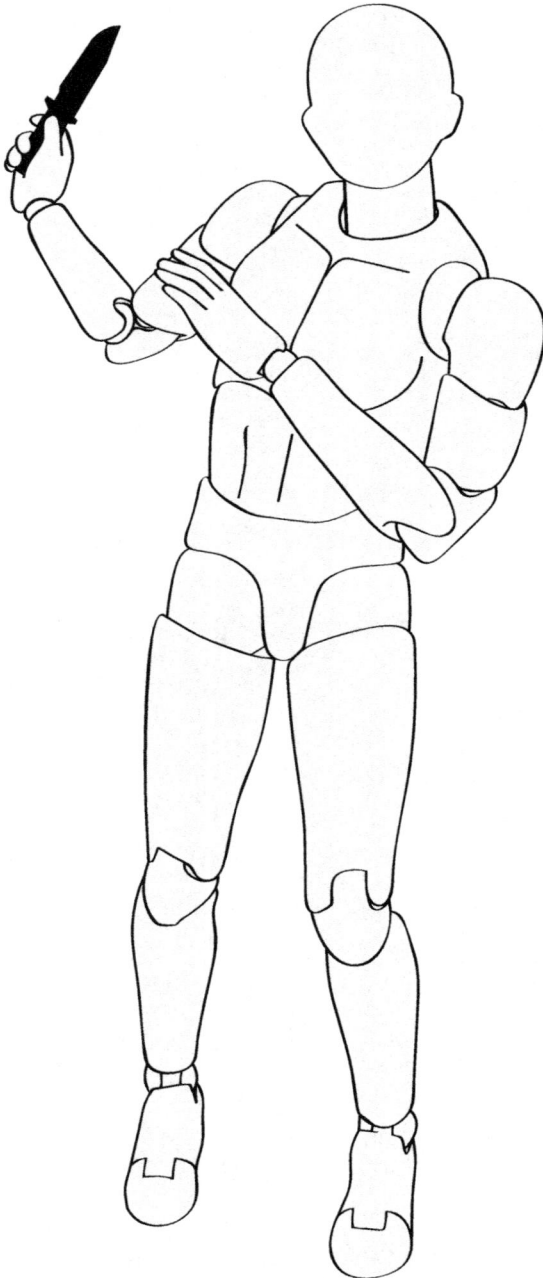

A razor is a sharp instrument originally developed to shave. Characteristically, its handle can be folded and when it is closed it protects the blade, whose point is round. An open razor makes a 180 degrees angle with the handle, which is bigger than the blade. Although it is an ancient instrument, it can still be found and, currently, many knives can also be folded like a razor. The difference in a situation of attack with a razor is how it is handled and how the attack happens. The attacking movements end up by being circular and crossed. Next, you will see defenses against knife attacks with circular movements like those in a razor attack.

See in Volume 1 more defenses against Knife Attacks.

WARNING
Never use a real knife when practicing this exercise.

76 Defense Against a Razor Attack N°1

(A)

In this situation, the defensive reaction happens in advance and when the opponent becomes a threat (A), regardless of how high he is holding the razor or knife. The defense starts with an instinctive reaction with a regular kick on the opponent's groins (B) and, at the same time, the body tilts backward to stay away from the blade.

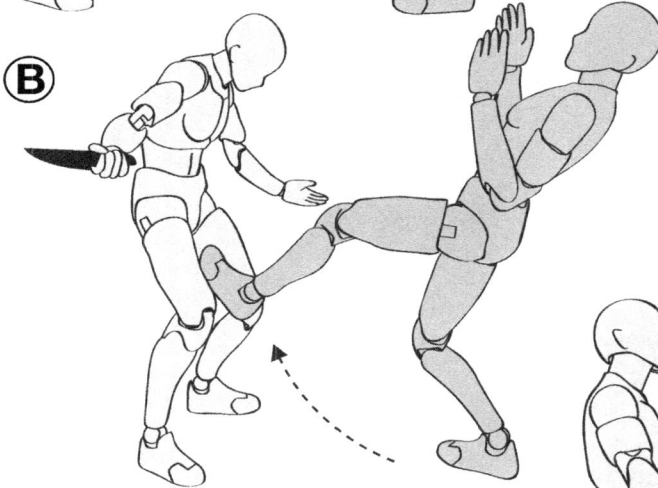

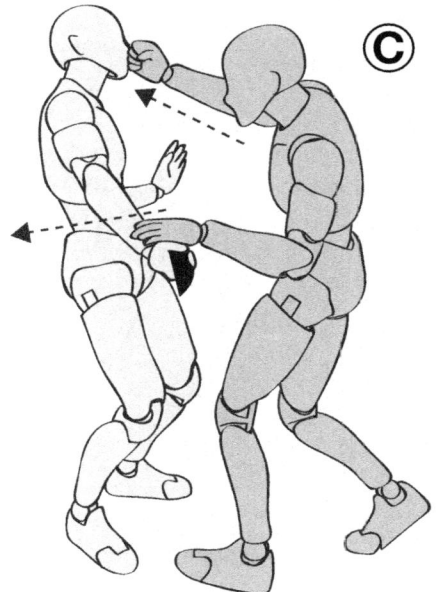

(B)

(C)

After the kick, the left hand grabs the opponent's arm and, at the same time, it moves the knife away by pulling the opponent's arm backward. Simultaneously, deliver right-hand boxing strikes on his face and do the necessary continuations (C).

Sergio Nisenbaum

77 Defense Against a Razor Attack N°2

(A)

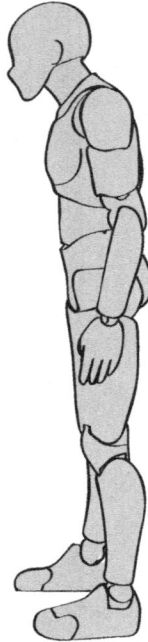

A razor attack can happen with a crossed movement, i.e., the opponent may be holding the knife upward, but attacking below the waistline, and vice-versa.
In a Defense Against a Razor Attack N°2, the blade is being held above you and the reaction does not happen in advance, as in the previous defense (A).

(B)

When the attack happens, the body tilts backward mainly to move the neck away from the blade. At that moment it is extremely important to have your hands below the line of attack so that you can prevent the hands and the arms from being hurt (B).

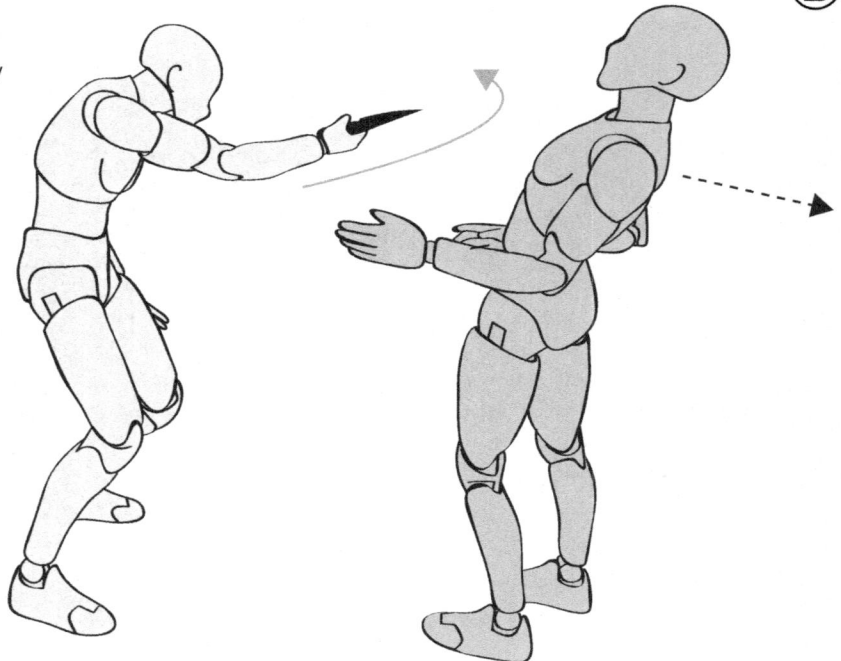

Ⓒ

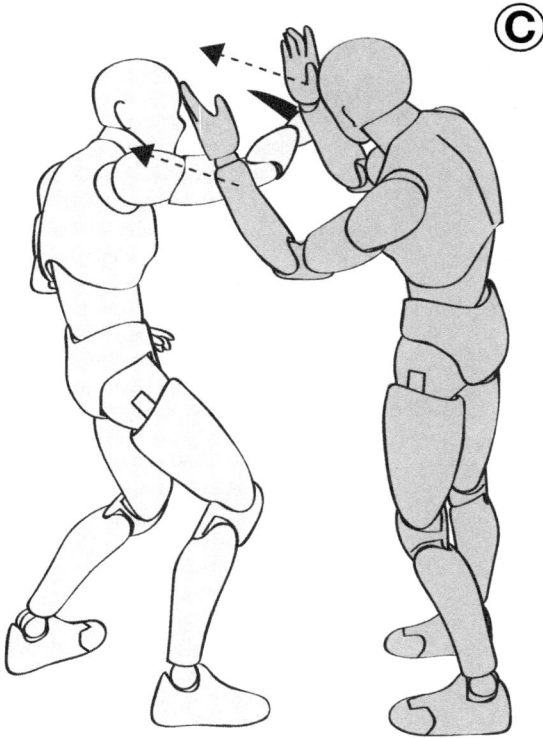

Once the type of razor attack is a circular and crossed movement, after the blade has passed by your side, before it makes its movement of return, both forearms make the block. One forearm blocks at the wrist level and the other, at the triceps level (C).

Ⓓ

After the block, the left hand goes down to grab at the opponent's fist level and push the arms with the knife toward the opponent. Simultaneously, deliver right-hand boxing strikes on the opponent's face (D).

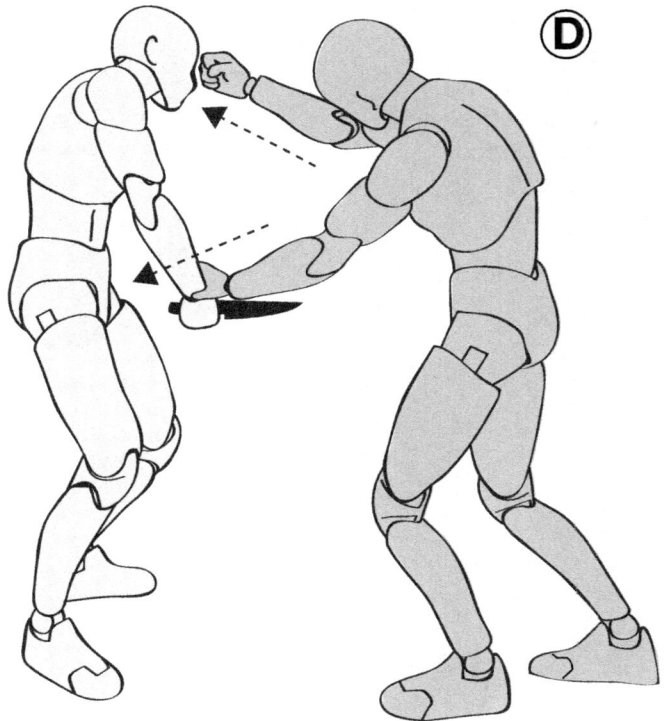

Sergio Nisenbaum

78 Defense Against a Razor Attack N°3

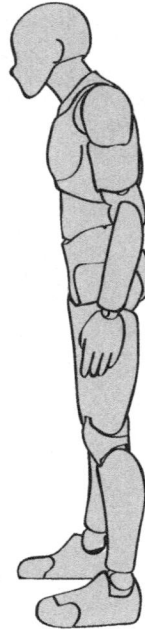

In this situation, the opponent is holding a knife or a razor with his right hand and his objective is to attack you at the abdomen level (A). In the moment of the attack, your feet make a small and quite fast movement to move the abdomen away from the blade and, at the same time, the hands also are moved away from the line of attack (B).

The razor attack is circular, and it starts from one side and goes to the other, a movement that can be repeated several times.

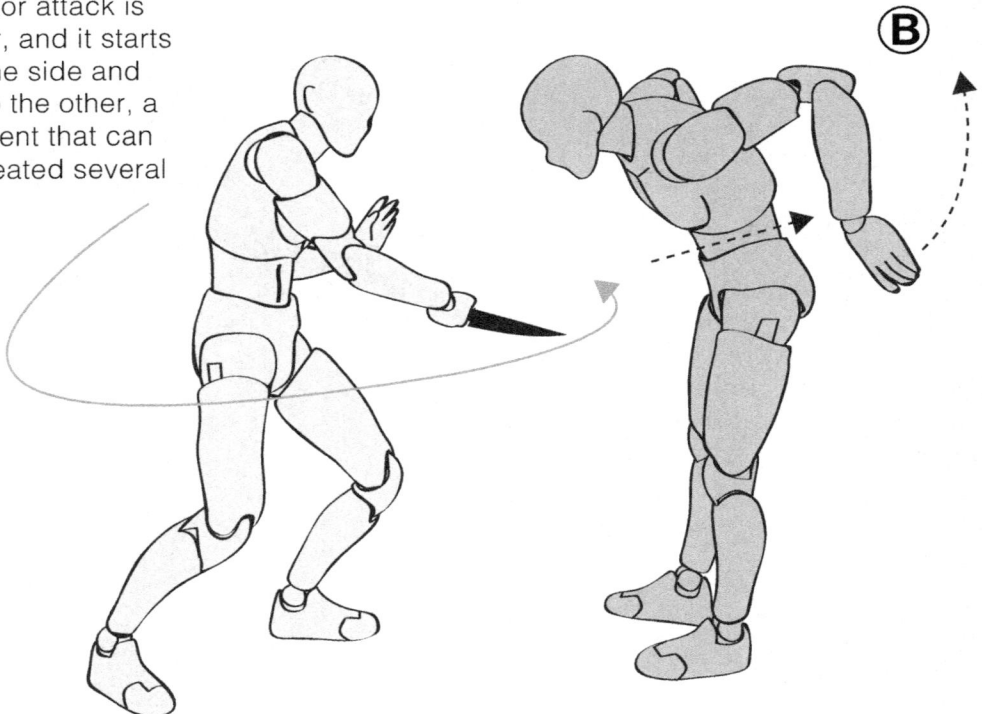

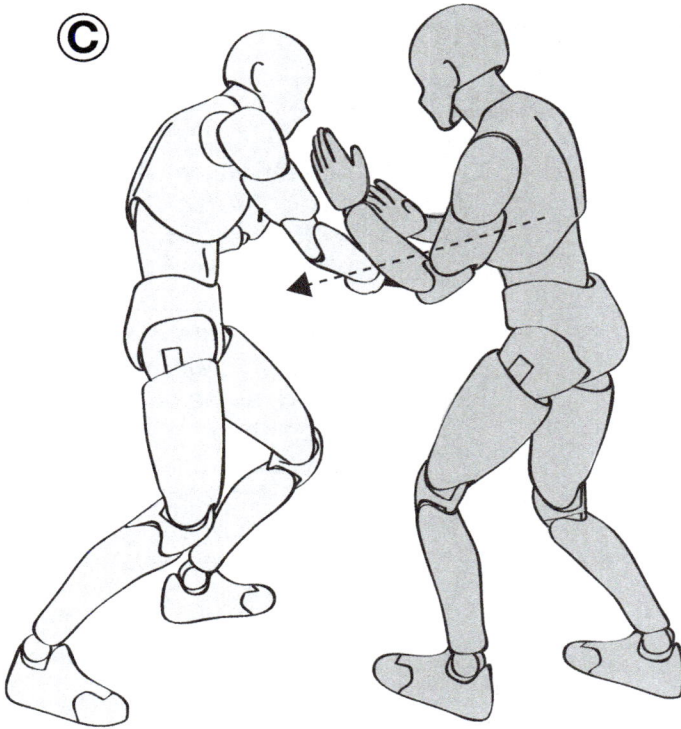

Immediately after deflecting the attack, your two forearms make the block to prevent the movement of return of the razor or knife (C).

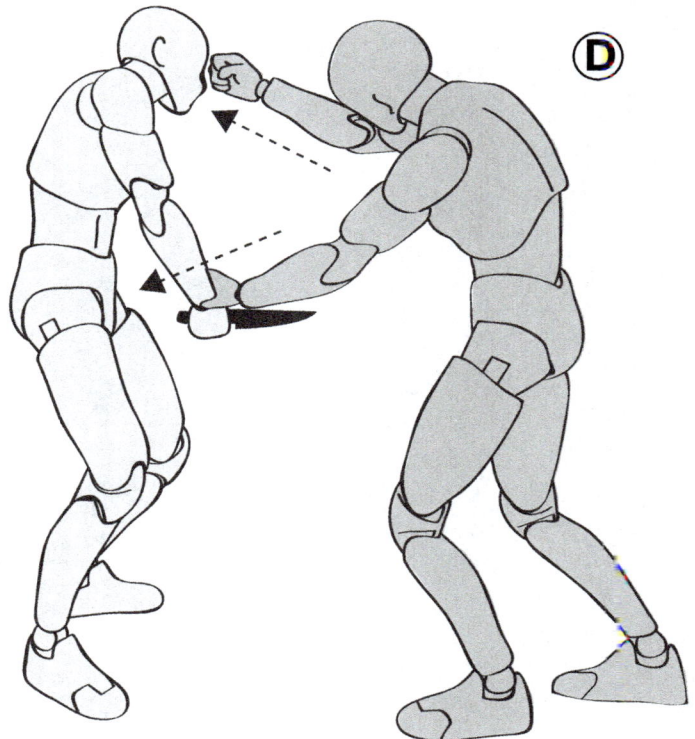

Next, and after the block, as seen previously, you must control the hand holding the knife. The left hand goes down to hold it at the wrist level and to pull the knife toward the opponent. Simultaneously right-hand boxing strikes are delivered on the opponent's face (D).

Sergio Nisenbaum

79 Defense Against a Razor Attack N°4

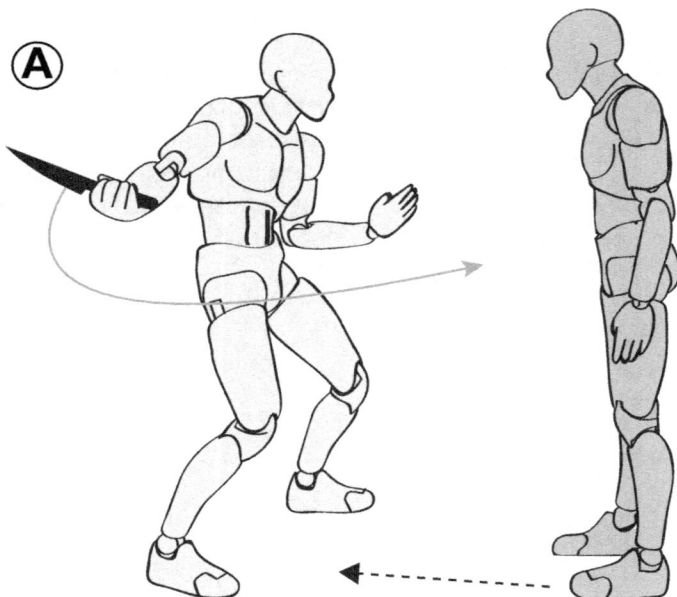

(A)

In a Defense Against a Razor Attack N°4, the opponent holds a knife with his right hand (A). The line of attack is also low. The defense is done with the left forearm and, at the same time, a right-hand boxing strike is delivered (B). After the block, the left hand holds the opponent's arm and simultaneously moves the knife away by pushing the arm backward. The boxing strikes continue (C).

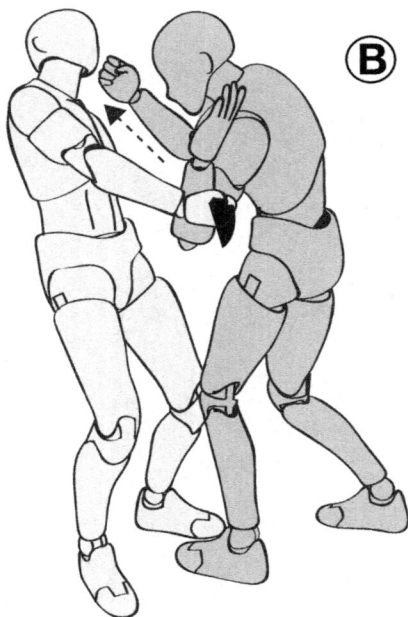

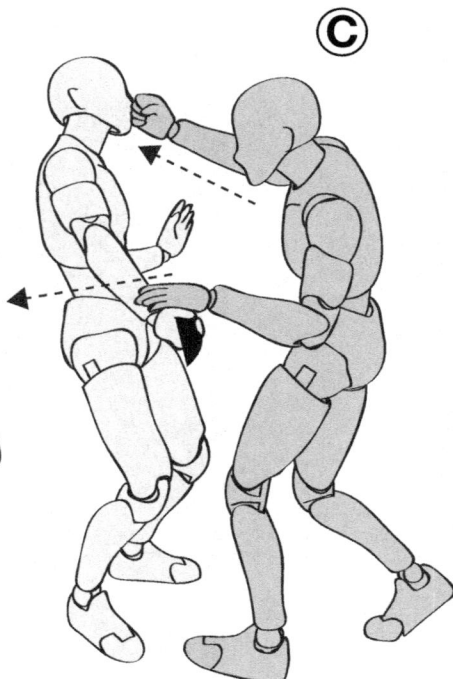

(B)

(C)

See in Volume 1 the complete didactical explanation of the 360 Defense used in the moment of the defense in figure B.

Defenses Against Stone Attacks

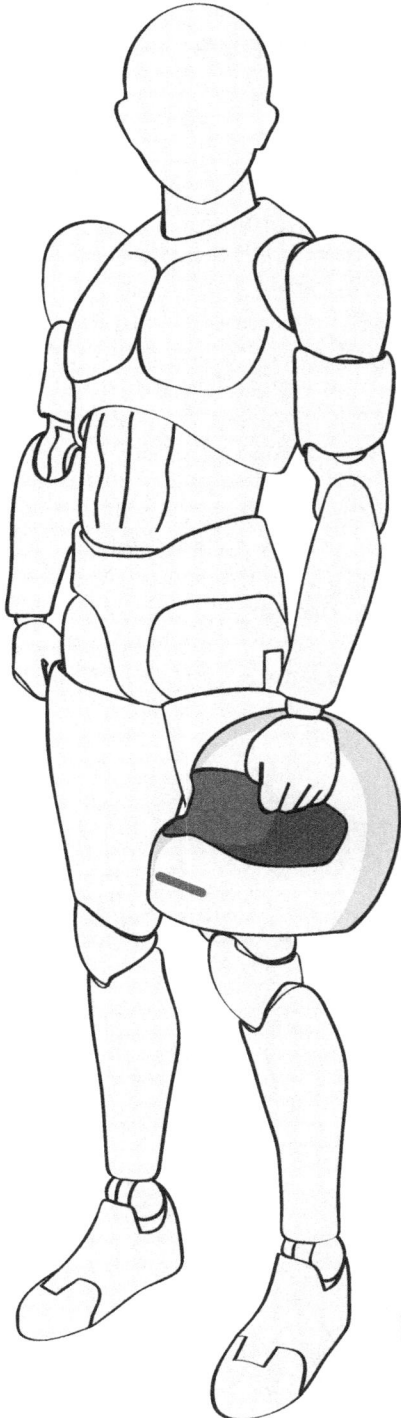

The following defenses approach attacks that happen when the opponent is holding a stone intending to hit someone's face or head. The defenses are done at a short distance, and they serve also to defend against other types of objects (brick, glass, bottle, helmet, etc.)

In many situations, in the moment of the defense, the stone can escape from the opponent's hand. Pay attention to the set of movements of deflection of the attacks combined with the deflection of the body and head in every exercise.

WARNING

Never use an object in the training that can cause some physical damage.

Sergio Nisenbaum

80 Defense Against a Front Attack with a Stone

Against an Attack from Above

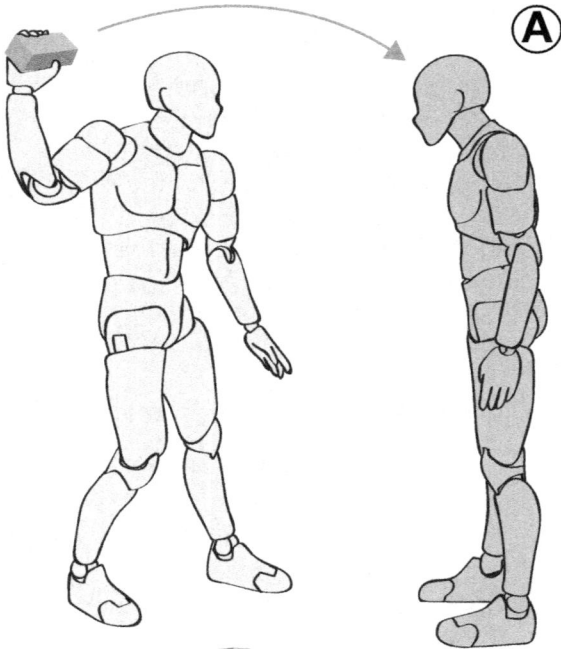

The opponent is holding a stone with his right hand intending to hit the head with a top-down attack (A). In the beginning of the attack, you take a step ahead with the left leg and, at the same time, the left arm stretches toward the attack. Simultaneously, deliver a boxing strike on the opponent's face (B). Next, the left hand grabs the opponent's arm, and the right leg rotates outwards to get off the line of attack of the stone. At the same time, deliver elbow strikes, make continuations with knee strikes, and other necessary moves (C).

81 Defense Against a Front Attack with a Stone

Against a Straight-Line Attack

Ⓐ

Ⓑ

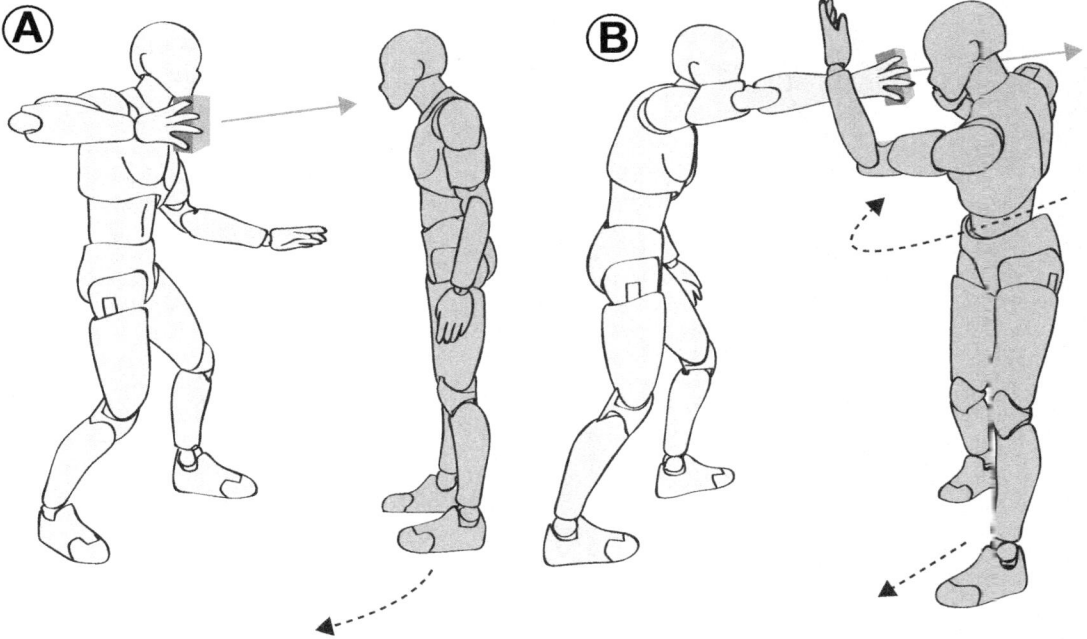

The opponent is holding a stone with his right hand and the line of attack is frontal toward the center of your face (A). To deflect the attack, the hips rotate to get the face away from the line of attack and, at the same time, to transfer the weight for the left forearm to deflect the stone to the other side. I. e., the head is moved to the left and the attack is deflected to the right (B). After the deflection, the left hand immediately grabs the opponent's arm and simultaneously delivers right-hand boxing strikes (C).

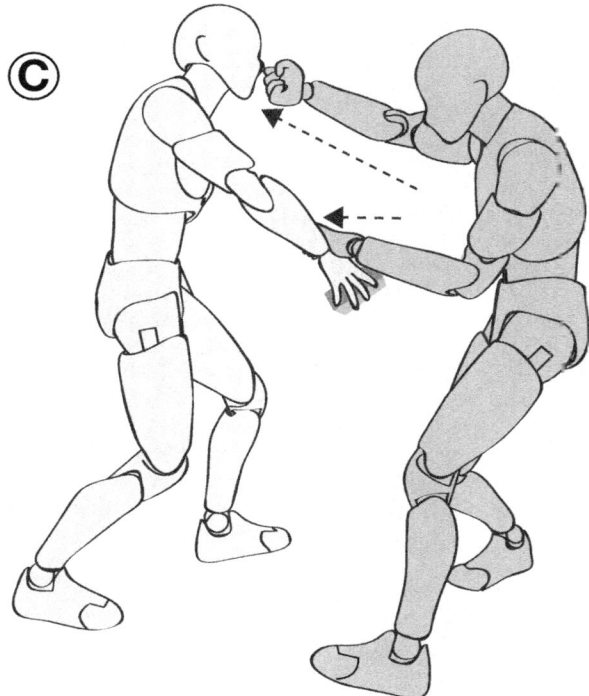

Ⓒ

Sergio Nisenbaum

82 Defense Against a Front Attack with a Stone

Against an Attack from the side

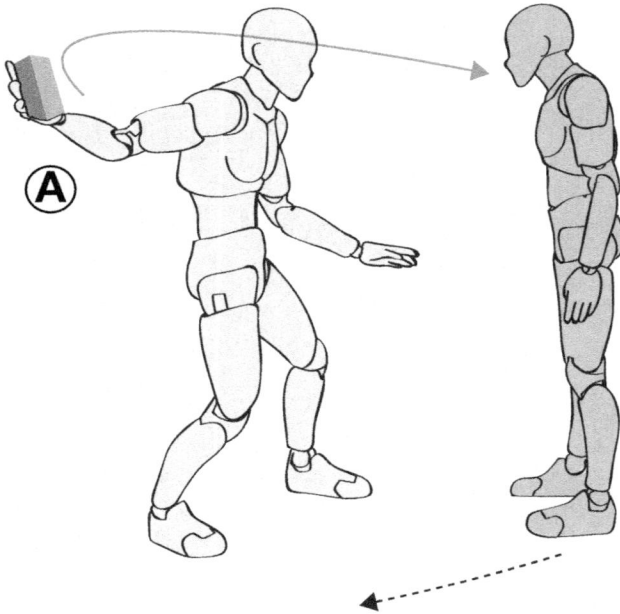

(A)

In this situation, the opponent is positioned in front of you, but the attack is circular to reach the side of your face (A). The exercise starts with a diagonal step forward and the left forearm does the defense against the attack. At the same time, deliver a right-hand boxing strike exactly like in the 360 Defense (B). Quickly, in the moment of the defense, the left hand grabs the opponent's arm and the right leg rotates outwards to move away from the line of attack of the stone. Simultaneously, deliver elbow and knee strikes, and other necessary moves (C).

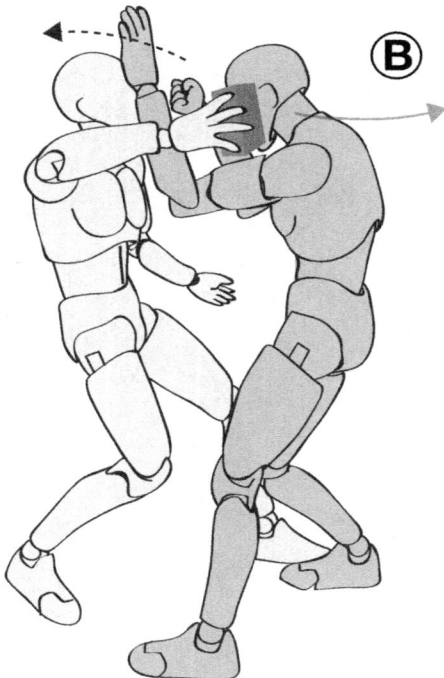

(B)

360 Defense

(C)

83 Defense Against a Side Attack with a Stone

Against an Attack from Above

(A)

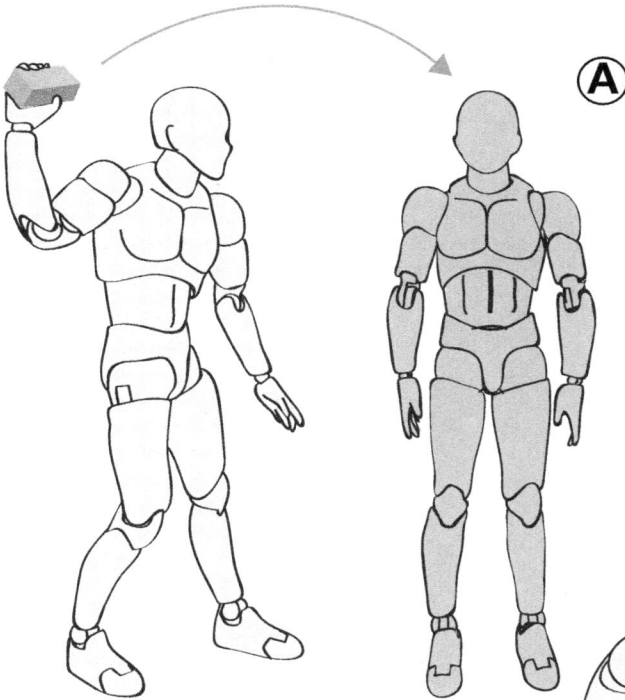

The opponent is positioned sideways and holds a stone with his right hand with the objective of hitting the head with a top-down attack (A).

(B)

To do the defense, take a diagonal step forward with the left leg to get out of the line of attack. At the same time, the right arm stretches to deflect the stone (B).

Ⓒ

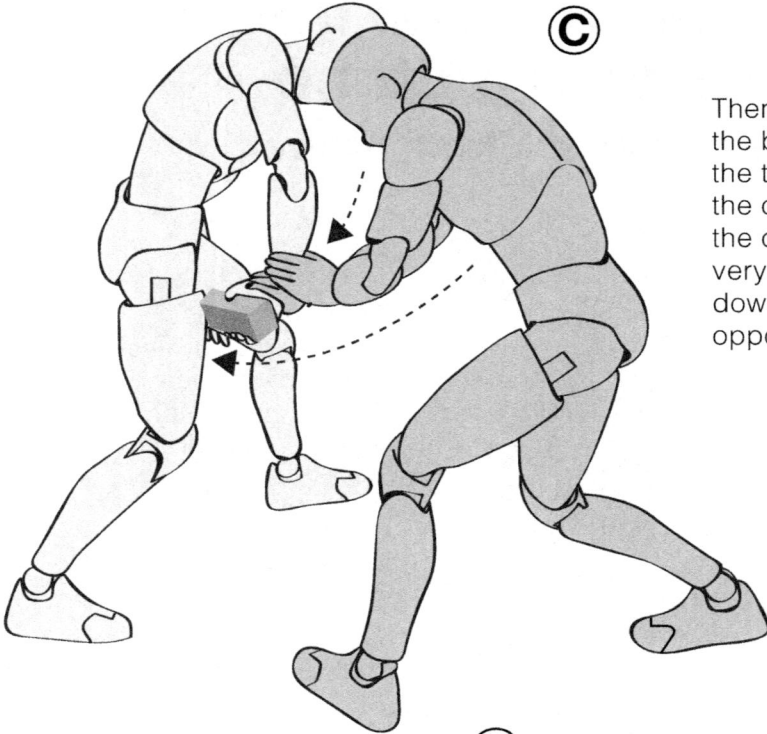

Then, after the deflection, the body turns around and the two hands quickly hold the opponent's arm with the objective of using the very stone's movement downward to reach the opponent's groins (C).

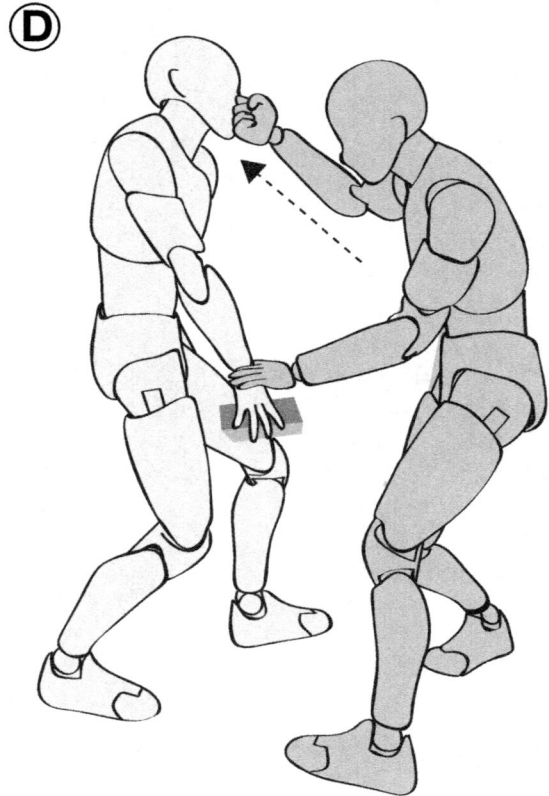

Ⓓ

Continue holding the opponent's arm with your left hand and deliver right-hand boxing strikes on his face (D).

84 Defense Against a Side Attack with a Stone

Against a Straight-Line Attack

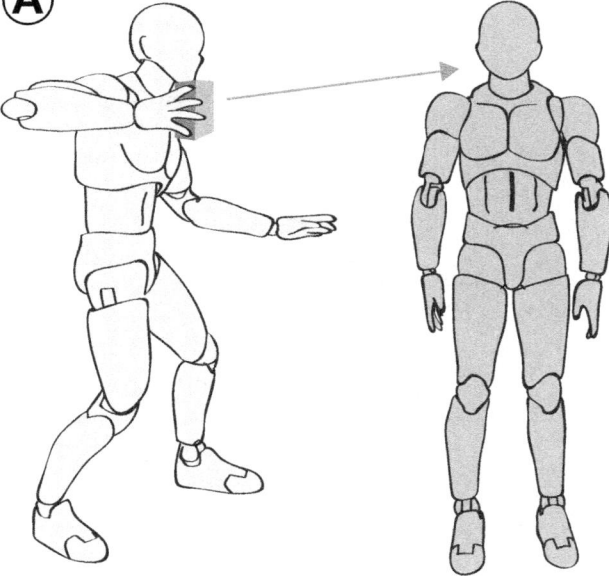

In this situation, the line of attack is frontal toward the right side of the head (A). Instinctively, the body moves backward to take the face out of the line of attack and, at the same time, the right forearm makes the deflection and the right foot moves backward (B). Immediately, the right hand grabs the opponent's arm and simultaneously left-hand boxing strikes must be delivered (C).

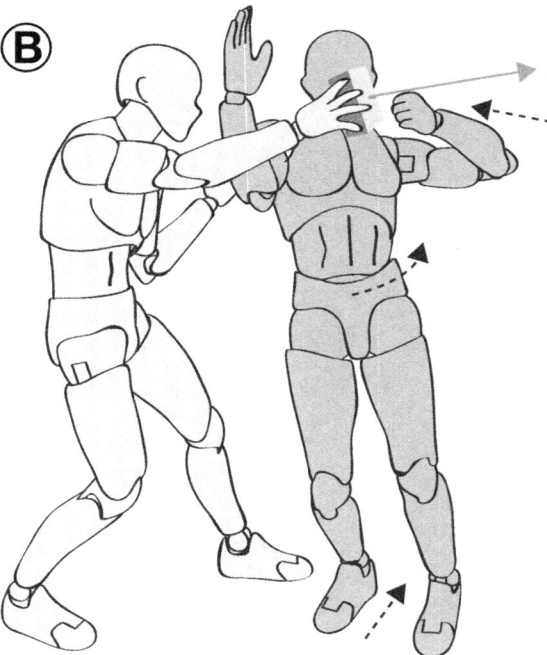

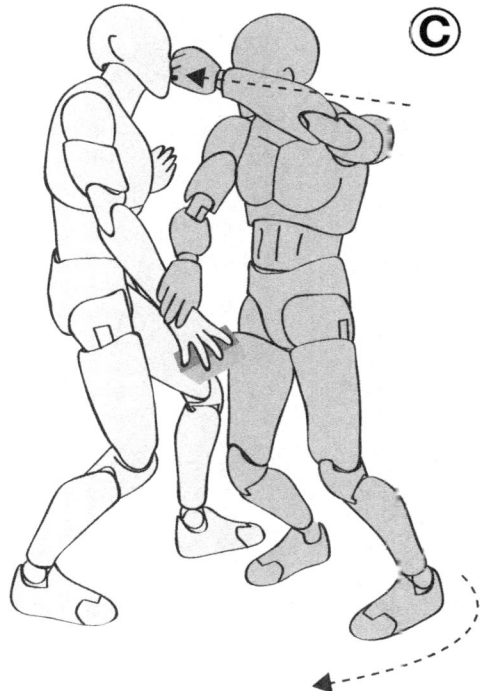

85 Defense Against a Side Attack with a Stone

Against a Side Attack

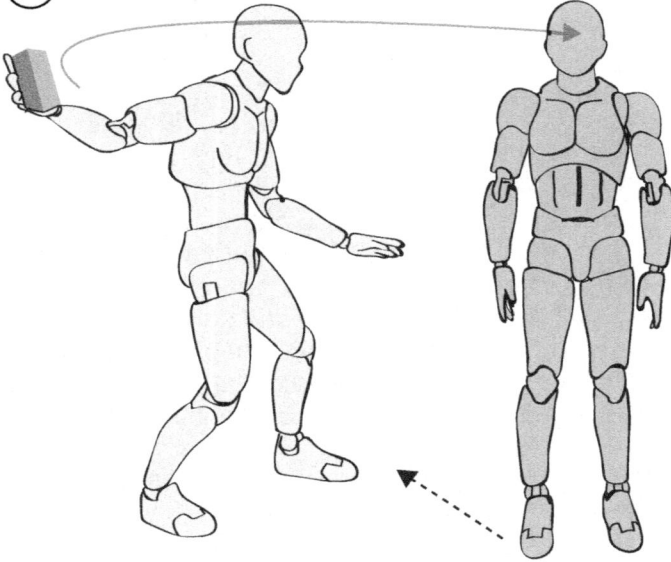

Here the opponent is by your side, but the attack is circular to hit your face (A). The defense starts with a diagonal step backward taken with the right foot and both forearms do the defense against the attack. Together with the step, the body moves to get out of the line of attack (B). The left hand holds the opponent's arm and, at the same time, boxing strikes are delivered, and continuations with kicks and other necessary moves (C).

Using a Stick in Attacks and Defenses

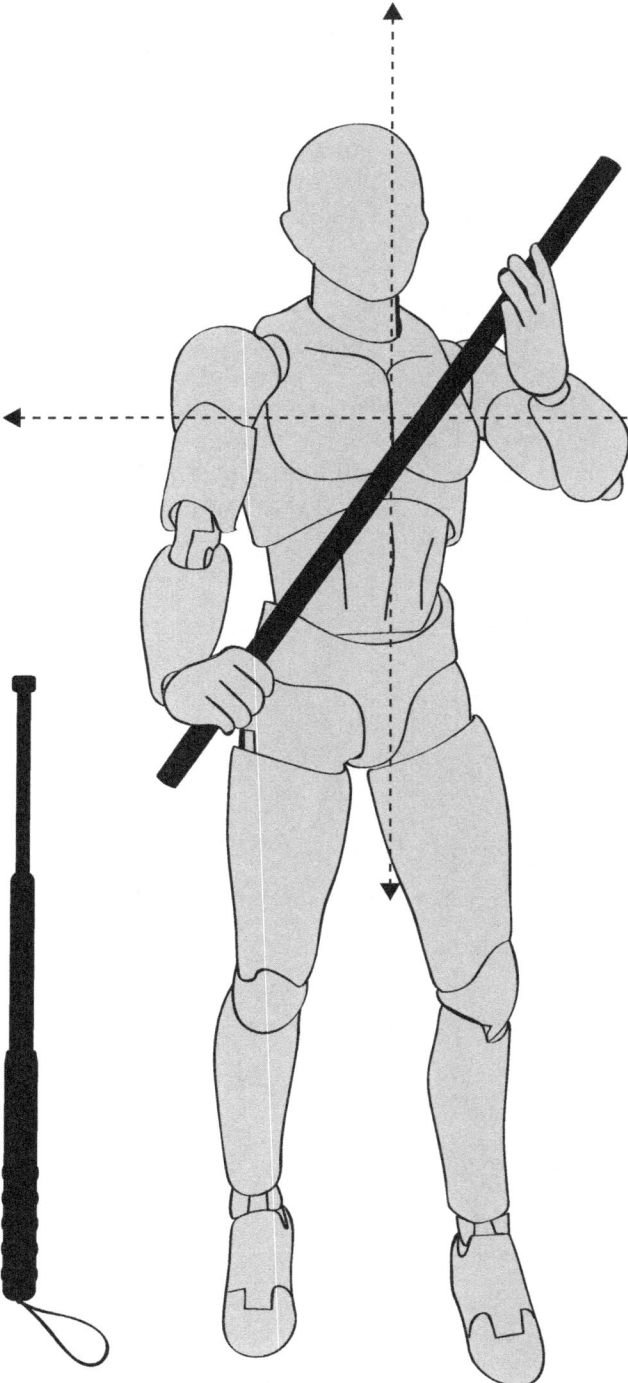

In Krav Maga, a stick is deemed an extension of the arms and it can be used as a defense and attack tool at all angles and directions.

Next, you will see the exercises divided into two parts.
The first part shows how to use a stick to defend yourself when an opponent is preparing for an attack. The second part shows how to use a stick to defend yourself against an ongoing attack.

The stick can vary as to size and thickness, and other objects with similar shapes can also be handled with the same technique and function.

SEE IN VOLUME 1 OTHER DEFENSES AGAINST STICK ATTACKS

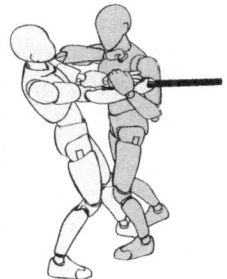

86 Sequence of an Attack with a Stick
Horizontally, toward the Neck

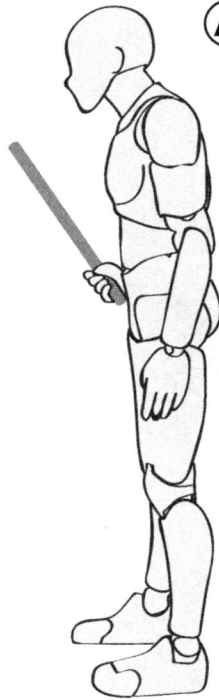

(A)

The following six exercises show variations of how to use a stick beforehand to prevent an imminent attack.

The defense stance is with the left hand holding the stick upwards, and the right hand down (A). To start the attack, the left hand goes down and, simultaneously, the right hand goes up.

(B)

At the same time, the hands move to put the stick in the horizontal position, simultaneously the body moves forward with the arms stretched to hit the opponent's neck with the center of the stick (B). This same movement can be used to hit the chest just to push away from the opponent and do the continuations with kicks and other attacks.

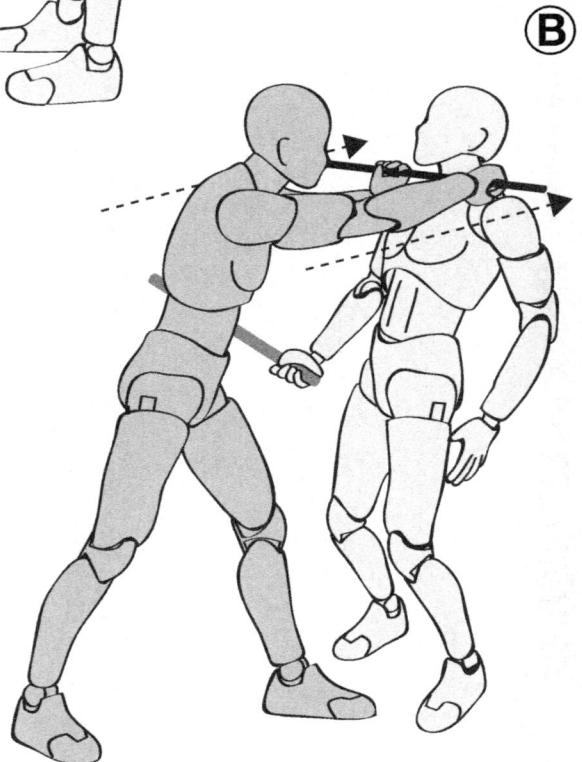

87

Sequence of an Attack with a Stick
Frontally, toward the face's center

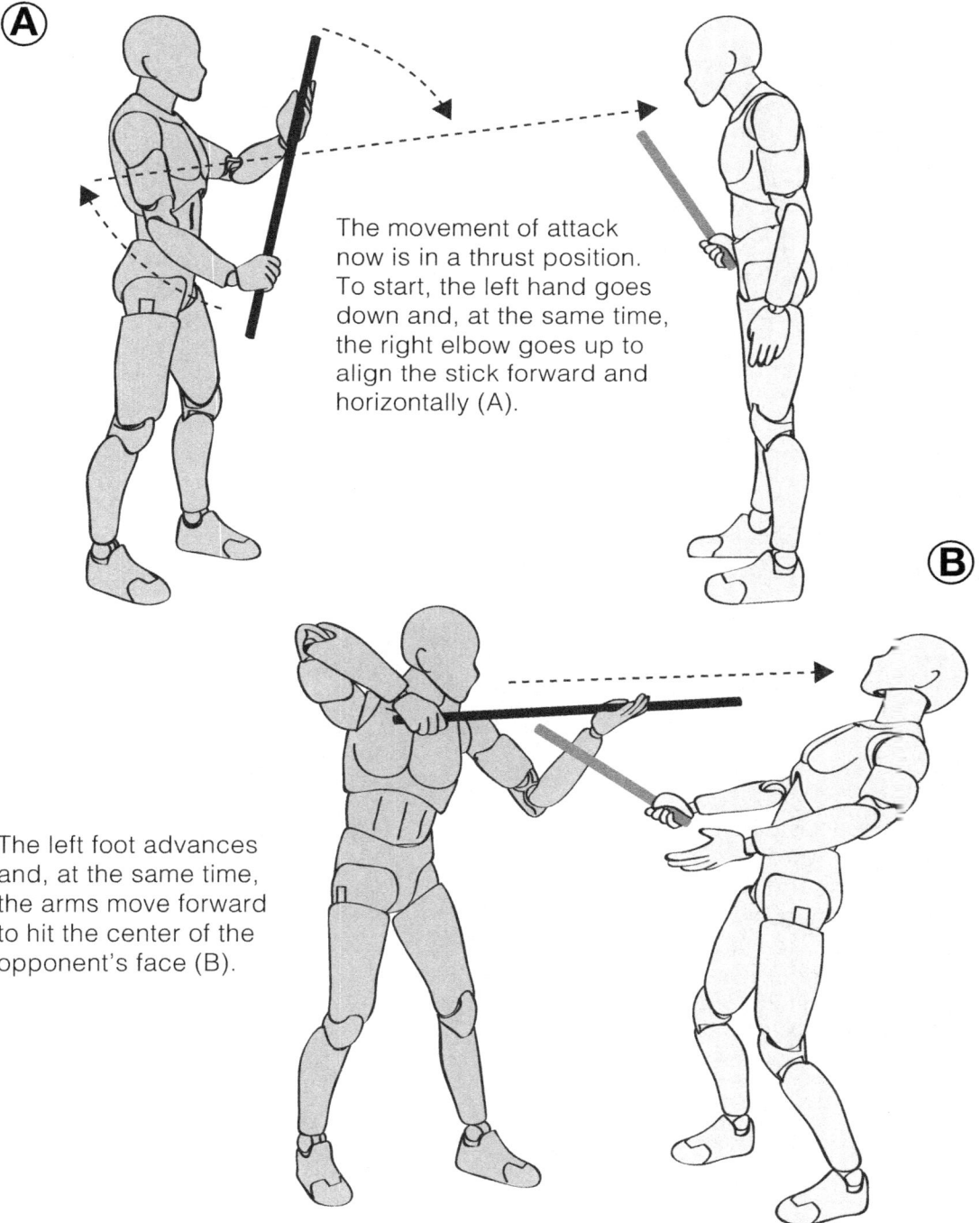

(A)

The movement of attack now is in a thrust position. To start, the left hand goes down and, at the same time, the right elbow goes up to align the stick forward and horizontally (A).

(B)

The left foot advances and, at the same time, the arms move forward to hit the center of the opponent's face (B).

88 Sequence of an Attack with a Stick
Sideways, to the Face's Right Side

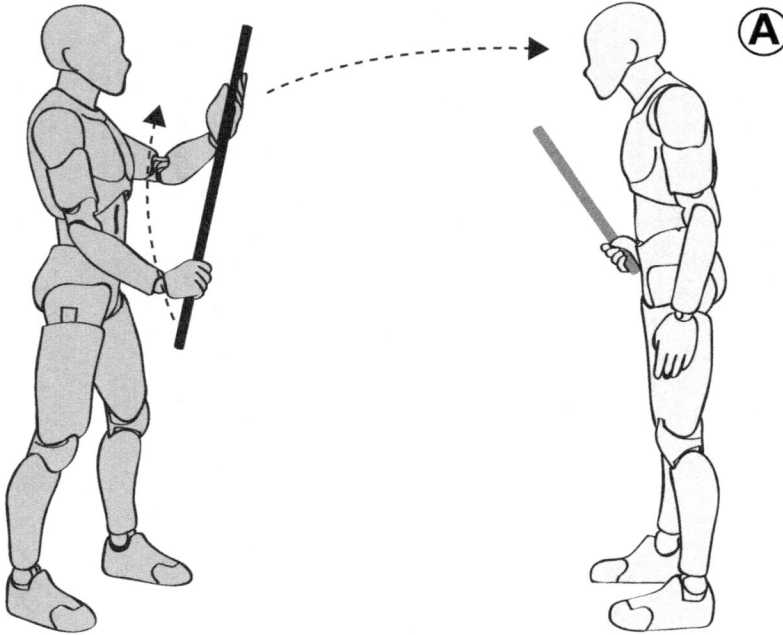

Ⓐ

In this movement, the left hand moves forward and outwards and, at the same time, the right hand goes up (A).

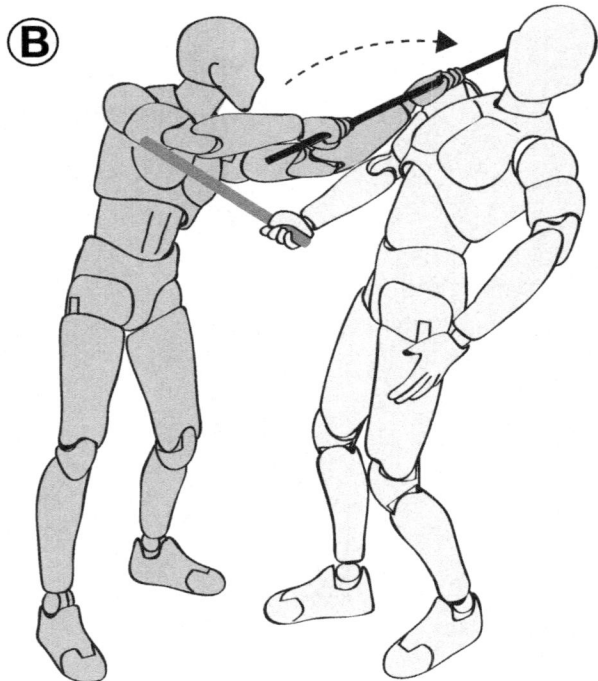

Ⓑ

The left foot advances diagonally toward the opponent's "dead" side. Simultaneously, the arms move forward with a short and circular movement to hit the face's right side (B).

89 Sequence of an Attack with a Stick
Sideways, toward the Face's Left Side

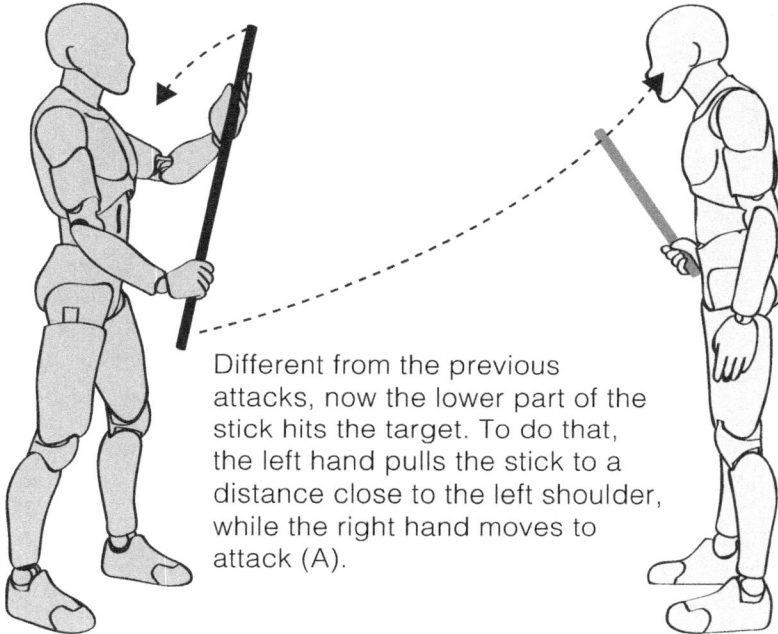

Different from the previous attacks, now the lower part of the stick hits the target. To do that, the left hand pulls the stick to a distance close to the left shoulder, while the right hand moves to attack (A).

The right foot advances diagonally to the right and, at the same time, the right hand goes up with a circular movement to hit the side of the opponent's face (B).

Sergio Nisenbaum

90 Sequence of an Attack with a Stick
Frontal, toward the Groins

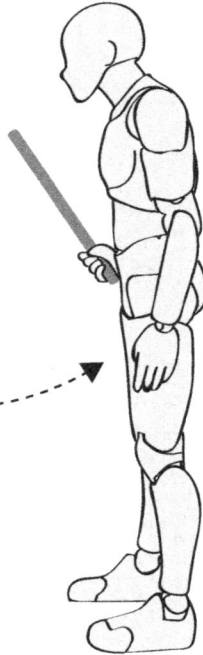

Ⓐ

Like in the previous attack, the lower part of the stick hits the target. The left hand pulls the stick outwards to a distance close to the left shoulder (A).

Ⓑ

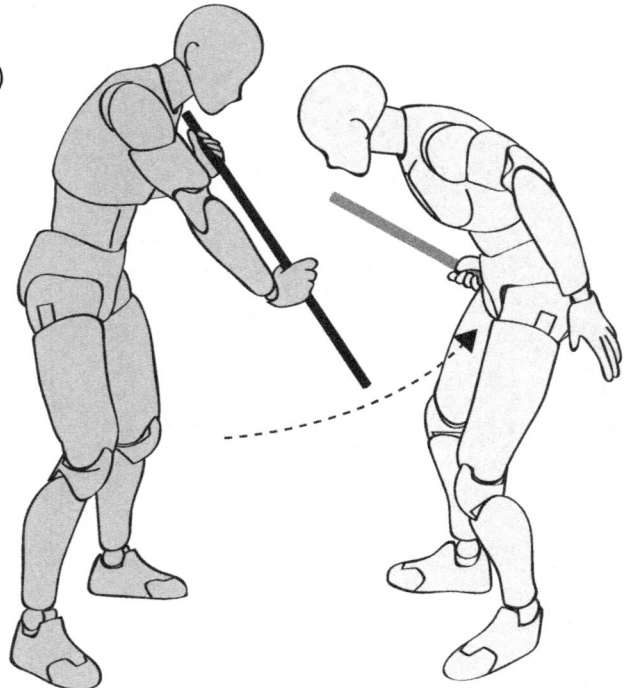

The right hand makes a quick, frontal, and circular movement with the lower tip of the stick to hit the opponent's groins (B).

91
Sequence of an Attack with a Stick
Top-down, toward the Center of the Face

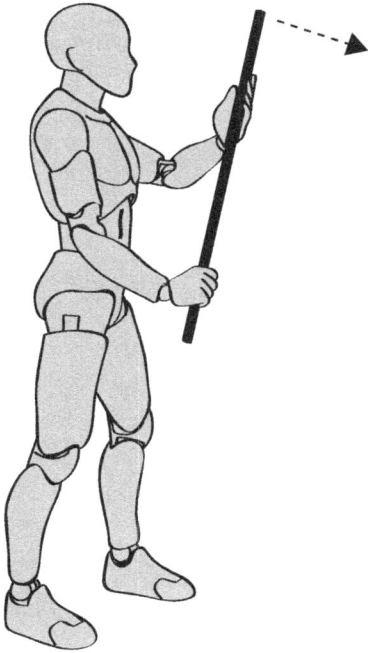

Ⓐ

In this last movement of the sequences, the left hand moves the tip of the stick forward (A). The left hand goes down with the stick's upper part to hit the center of the opponent's face with a top-down movement and, at the same time, the right hand makes a short movement upward with the lower part of the stick (B).

Ⓑ

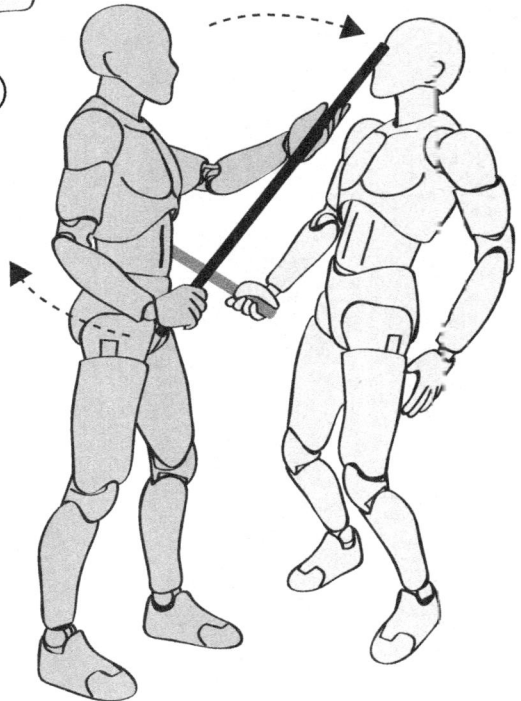

HINT: In all options, regardless of the type of attack, both hands always work together. One hand transfers the weight to the target while the other counterpoints to strengthen the movement of attack.

92

Defense Against an Attack with a Stick
Top-down Movement

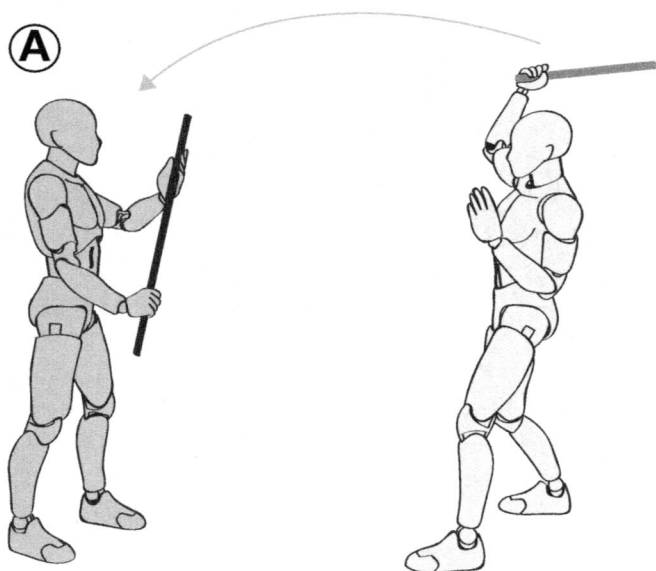

(A)

The following exercises use a stick to defend against an attack that is already happening. The six previous variations will be used for sequences and continuations of the defenses.

In this situation, the opponent attacks with a stick with a top-down movement toward the head's center (A).

(B)

To do the defense, the priority is to protect the head. To do that, both hands move the stick up and frontally, in a horizontal position (B).

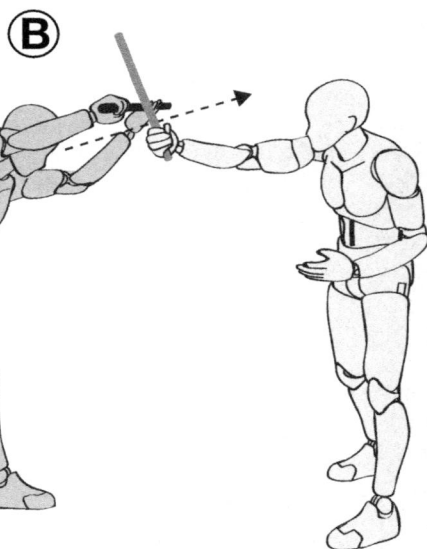

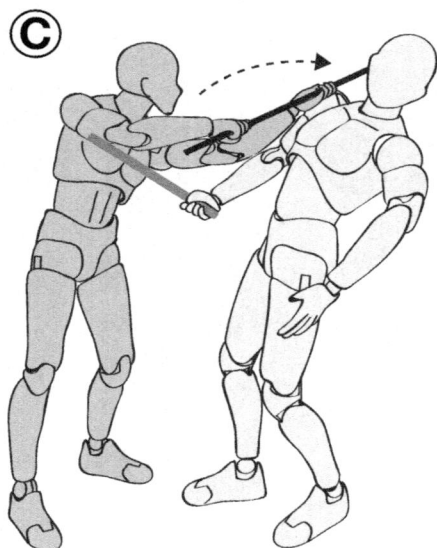

(C)

Immediately after the block, the attack is deflected, and a short and circular movement is made to hit the right side of the opponent's face (C), as described in exercise 88.

93

Defense Against an Attack with a Stick
Down-top movement

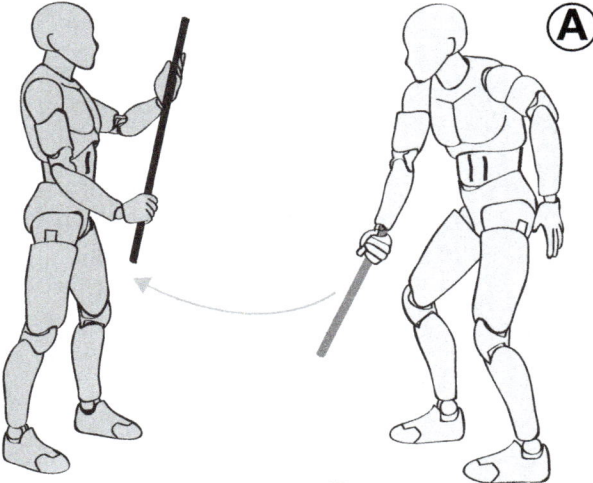

(A)

In this defense, the opponent attacks with a stick in a down-top movement toward the opponent's groins (A).

Defense is also done with the stick positioned horizontally. Both hands lower the stick diagonally toward the attack to block it (B).

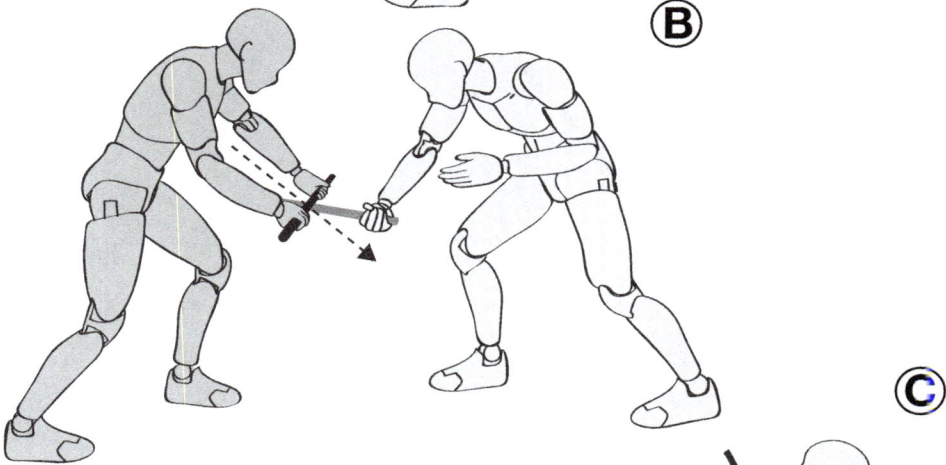

(B)

(C)

After the block, both hands move the stick horizontally toward the opponent's neck (C).
See the movement in exercise 86.

Sergio Nisenbaum

94 Defense Against an Attack with a Stick
Frontal thrust

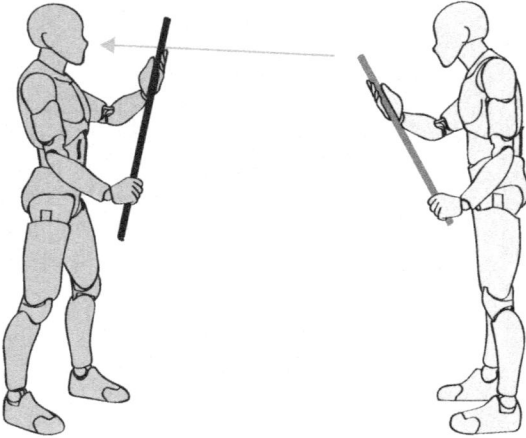

(A) The opponent attacks with the stick in a straight line toward the center of the face. This movement is called thrust (A).

In the moment of the attack, the left hand pushes from the outside in the upper part of the stick to do the deflection (B).

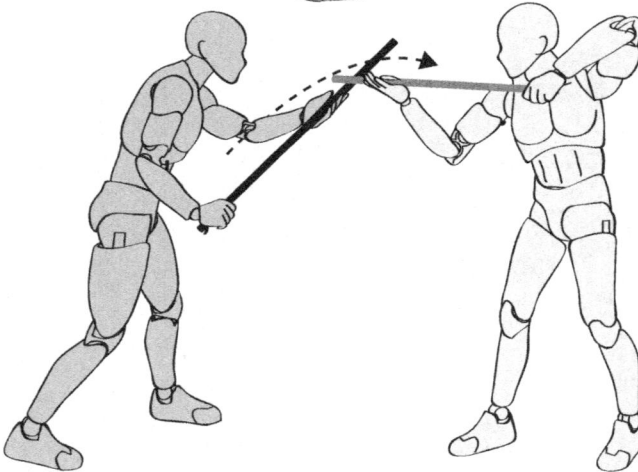

(B)

(C) At the same time, a deflection is done to the "dead" side, and also with a thrusting movement, the arms move forward to hit the center of the opponent's face (C).
See exercise 87.

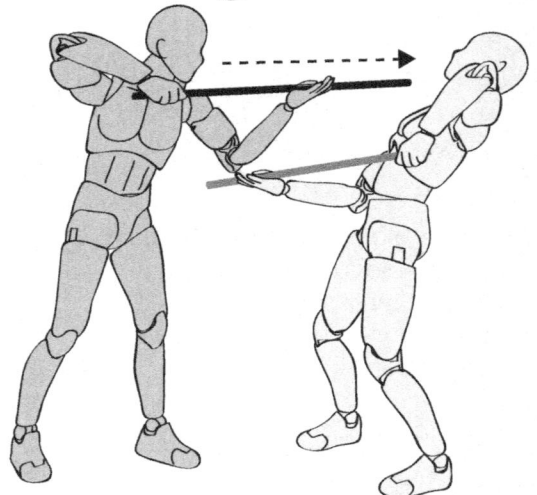

95

Defense Against an Attack with a Stick
From the Left Side

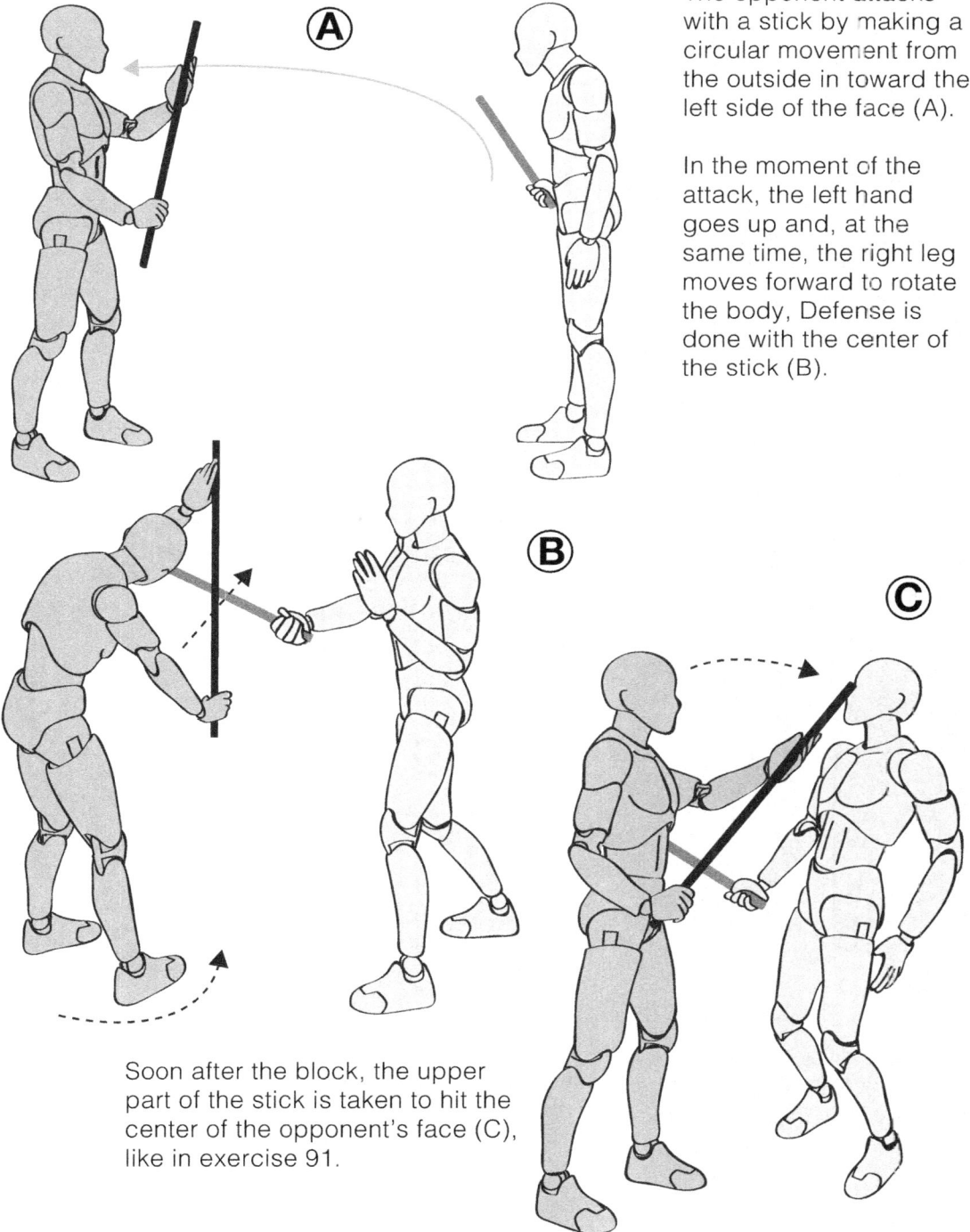

The opponent attacks with a stick by making a circular movement from the outside in toward the left side of the face (A).

In the moment of the attack, the left hand goes up and, at the same time, the right leg moves forward to rotate the body, Defense is done with the center of the stick (B).

Ⓐ

Ⓑ

Ⓒ

Soon after the block, the upper part of the stick is taken to hit the center of the opponent's face (C), like in exercise 91.

96

Defense Against an Attack with a Stick
From the Right Side

(A)

Now the opponent attacks with a stick by making a circular movement from the outside in toward the right side to hit the abdomen (A).

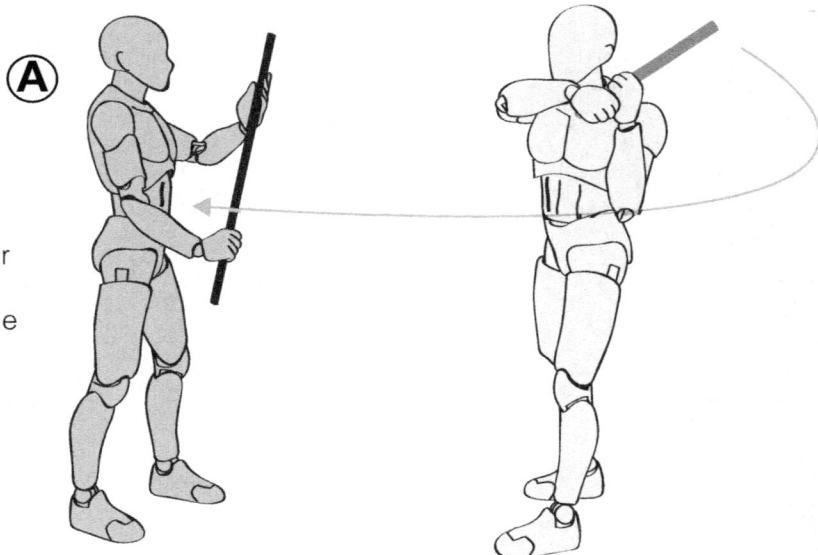

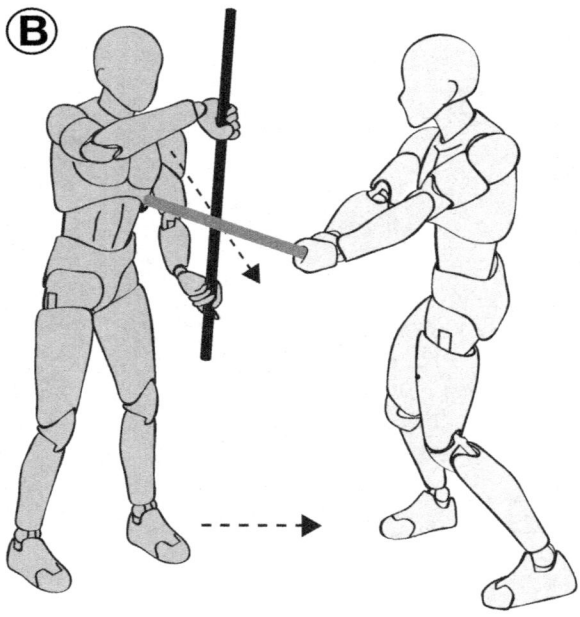

(B)

To do the defense, the right hand moves up and the left hand moves down, placing the stick in a vertical position, while the left leg advances forward (B).

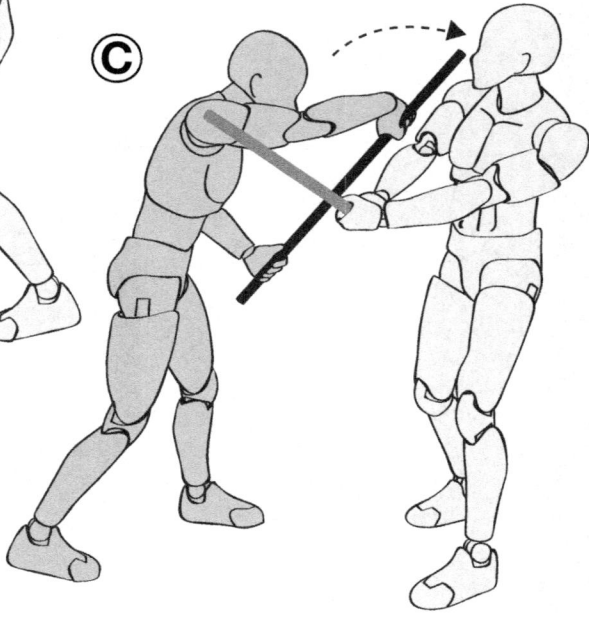

(C)

Next, the right hand moves the upper part of the stick to the center of the opponent's face (C).

97

Defense with a Stick
Against a Regular Kick N°1

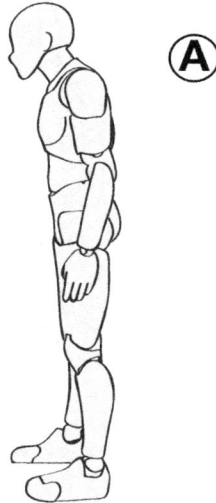

(A)

In this situation, the stick is used as a tool to defend yourself against varied attacks. In this case, against a kick attack (A).

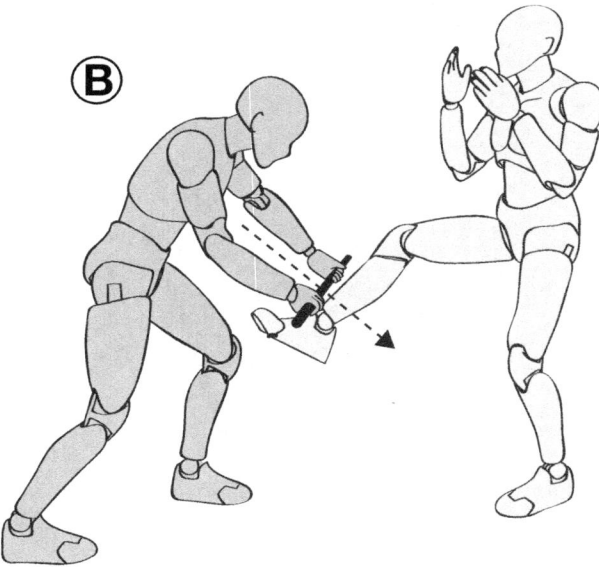

(B)

In the moment of the kick, the left foot advances diagonally outwards and both hands lower the stick diagonally toward the opponent's shin (B).

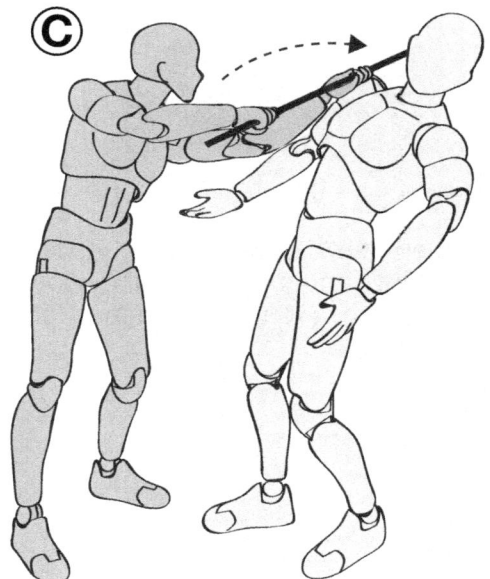

(C)

Now the stick is used to do continuations of attacks (C), which can also include sequences of kicks. For instance, the stick hits the opponent's face and, next, a regular kick is delivered on the opponent's groins.

Sergio Nisenbaum

98 Defense with a Stick
Against a Regular Kick N°2

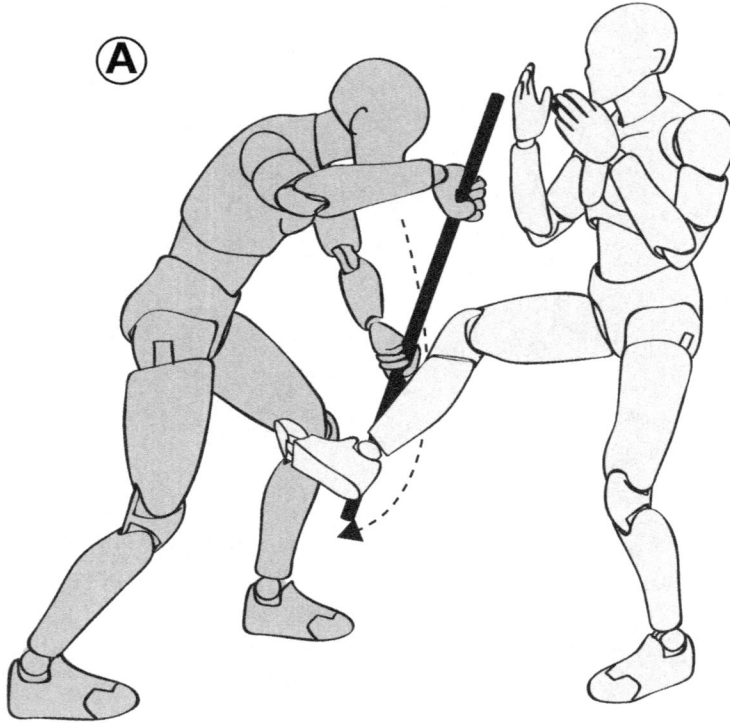

A

In this alternative for the same attack with a regular kick, the stick does the deflection from the outside in. In the moment of the attack, the left foot advances diagonally outwards to get out of the kick line. The left hand moves down quite quickly to deflect the kick from the side (A).

B

Immediately after deflecting the kick, the right hand moves the upper part of the stick toward the opponent's face (B).

99 Defense with a Stick
Against a Boxing Strike

Now the stick is used to defend against a right-hand boxing strike (A).

As the boxing strike comes in a straight line, the defense is done as if it were a deflection from a thrust. The advantage in this defensive situation against a boxing strike is that the stick works as an extension of the arm and keeps you at a safe distance from the attack. In the moment that the strike is delivered, the left hand deflects the opponent's arm from the outside in (B).

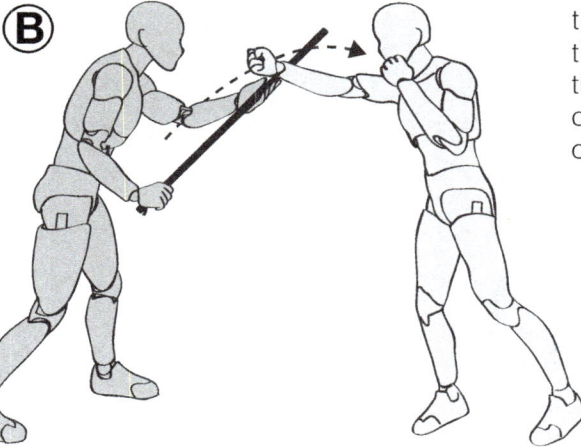

Next, with a thrusting movement, the stick moves to the center of the opponent's face (C).

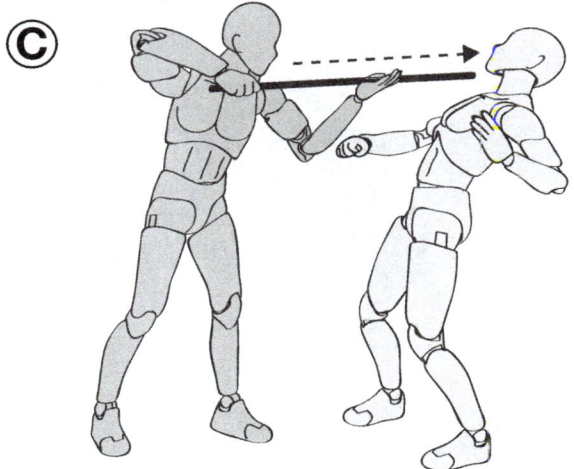

Defense Against Gun Threats

Once this is a high-risk defense, the whole practice for threats involving guns requires strong self-control and technical capacity to do it precisely. Additionally, it is indispensable the supervision of a duly qualified instructor to teach this defense. Regardless if the attack involves a pistol or a revolver, all defenses to be followed consist of deflecting the body together with deflecting the gun, and doing the necessary continuations to disarm the opponent.

See below some basic characteristics of a revolver and a pistol.

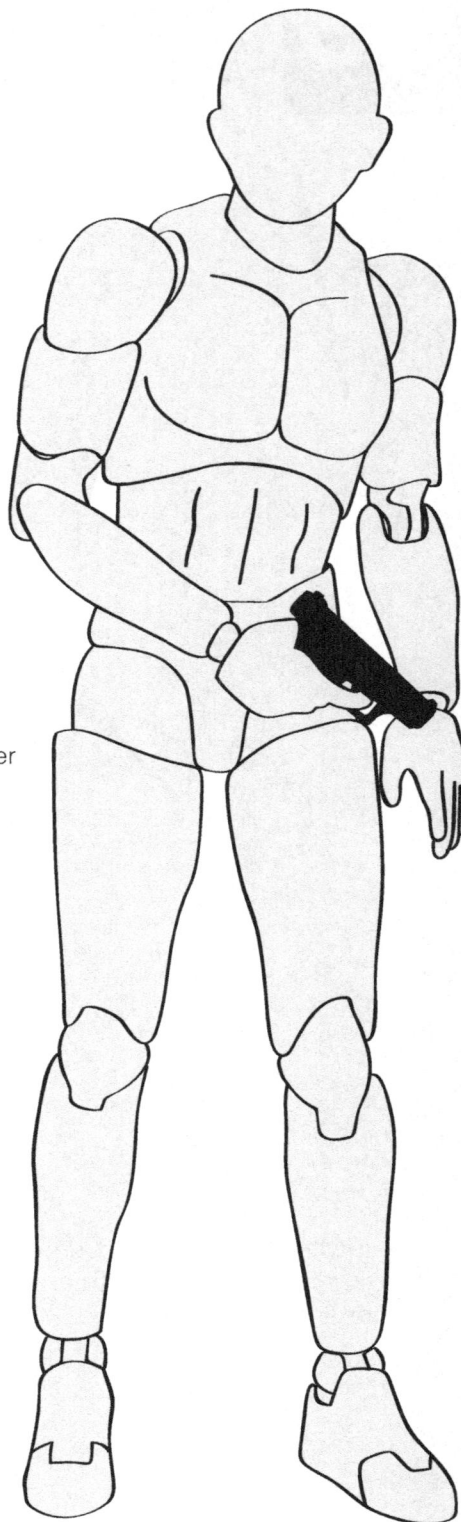

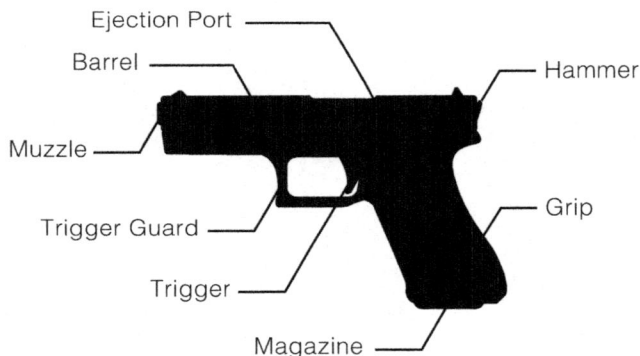

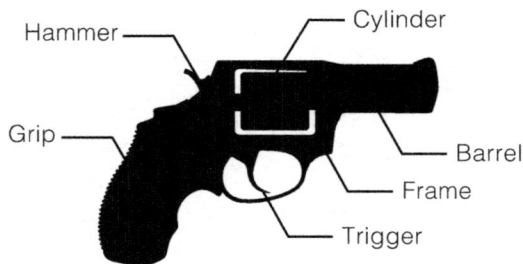

Ejection Port

Barrel

Hammer

Muzzle

Trigger Guard

Grip

Trigger

Magazine

Hammer

Cylinder

Grip

Barrel

Frame

Trigger

⚠ **WARNING**
Never use a real gun
in your practice.

100 Defense Against a Gun Threat
On the head, frontally

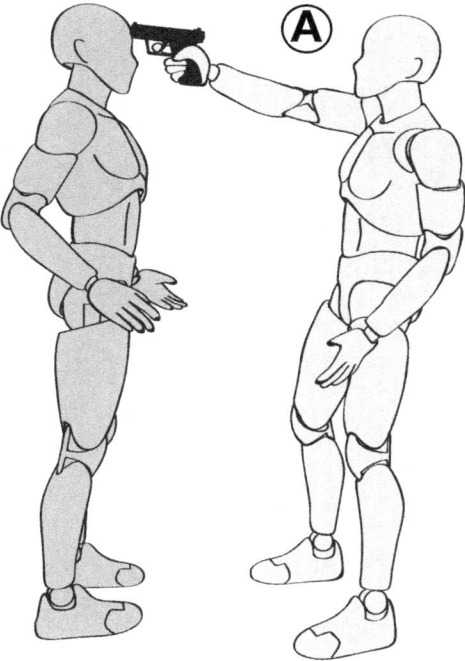

Carefully observe, in the defenses showed next, the set of defensive movements and attacks necessary to dominate and reverse the situation. In this threat, the opponent puts the gun barrel against your head (A). The defense starts with two simultaneous movements. Deflecting the head from the line of fire and deflecting the gun. For those purposes, both hands together raise the gun from below and, at the same time, raise the chin. Together with the deflecting movement, a regular kick can be delivered on the opponents' groins (B).

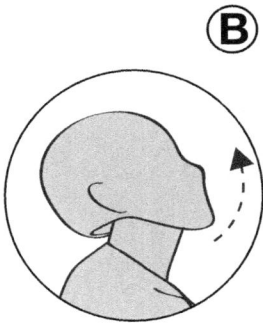

The chin raises quickly together with the hands to deflect the head out of the line of fire.

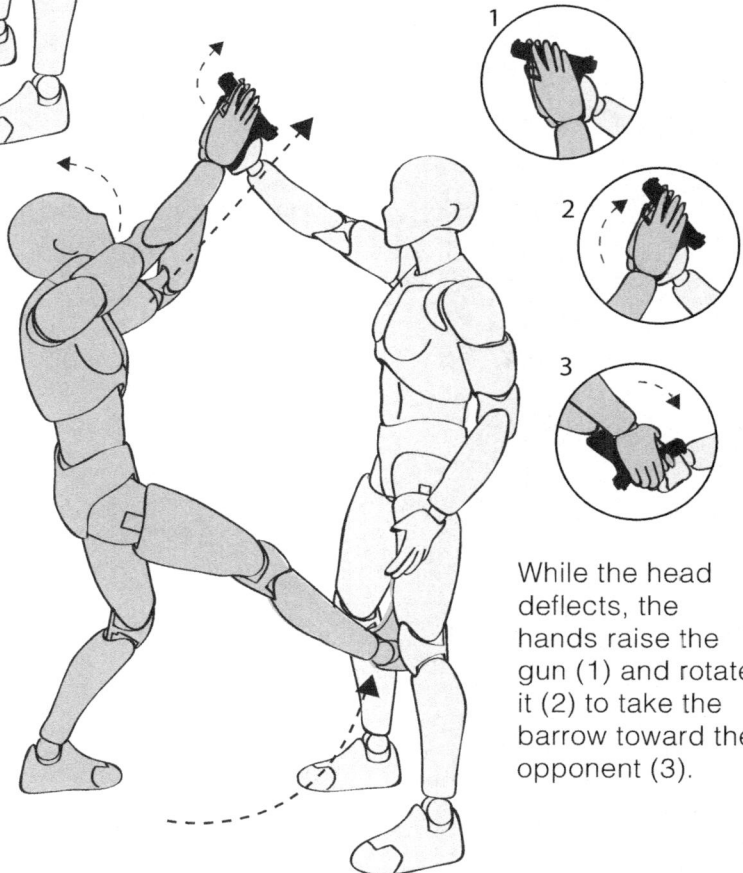

While the head deflects, the hands raise the gun (1) and rotate it (2) to take the barrow toward the opponent (3).

The hands hold steadily, from below to the top, in the gun's center from the trigger guard to the barrel or chamber and, after the kick, they make a movement down and backward (C).

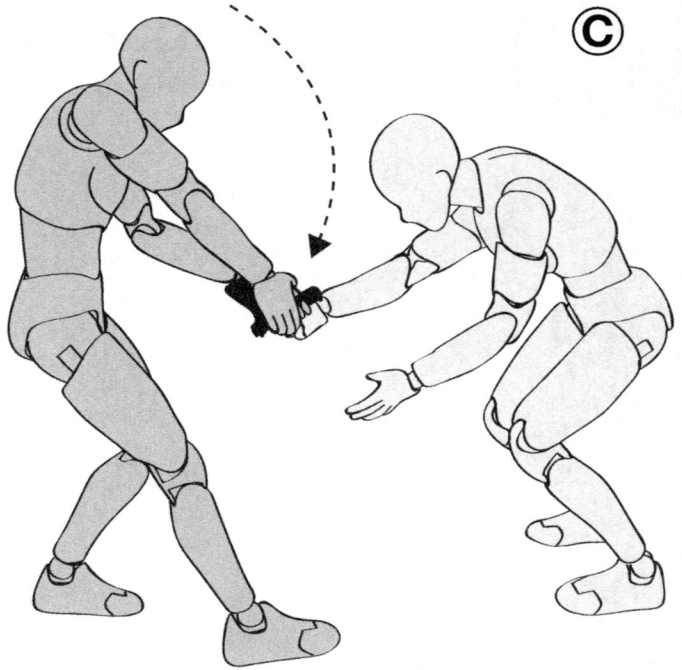

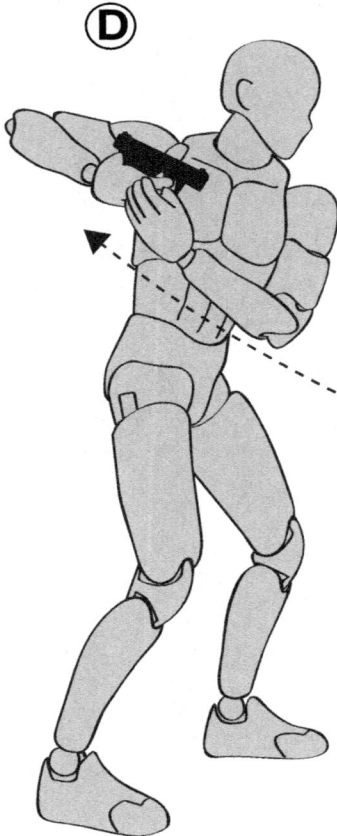

The gun is removed from the opponent's hand and, finally, you position yourself at a safe distance (D). It is extremely important that all the final movements be made with the gun barrel always pointing at the opponent.

101 Defense Against a Gun Threat
Frontally, at the Waist Level

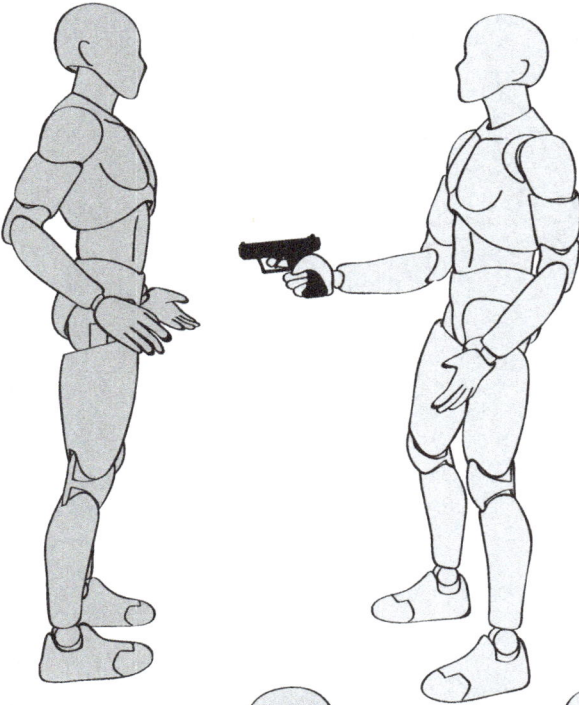

(A)

Here the opponent threatens with a gun at the level of your waist at a short distance (A).

The defense starts with two simultaneous movements. The heel of the hand deflects the gun from outside in and, simultaneously, the hips rotate outwards to get out of the line of fire (B). Immediately, together with the deflection of the body, the right hand goes up to reach the opponent with attacks with boxing strikes.

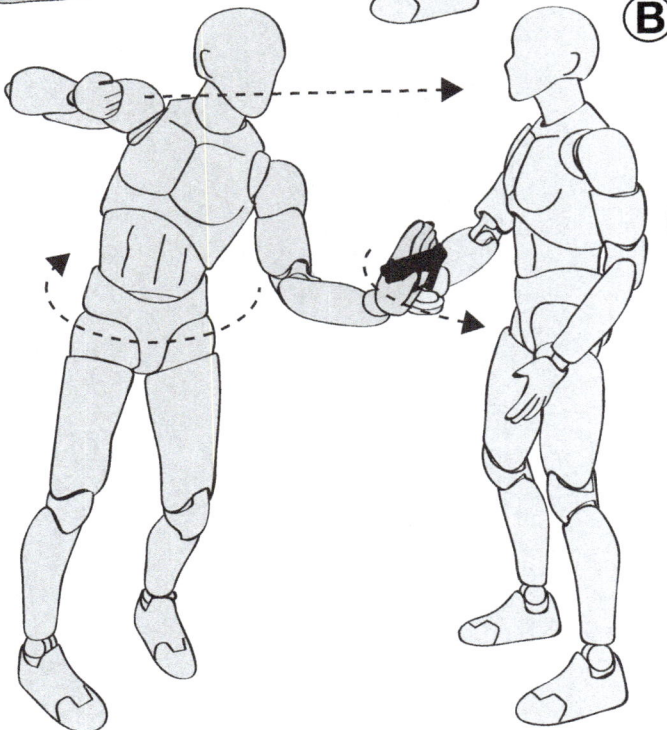

(B)

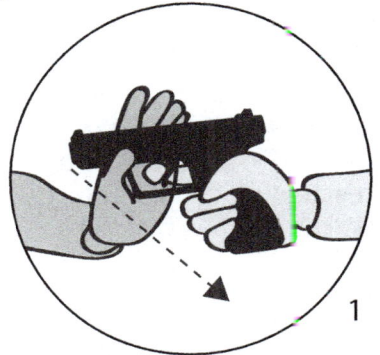

The heel of the hand is positioned right in the center to block the gun chamber or to lock the cylinder in the case of a revolver (1).

C

With your arms strongly stretched, the left hand holds the gun, and the body weight is taken forward and downward. At the same time, you start the attacks with boxing strikes on the opponent's face (C).

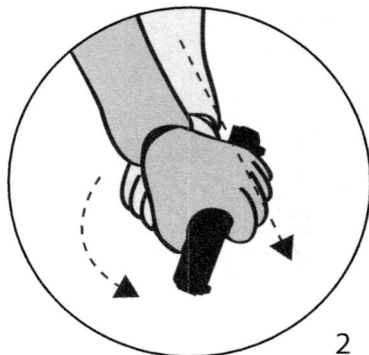

2

The gun barrel is deflected to the side at the same time the hand transfers the body weight to the hand holding the gun (2).

After the boxing strikes, the right hand passes under the gun (3) and holds it at the hammer level (D). If the opponent still shows resistance, continue to deliver attacks of boxing strikes.

D

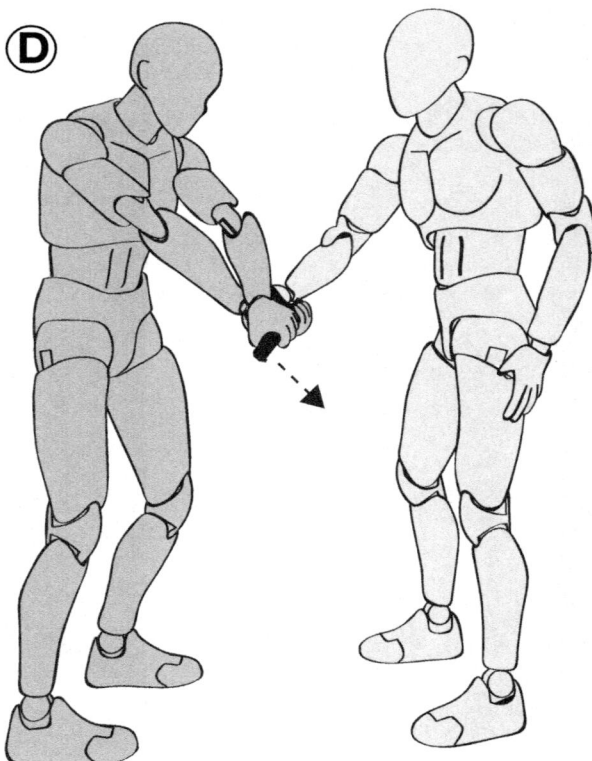

3

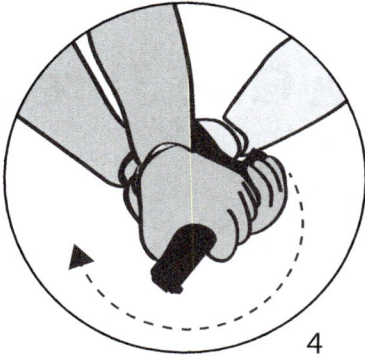

To disarm the opponent, the right hand pulls from below and, at the same time, takes a strong turn to make to gun's upper part turn downward (4).
(Even in this phase the barrel continues to point outward).

4

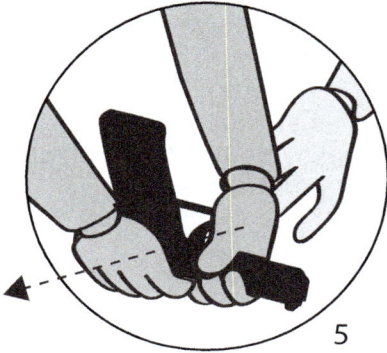

Both hands pull the gun strongly from the finger in the trigger (5).
Together with the pull, take some steps back to position yourself at a safe distance from the opponent (E).

5

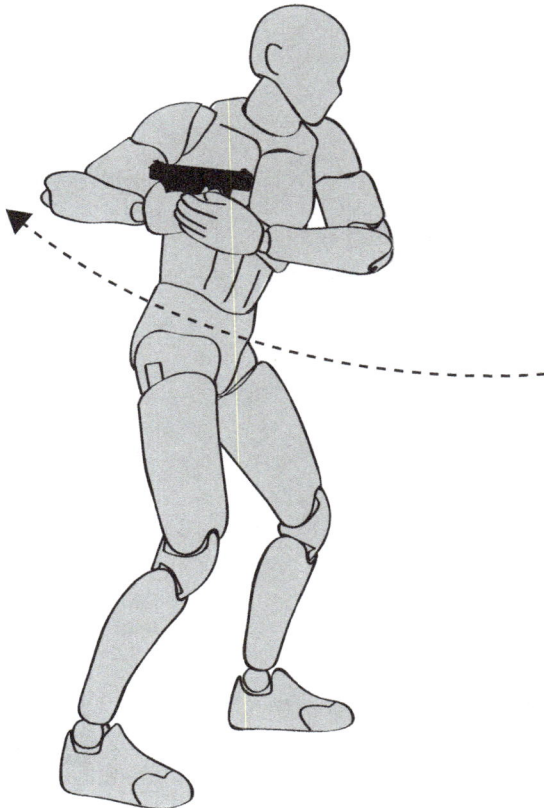

Ⓔ

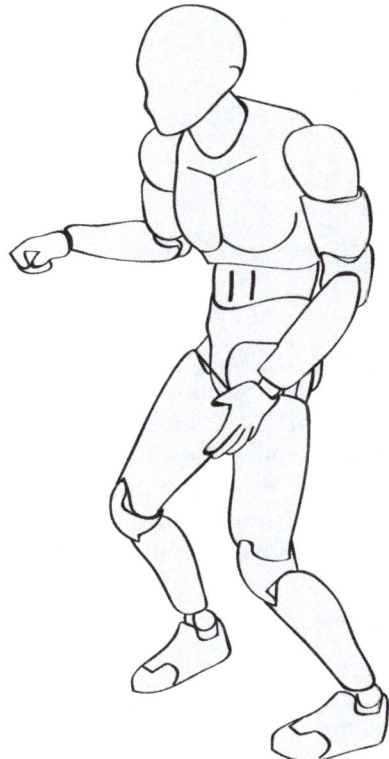

Sergio Nisenbaum

102 Defense Against a Gun Threat
From behind, at the back level

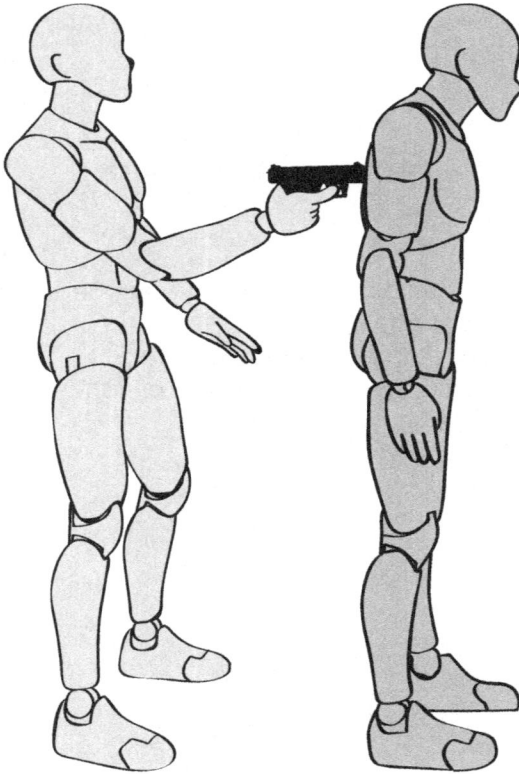

(A)

The threat here comes from behind, at the back level (A). First, before any defensive reaction, when you realize the threat, you must check which hand is holding the gun (B). To do that you must check discreetly both sides to be sure of the correct position.

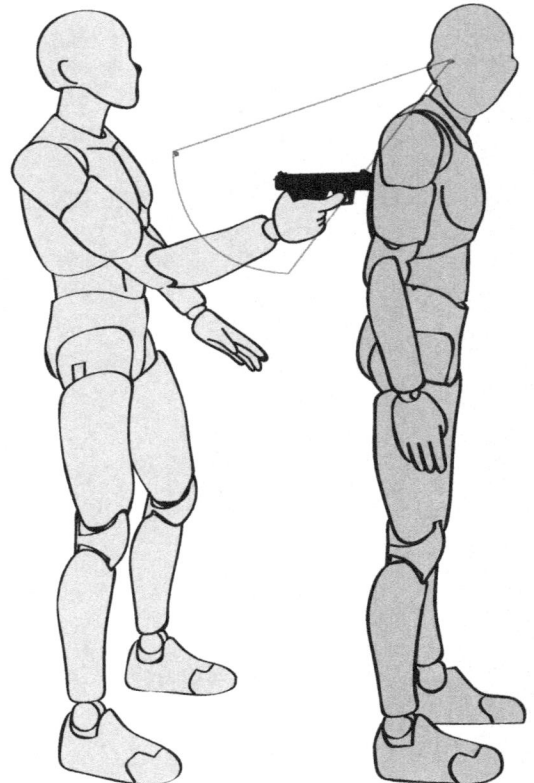

(B)

Even if at first glance you can already check which hand is holding the gun, it is also important to look at the other side and check where the other hand of the opponent is. Now, see the movements to get away from the line of fire and to recover control of the situation (B).

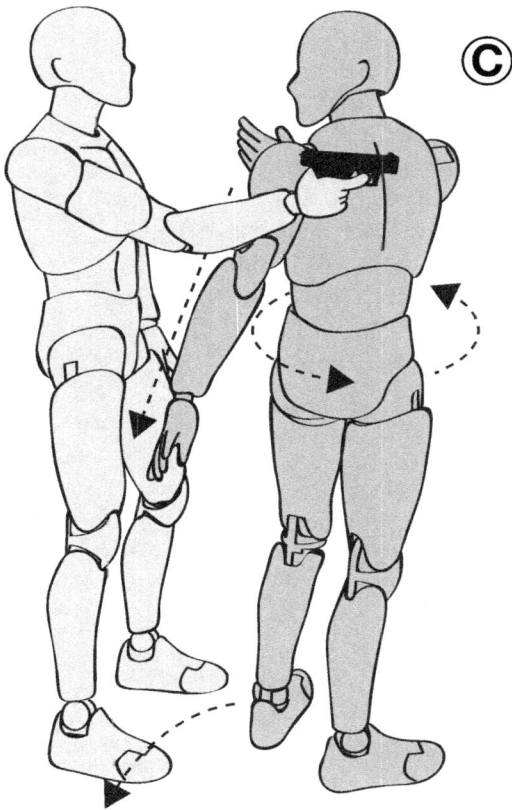

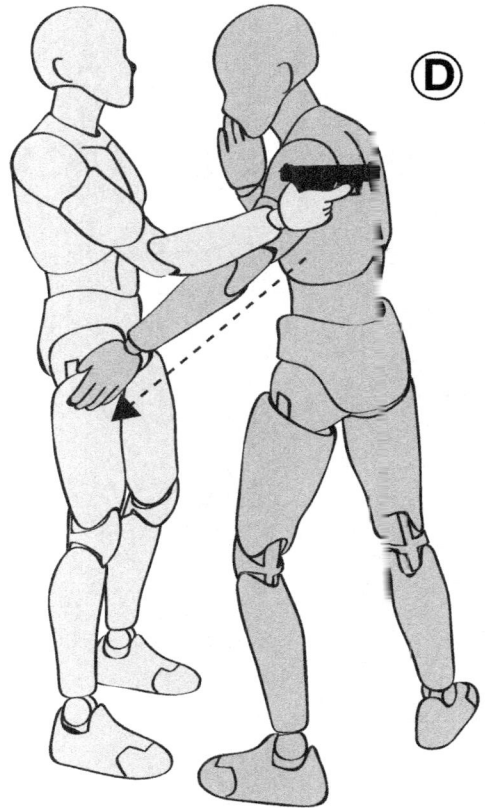

The defense happens as a chain reaction, i.e., a movement leads to another until the end. By taking advantage of the movement to look at the back, the left arm stretched deflects the gun and simultaneously the hips rotate to remove your back from the line of fire (C).

The left foot moves to the left and simultaneously the left arm passes diagonally under the opponent's forearm (D).

Now the left hand strongly holds the opponent's forearm, having his right hand holding the gun tightly pressed and close to his body so that he has no room to move the gun. At the same time, elbow strikes are delivered forward toward the opponent's face (E).

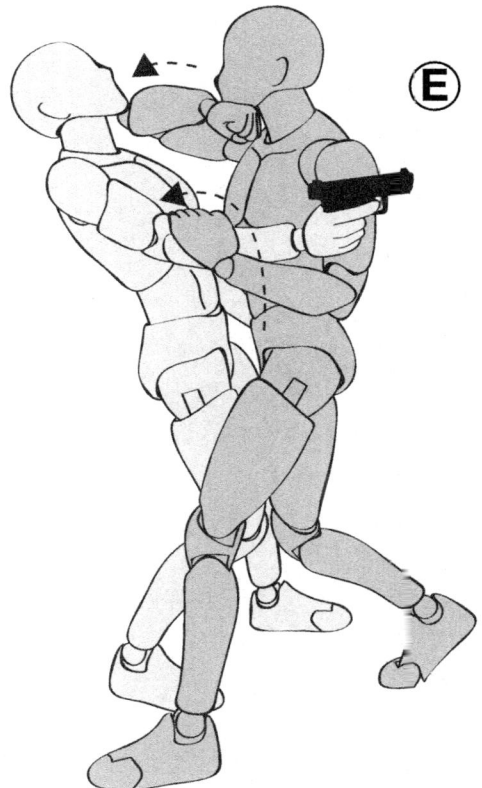

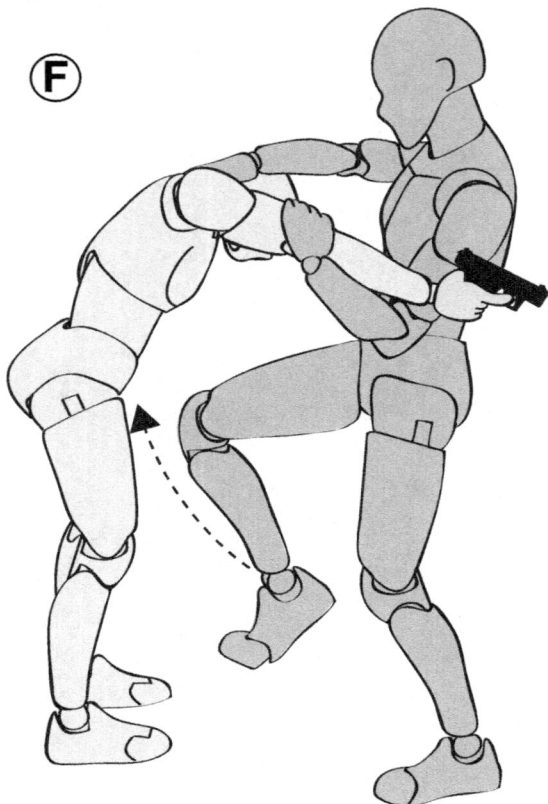

(F)

Immediately after the attack with an elbow strike, the right hand holds the opponent's shoulder to deliver a knee strike on his groins (F). The left hand continues strongly pressing the forearm to keep under control the hand that is holding the gun (F).

To remove the gun from the opponent, the body makes a short and quick movement to rotate the hips by taking the left shoulder back and the right hand over the gun (1) to grab the barrow and turn it toward the opponent (G).

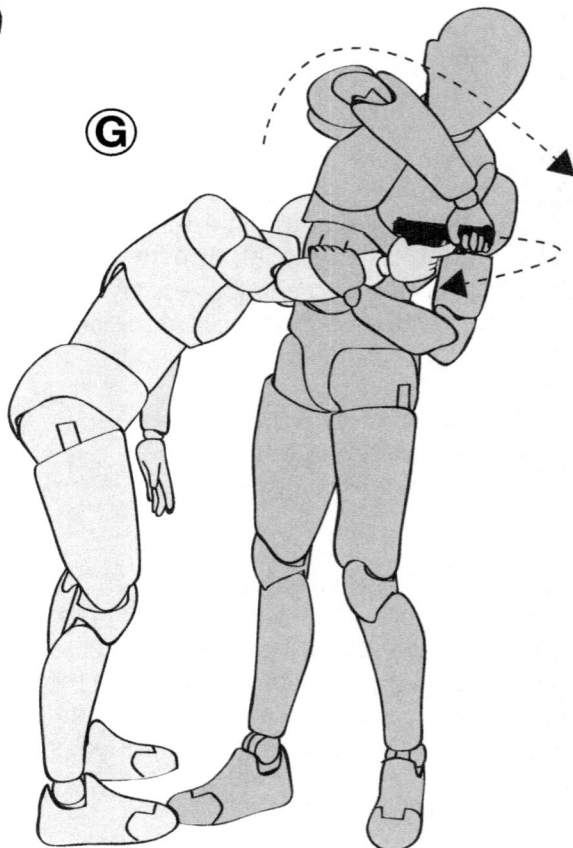

(G)

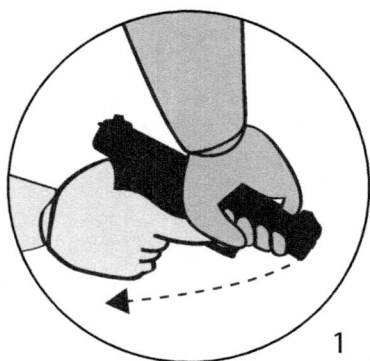

1

The right hand comes from above the gun to prevent the hand from passing in front of the barrow.

(H)

In this position, to disarm the opponent, the gun is pulled outward (2) and next a circular movement is made to hit the opponent's face with the right elbow, or even with the very gun grip (H).

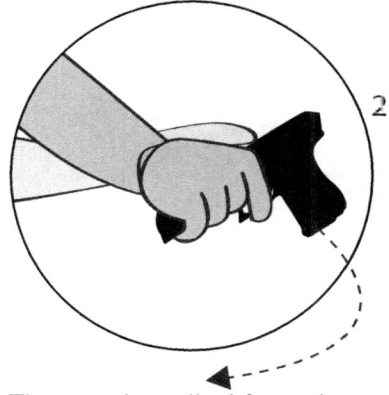

2

The gun is pulled from the opponent's finger that is still on the trigger (2).

(I)

The gun is removed from the opponent's hand and, finally, you must position yourself at a safe and defensive distance from him (I).

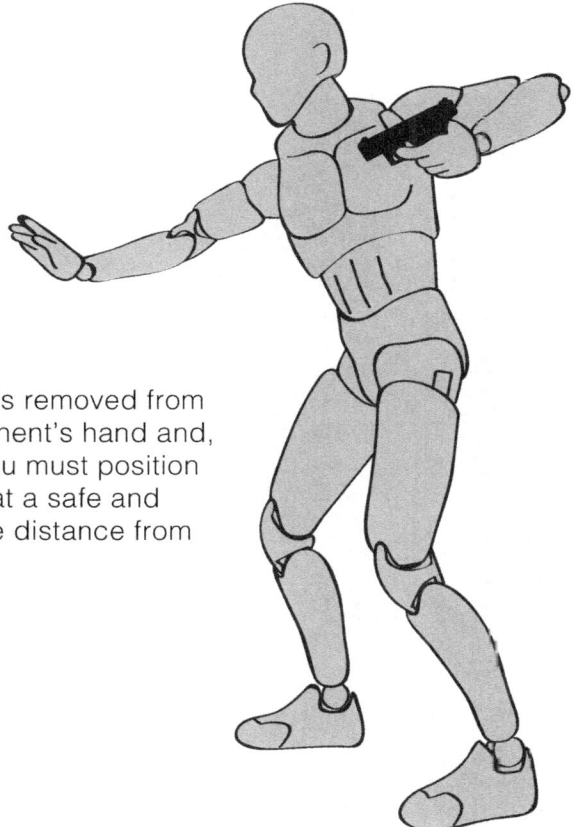

Sergio Nisenbaum

103 Defense Against a Gun Threat
Sideway, behind the Arm

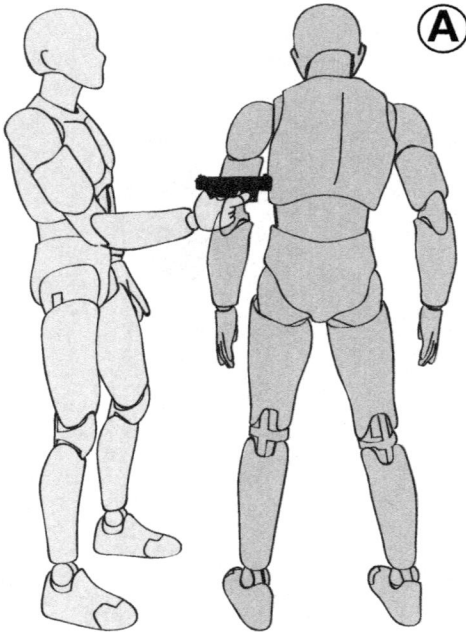

A

In this situation, the opponent threatens you with a gun placed against the left side of your body, behind the arm (A). Although the position is different, this defense happens virtually like the previous defense with a threat from behind. The left arm stretched diagonally deflects the gun and simultaneously the hip rotates to take the side of the body out of the line of fire (B). The left foot moves to the left and, simultaneously, the left arm passes diagonally under the opponent's forearm to strongly hold the opponent's forearm. At the same time, elbow strikes must be delivered toward the opponent's face (C).

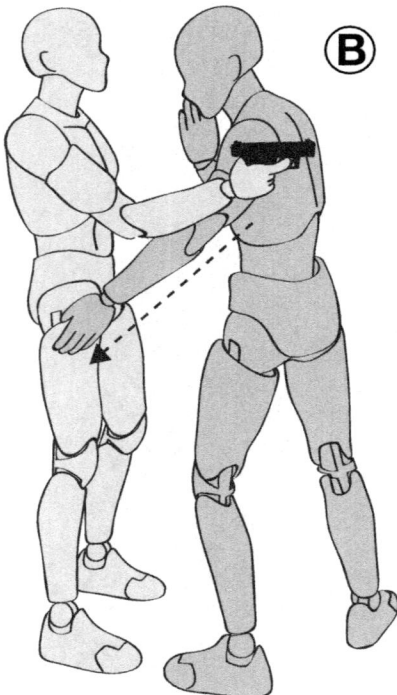

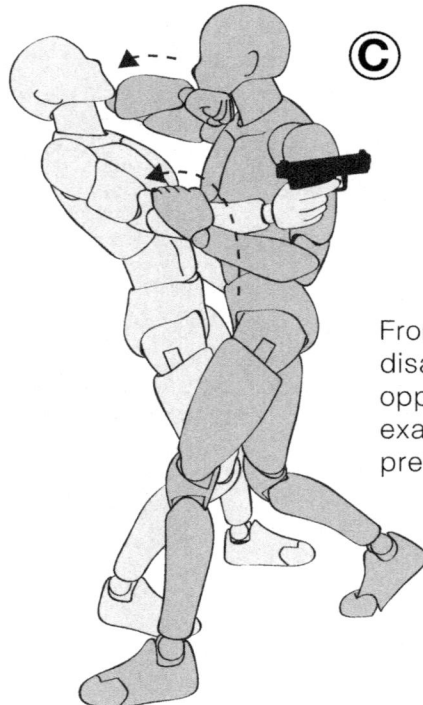

B

C

From this point, disarming the opponent is done exactly like in the previous defense.

104 Defense Against a Gun Threat
Sideway, from the front of the Arm

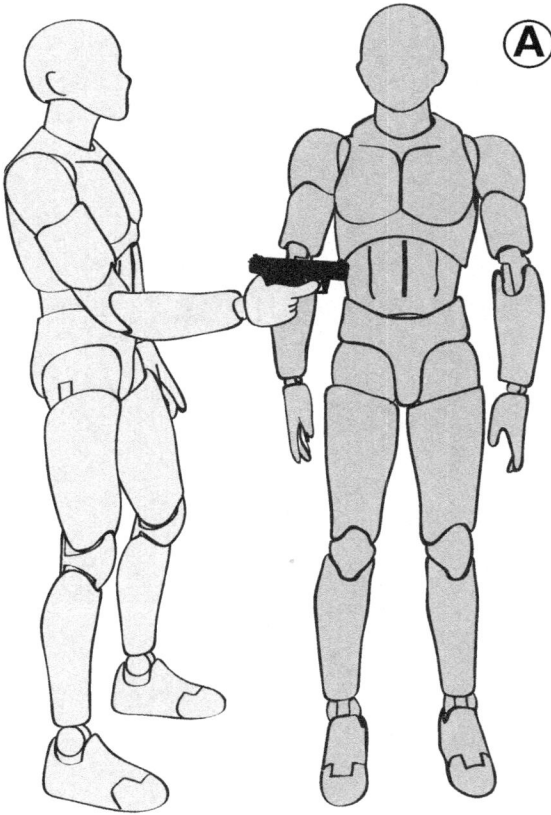

(A)

Now the opponent threatens on the right side of your body with a gun pressed in front of the arm (A). To deflect the gun and take the side of the body away from the line of fire, the right arm stretched makes a short movement forward to deflect the gun. The heel of the hand is positioned outward. At the same time, the body is moved backward in the opposite direction of the deflection of the gun (B).

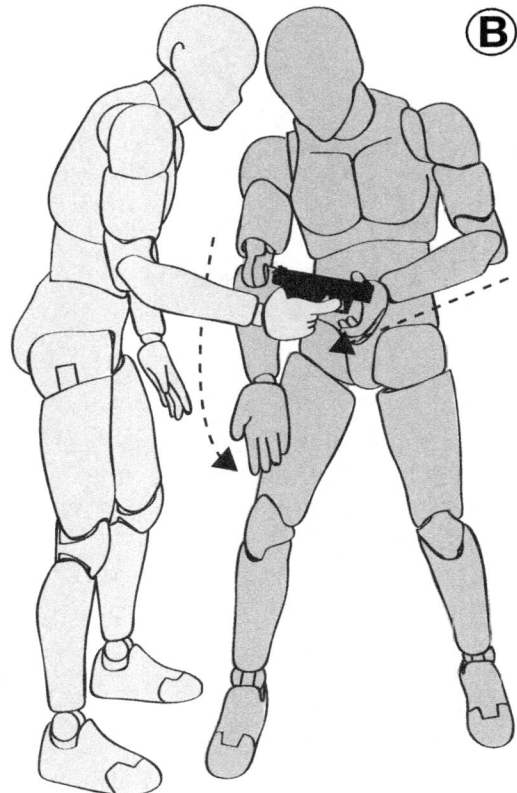

(B)

After the simultaneous deflection of the gun and the body, the left hand raises and moves to grab the gun from behind.

C

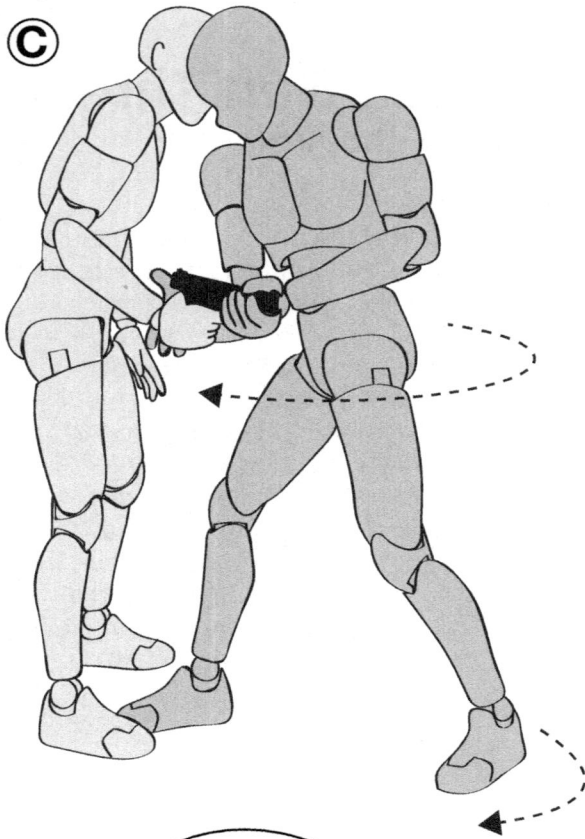

Now the gun needs to be turned toward the opponent. To do that, three movements are made simultaneously. The left hand holds tightly the gun barrow and the right hand raises to hold the wrist (1). The left foot rotates outward together with the hips (C).

1

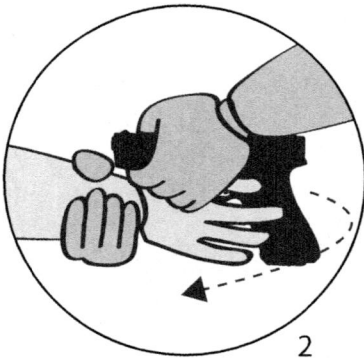

2

D

The rotation of the hip and the heel of the left foot, transfer the body weight to turn the gun strongly (D).

At this moment, the finger on the trigger can sustain a fracture (2).

(E)

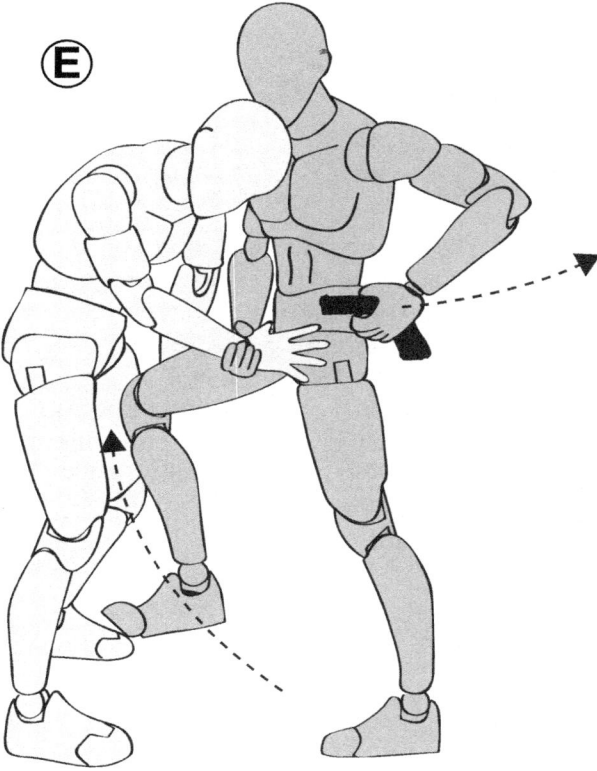

The right hand keeps on holding the wrist, and the left hand disarms the opponent by pulling the gun out and backward. At the same time, knee strikes must be delivered on the opponent's groins (E).

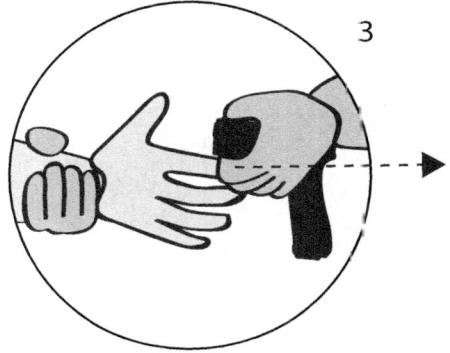

3

The gun is pulled out and backward (3).

(F)

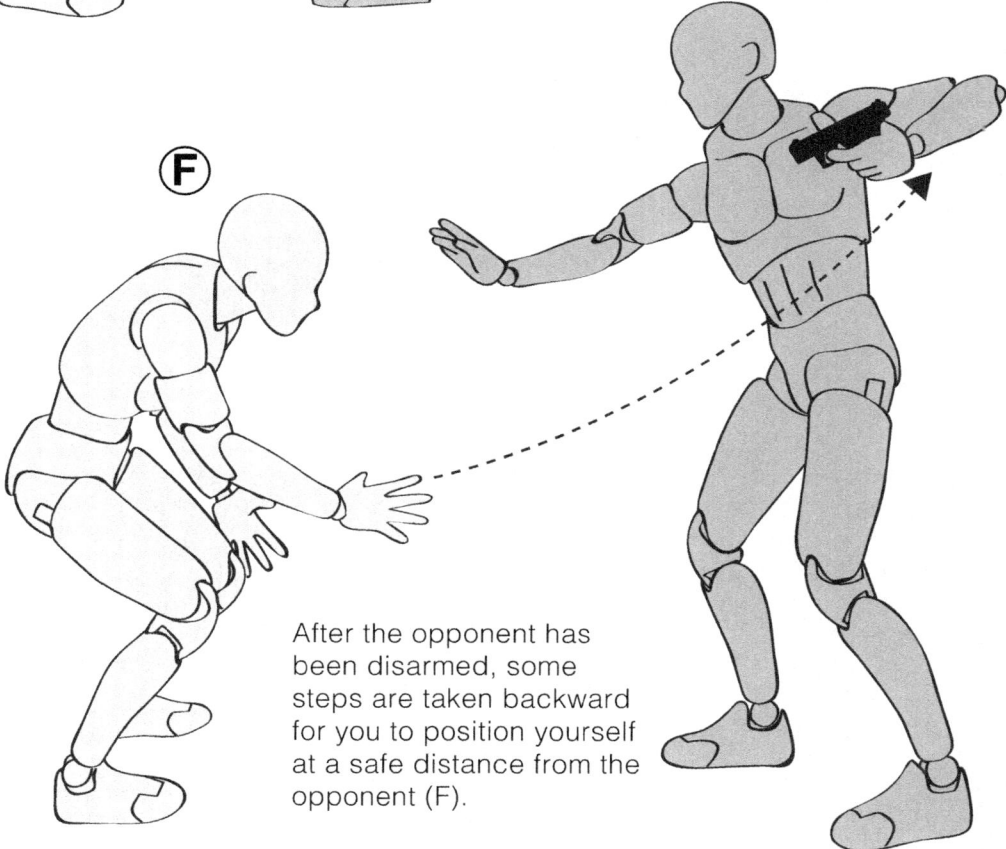

After the opponent has been disarmed, some steps are taken backward for you to position yourself at a safe distance from the opponent (F).

105 Defense Against a Gun Threat
Sideway, on the Head

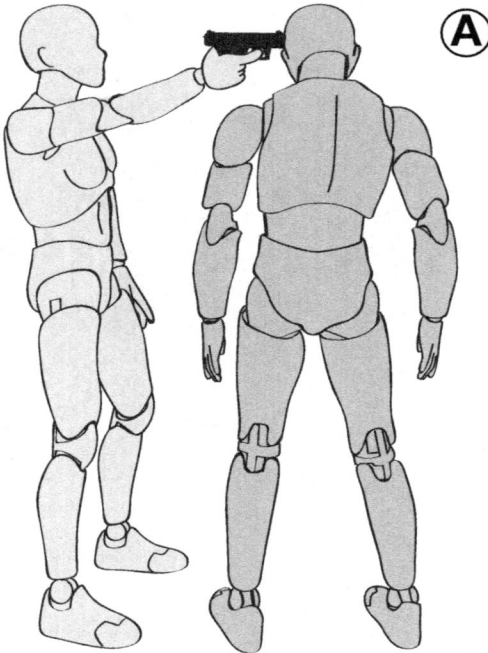

(A)

The opponent threatens with a gun to the left side of your head (A). The defense starts with you deflecting the gun and deflecting your head from the line of fire. The head rotates to the right and the body tilts backward to get out of the line of fire. Simultaneously, the left hand turns the gun forward (B).

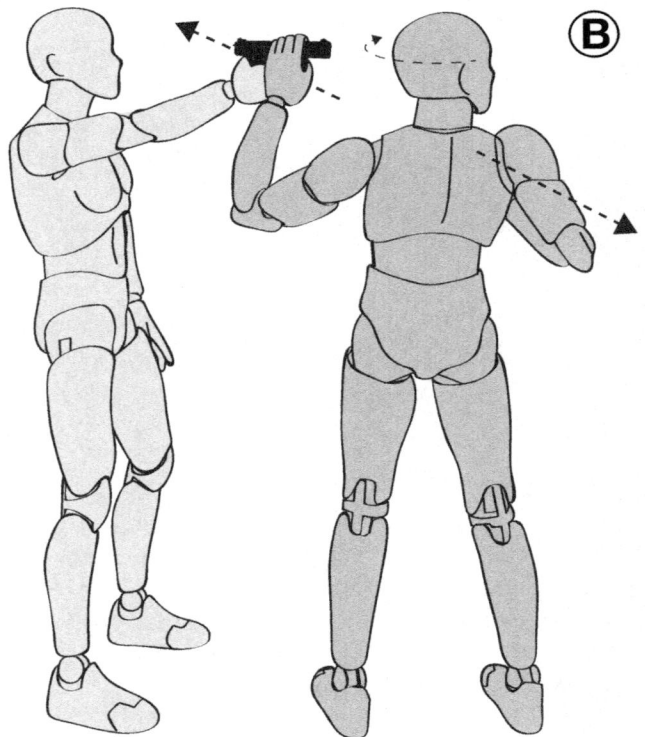

The gun can be pressed against your head or quite close to it. If it is pressed, turning your head helps, even more, to deflect the gun as seen in figures 1 to 3.

(B)

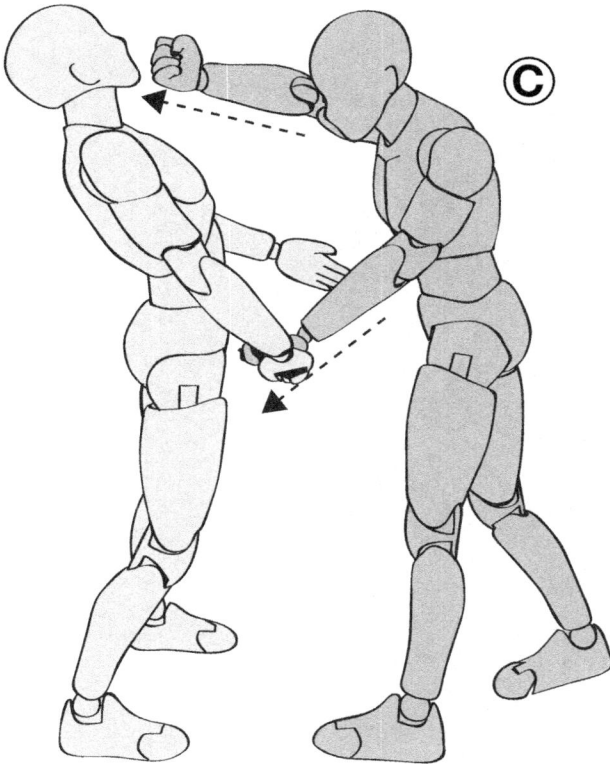

The left hand continues to hold the gun and the body rotates to become in front of the opponent. At the same time, right-hand boxing strikes must be delivered on the opponent's face (C).

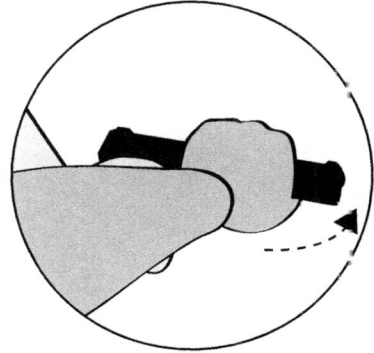

The body weight must be transferred to the left hand that holds the gun tightly. At the same time, the hand keeps the barrow pointed outward.

(1) The gun is pressed against the side of the head.

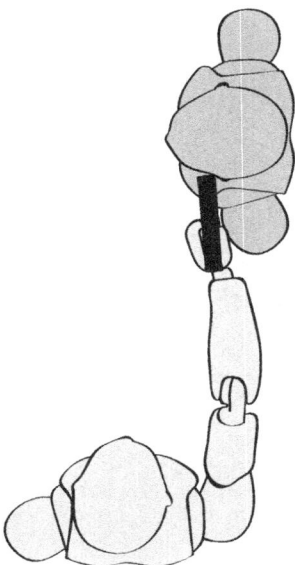

(2) The head rotates to deflect the gun.

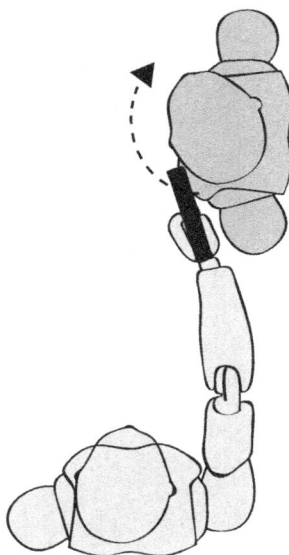

(3) The hand pulls the gun forward and you move your body away backward.

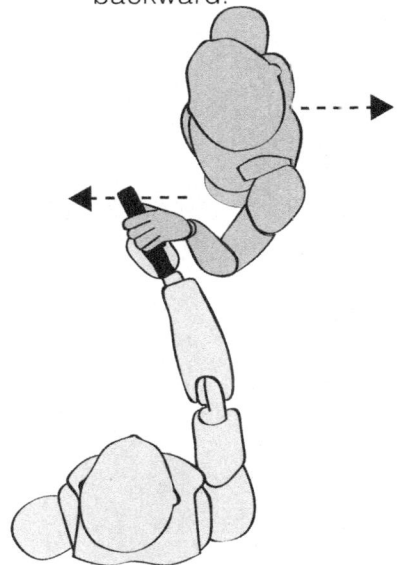

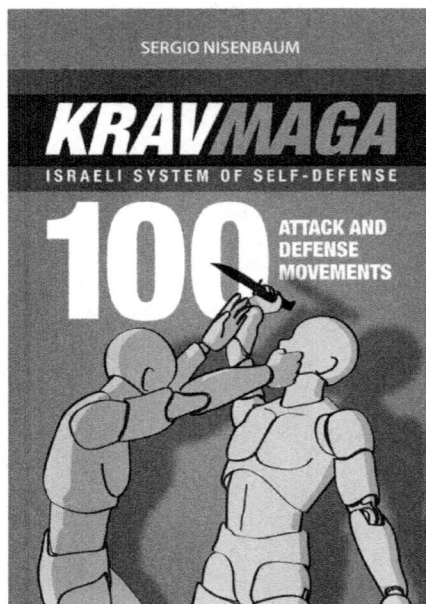

SERGIO NISENBAUM

KRAVMAGA
ISRAELI SYSTEM OF SELF-DEFENSE

100 ATTACK AND DEFENSE MOVEMENTS

Volume 1 brings the basic, intermediate, and even some more advanced techniques of Krav Maga self-defense: stances, boxing strikes, elbow strikes, kicks, knife defenses, stick defenses, etc. For you to enjoy Volume 2's contents fully, reading Volume 1 is essential. Volume 1 is a truly practical and objective guide that allows you to understand the movements easily. Fully illustrated, you will learn the technical details of every situation. After all, in situations of attack, well-executed details make all the difference. For Krav Maga practitioners, it is an excellent didactic material to study its fundamentals. It is also indicated to everyone who is willing to learn the Israeli defense art.

Afterword

If you have a dream, the only way to find out whether one day it will come true is to fight for it, to be patient and persistent.

Printed in Great Britain
by Amazon

62808063R00132